Health Care
and
Its Costs

THE AMERICAN ASSEMBLY was established by Dwight D. Eisenhower at Columbia University in 1950. Each year it holds at least two nonpartisan meetings which give rise to authoritative books that illuminate issues of United States policy.

An affiliate of Columbia, with offices at Barnard College, the Assembly is a national, educational institution incorporated in the state of New York.

The Assembly seeks to provide information, stimulate discussion, and evoke independent conclusions on matters of vital public interest.

CONTRIBUTORS

DREW E. ALTMAN, Commissioner of the New Jersey Department of Human Services

H. DAVID BANTA, Chair, Commission on Future Health Technologies in the Netherlands

ROBERT J. BLENDON, Senior Vice President of the Robert Wood Johnson Foundation

DONALD R. COHODES, Executive Director of Policy, Blue Cross and Blue Shield Association

ROBERT EBERT, Special Advisor to the President, Robert Wood Johnson Foundation

SUSAN FEIGENBAUM, Chief of Methodology Division, Maryland Health Services Cost Review Commission

ANNETINE GELIJNS, Senior Researcher, Project on Future Health Technology in the Netherlands

KENNETH G. MANTON, Senior Fellow, Center for the Study of Aging and Human Development, Duke University Medical Center

STEVEN C. RENN, Research Associate, Center for Hospital Finance and Management, Johns Hopkins Medical Institutions

DIANE ROWLAND, Research Associate, School of Hygiene and Public Health, Johns Hopkins University

CARL J. SCHRAMM, Director of the Johns Hopkins Center for Hospital Finance and Management

THE AMERICAN ASSEMBLY
Columbia University

Health Care
and
Its Costs

CARL J. SCHRAMM
Editor

W·W·NORTON & COMPANY
New York   London

The text of this book is composed in Baskerville, with
display type set in Baskerville. Composition and
manufacturing by The Haddon Craftsmen, Inc.

First Edition

ISBN 0-393-02437-7

ISBN 0-393-95671-7 PBK

W. W. Norton & Company, Inc.
500 Fifth Avenue, New York, N. Y. 10110
W. W. Norton & Company Ltd.
37 Great Russell Street, London WC1B 3NU

1 2 3 4 5 6 7 8 9 0

Contents

Preface

STEPHEN STAMAS

The health care system has been a major concern of most Americans in the postwar period. The passage of Medicare and Medicaid in the 1960s resolved a long national debate by providing insurance to older citizens and to the poor. Since then, however, other important issues have emerged. The cost of health care has increased so rapidly that it now takes a significantly greater percentage of our gross national product than it did in the mid-1960s. More than $425 billion each year goes for such expenditures, 90 percent of which are paid by private insurers or Medicare/Medicaid.

This has led private insurers and employers, as well as the federal government and the states, to seek ways to limit increases in health care charges by hospitals and physicians. At the same time, new health care providers, such as health maintenance organizations, have come into the field as payers, and patients seek alternatives to the traditional health care delivery systems. Hospitals have been adversely affected by these trends, raising questions about surplus facil-

---

STEPHEN STAMAS is president of The American Assembly.

ities, and a possible surplus of physicians.

With the rapid changes in health care institutions and financing, questions have been raised about the ability of the system to maintain the high quality of health care and access to it by those who do not have insurance coverage. Some believe that government should take a more active role to ensure that private or other insurance is available to the 37 million or more Americans who now are not covered. Others believe that the present trend toward diverse health delivery and private insurance plans ultimately will lead to adequate coverage of our citizens, with high quality health care at the lowest possible cost.

Most agree that future health care cost increases must be moderated and related to our other societal priorities, but there is no agreement on how to do so.

To discuss these issues, The American Assembly undertook a program that began with a meeting at Arden House, in Harriman, New York, from November 13–16, 1986. This meeting, the Seventy-second American Assembly, brought together distinguished Americans from various sectors of our society. They discussed an agenda prepared by Dr. Carl Schramm of Johns Hopkins University, who acted as director of the Assembly. As background for their discussions, they had papers prepared under Dr. Schramm's direction. Before leaving Arden House, the participants issued a report, which is included as an appendix to this book.

The background papers used by the participants have been compiled into the present volume. They are made available in the hope that a wider group of interested citizens will use them to establish their own views on the difficult choices our nation faces in regard to the health care system.

Funding for this project was provided by the Coca-Cola Foundation and the M.R. Bauer Foundation. The opinions addressed in this volume are those of the individual authors and not necessarily those of the funders nor of The American Assembly, which does not take stands on the issues it presents for public discussion.

Health Care
and
Its Costs

Introduction

CARL J. SCHRAMM

This collection of essays attempts to illuminate one of the most important contemporary domestic problems facing all Americans. Health care delivery and finance has been a topic of continuous concern since the advent of modern medicine. Several themes have characterized deliberations on the issue through the years. Formal policy attention was first paid to the subject in the 1930s, when the cost of care emerged as the most important aspect of medicine. Following World War II, government focused on the distribution of care by encouraging the development of the nation's hospital network through the Hill-Burton hospital building program. In the 1960s, when the cost of care had risen to such an extent that

CARL J. SCHRAMM is director of the Johns Hopkins Center for Hospital Finance and Management and is an associate professor in the School of Hygiene and Public Health at Johns Hopkins University. He serves as senior program consultant for The Robert Wood Johnson Foundation and served nine years as a member and chairman of the Maryland Health Services Cost Review Commission. Dr. Schramm's research interests and publications have included a broad range of health care issues, with specific emphasis on hospital finance.

the elderly and the poor often were being denied hospital care, the government funded care for these populations through the Medicare and Medicaid programs. Of course, containing hospital costs has been the focus of virtually all policy since the 1970s, when inflation in the health sector of the economy overwhelmed that of all other goods and services.

Throughout this long period of public discussion and action on the question of health care delivery and finance, two phenomena seem to characterize the debate. The first is the need for a deeper understanding of health care as an incident of modern citizenship. How does an individual's claim to equal and appropriate access to health care fit into the structure of societal rights and responsibilities? The passage of Medicare and Medicaid enfranchised the elderly and poor with a virtually unqualified right to obtain care without regard to their individual resources. We extended this right at a time when our economy was enormously robust and our public budgets were flush. In the 1960s we were, as a nation, also engaged in the widest discussion of individual rights and liberties since the founding of the republic. In such a circumstance, it seemed normal for government to take the role of actor.

The second theme that has evaded our collective discussion of health care relates to what its future will be. Reflecting an attitude that we cannot collectively create our medical future (rather, it will evolve on its own momentum), there is little interest in speculating on how we can positively change the delivery and financing system to make it more effective. Inevitably, such a view requires a crisis situation before systematic policy action can result.

This volume offers some thoughts on how the past may influence the future of the health care delivery system. It does not abandon a role for government and other forces in shaping the future; indeed, it is the thrust of these chapters that something must be done to preserve the system's best aspects and to detect underlying pressures that will inevitably change it. Given that the volume takes as its overarching job the stimulation of informed debate, the authors lay a solid historical and factual base so that a reader not enormously conversant with health care can be prepared to responsibly consider its future.

More specifically, the chapters attempt several tasks. For the average reader, the book should provide a sound foundation in the issues surrounding the question of how we finance medical attention. Not only does Steven Renn lay out a set of the most important basic facts, but Robert Blendon and Drew Altman, relying on broad-based population surveys, provide the reader with a sense of what the American people feel about matters such as the high cost of health care and what should be done about it.

The book examines the major forces that are in flux and how they will influence change in the years ahead. Two chapters of a more general nature lay the foundation for what the book, taken as a whole, attempts to do. Donald Cohodes provides an overview of the changes that have occurred in the last twenty years and speculates on the seeds for future changes in the health system. Susan Feigenbaum provides the reader with a most interesting look into the question of risk in the medical marketplace. Perhaps the key to understanding the past from the perspective of paying for medicine is to appreciate the concept of economic risk. To develop a thoughtful sense of what we should do, we must settle on a workable system of apportioning risk sharing among government, the individual, the institutions that provide care, insurance companies, and family members.

Robert Ebert, formerly dean of the Harvard School of Medicine, discusses the physician's role in the health care delivery system and pays particular attention to how the physician is trained. Through a thorough discussion of the American physician's professional and social evolution, Ebert equips the reader with a perspective to appreciate the change that has characterized the physician and his or her training in the last twenty years. Ebert argues that the various relations physicians enjoy with hospitals, insurers, patients, government, and each other will be greatly upset in the years ahead.

Kenneth Manton, a distinguished student of population dynamics and medical care, discusses the importance of demo-

graphic shifts in the population and how they may eventually
change demand for medical care. Manton's critical point is that
past patterns that link demand with various aging phenomena
in the population are of little assistance in understanding contemporary and future demands for medicine. Diane Rowland
provides an important examination of the ways in which the
fastest growing portion of the population—the elderly—has
impacted the health care system. She also speculates on what
the future will bring and leaves us with a sense of unprepared-
ness regarding what public and private policy should do to
accommodate future needs. Finally, David Banta and Annetine
Gelijns discuss the importance and growth of medical technology as a part of medicine itself. They assert that the very nature
of medicine is tied to technology and that the future of medicine is dependent on the development of technology.

Throughout the essays there is one consistent theme. If we
are to know what has transpired in the health care past and to
prepare for the medical future, we must understand the nexus
between our mechanisms for financing care and the nature of
the components of delivering care. Modern medicine is a classic case of seeing the world as shaped by dollars, and each of
our authors, save Manton, has examined, to some extent, the
importance of the finance system on the very nature of the
delivery system beneath it.

This book is about the future as well as the past. The operating premise among all the authors' works is that a snapshot
taken in the mid-1980s tells us very little about two fundamental questions concerning the finance of health care. The first
is: can we establish a public debate as a prelude to developing
a more efficient structure for the finance of health care? As in
all things, we have an obligation to create an optimal system
of producing medical attention. The second question must be
answered collectively prior to reordering the system: should
we, as a people, be dedicated to the notion that health care
should be enjoyed equally by all, regardless of personal resources? Health care is an incident of citizenship, and we
should seek a consensus on how we develop this right in the
future. Each author has attempted to push the boundary of our

knowledge about the future a bit further in order to anticipate forces that will shape the deliberations. I hope that this volume may guide the inevitable debate over how we will structure the American system of medicine.

1

The Structure and Financing of the Health Care Delivery System of the 1980s

Introduction

An author charged with using 10,000 words to describe the structure and financing of the health care delivery system of the 1980s soon realizes his or her dilemma: given the luxury of an abounding wealth of material, how does one present, in a comprehensive and timely manner, the complexities, subtleties, and interactions of an industry in violent flux, while at the same time focusing concisely on those trends that are the most reliable harbingers of the future? The solution attempted here is to portray the salient features of the current delivery and financing landscape, how they evolved, and how the terrain may continue to change.

STEVEN C. RENN is a research associate with the Center for Hospital Finance and Management at the Johns Hopkins Medical Institutions. He also serves as assistant professor in the Department of Health Policy and Management at Johns Hopkins University. Mr. Renn has authored or coauthored a number of articles regarding health care finance and hospital management.

The author gratefully acknowledges the assistance of Renee Bryant in the preparation of this chapter.

This chapter has three goals. First, it seeks to summarize the basic, essential information about the status of the U.S. health care financing and delivery system in the mid-1980s. Second, it tracks the course of evolution the industry has followed since 1930, in deference to the aphorism that the past is prologue. Finally, since, without any editorializing, the descriptive, experiential approach employed to achieve the first two objectives would make for an arid recapitulation, the chapter indulges in some prophesying. While no prescriptions for change are offered, the trends most likely to influence the financing and delivery system of the future are speculated upon.

The Providers of Health Care Services

Health care services are delivered in myriad institutional settings, ranging from ambulatory clinics, physician offices, and hospital emergency rooms to substance abuse and detoxification facilities, nursing homes, and hospices. As with other service oriented sectors of the economy, the health care industry is also labor intensive: over two-thirds of health care expenditures are devoted to medical personnel. The primary groups of health care workers include independent practitioners (such as physicians, dentists, chiropractors, podiatrists, and optometrists) and dependent practitioners, authorized by law to deliver a specified range of services under the supervision of an independent practitioner (including registered and licensed practical nurses; physicians' assistants; certified registered nurse anesthetists; psychologists; social workers; and speech, occupational, and physical therapists). Independent and dependent practitioners are assisted by a large group of health care workers who less frequently provide direct, patient care services; the support staff includes laboratory, radiological, and other medical technicians; nurses' aides; dental assistants; and administrative, clerical, maintenance, housekeeping, and dietary workers. Since the most visible providers of care—physicians and community hospitals—consume 60 percent of health care resources, they have been the target of most cost-containment initiatives and will be the focus of the remainder of this section.

The Structure and Capacity of the Hospital Industry

The earliest hospitals were institutions that rendered care, not cure, and the modern hospital's inheritance has been more than vestigial. Hospitals are still, by and large, charitable, eleemosynary institutions, often with religious affiliations, that were founded by and are still responsive to their local communities. Despite their heritage, however, hospitals are no longer a cottage industry.

By the end of World War II, advances in medicine and technology, such as the discovery and development of anesthesia, aseptic surgery, insulin, and antibiotics, began to shape the modern role and size of the industry. The Hill-Burton program, begun in 1946, provided a massive infusion of federal and state governmental monies, and helped construct over 400,000 hospital beds between then and the early 1970s, or nearly half of those beds in use today. The contemporaneous expansion of third-party health insurance fueled the industry's growth, although it was more evident in the number of services offered and types of patients treated than in the size of the industry.

From 1950 to 1965, the *total* number of hospital beds in the United States grew at an annualized rate of 0.5 percent, to a peak of about 1.7 million beds, or 8.8 beds per 1,000 persons in 1965. Total U.S. beds per capita gradually declined in each year subsequent to 1965 to a low of 5.9 beds per 1,000 persons in 1984.

While the number of *total* beds was growing from 1950 to 1965, federal hospital, nonfederal tuberculosis, and nonfederal long-term general and other special beds were declining in number. This decline was more than offset by the growth in total nonfederal short-term general and other special beds, or *community* hospital beds, which increased from 3.3 beds per capita to 4.2 beds per 1,000 persons between 1950 and 1965. Thus the nature of the hospital product changed substantially after World War II. The decline in the number of *total* hospital beds per capita was primarily the result of the deinstitutionalization of the mentally handicapped, which closed many psychiatric hospitals and dramatically reduced the number of admissions to psychiatric hospitals. Much of the increase in the number of short-term general hospital beds occurred in rural areas and was attributable to the Hill-Burton program.

Community hospitals also became noticeably larger over time. The average size of general acute care hospitals increased from 100 beds in 1950 to 175 beds by 1985, in part in response to the changing technological environment that enabled hospitals to perform many more functions than they could in 1950. Many services that are fairly routine today, such as CT scanning and open heart surgery, were not available in 1950.

One characteristic that changed little since 1950 is hospital ownership. The relative shares of hospital beds operated by for-profit organizations, not-for-profit organizations, and state and local governments have remained essentially constant during this period. In 1985 not-for-profit institutions controlled approximately 70 percent of all community hospital beds, state and local governments operated 20 percent, and for-profit organizations owned the remaining 10 percent.

The most recent data indicate that there are now just under 5,800 community hospitals, containing nearly 1 million beds, or about 4.2 beds per 1,000 persons. Community hospitals admitted slightly less than 36 million patients in 1985, or 152 per 1,000 persons, with an average length of stay of 7.4 days. The average hospital's occupancy rate, a measure of the industry's capacity being utilized, was 64 percent. Hospitals now employ 3.6 million people, or about one out of every thirty U.S. workers.

Aggregate and average measures conceal the wide diversity that exists among hospitals. For example, Big Sandy Medical Center in Chouteau County, Montana has nine beds and provides the following services: an emergency department, obstetrics, and dental care. Baptist Memorial Hospital in Memphis, Tennessee, with 1,805 beds, offers the same services, in addition to the following facilities: ambulatory surgery, an intensive care unit, open heart surgery, a pharmacy, ultrasound, X-ray radiation therapy, megavoltage radiation therapy, radioactive implants, diagnostic and therapeutic radioisotopes, histopathology laboratory, organ transplant, blood bank, health promotion, respiratory therapy, a premature nursery, hemodialysis, a burn care unit, physical therapy, occupational therapy, inpatient and outpatient rehabilitation units, inpatient and outpatient psychiatric units, a psychiatric emergency room, clinical psychology, an organized outpatient department, social work, family planning, genetic counseling, podiatry, speech pathology, a hospital auxiliary, patient representatives, a neonatal intensive care unit, pediatric inpatient unit, CT scanner, and a cardiac catheterization laboratory.

The Consolidation and Commercialization of the Hospital Industry

Probably the most pronounced change underway in the hospital industry—and the first major trend of note—is the consolidation of hospitals into multi-institutional systems, especially those organized to deliver health care for profit.

Proprietary ownership of hospitals is not a new phenomenon; in the early part of this century, nearly half of the hospitals in the United States were investor-owned. However, of all community hospitals in the late 1960s, the proportion that were for-profit had dwindled to 13 percent, and has hovered at about that share since then. Further, since investor-owned hospitals tend to be smaller, the for-profits' share of beds has been even less, remaining a nearly constant 8 to 9 percent of all community hospital beds.

However, the fairly stable proportion of one hospital in seven being investor-owned masks an important structural change that has occurred within the for-profit sector. Prior to the inception of Medicare and Medicaid in 1966, there were no investor-owned hospitals that were affiliated with systems or "chains." By 1970 twenty-nine investor-owned chains had formed owning 207 hospitals, or less than 4 percent of all community hospitals at the time. Rapid growth of the investor-owned systems followed almost immediately; from 1970 to 1984 they doubled their share every seven years. Since 1975 investor-owned chains have added 500 hospitals to their systems, which translates into a 10 percent average annual rate of growth. Over the same period, the number of *freestanding* for-profit hospitals, usually owned by groups of physicians, declined at roughly 7 percent per year; put differently, nearly all of the growth in chain-affiliated investor-owned hospitals has been matched by the freestanding for-profits' demise. The four largest investor-owned hospital management companies —Hospital Corporation of America (HCA), American Medical International (AMI), Humana, and National Medical Enterprises (NME)—together owned or managed over 500 community hospitals (representing more than one-half of the total for-profit beds) in 1985.

Growth in the number of hospitals affiliated with *not-for-profit* multihospital systems has also been remarkable, although not as dramatic as that demonstrated by the investor-owned systems. While not-for-profit chains are more prevalent than investor-owned systems, they tend to have fewer numbers of hospitals, on average, in each system. Hospitals in not-for-profit systems, however, are twice as large as those in investor-owned systems, although because there are fewer, their orientation tends to be more regional than national. Finally, not-for-profit systems are more loosely structured, often entailing only joint purchasing agreements or shared service arrangements, whereas investor-owned chains are much more centralized, with individual member hospitals usually organized as operating subsidiaries of a parent corporation.

Among the many changes in the organizational structure of the hospital industry, few have been met with as much interest, consternation, and controversy as the emergence of investor-owned multihospital systems. In theory, the for-profit delivery of hospital care should result in its more efficient production and thus help alleviate cost inflation. Proponents of the for-profit model argue that it is more responsive to the needs of physicians and patients, better able to attract skilled management, more innovative, better poised to acquire capital, and most importantly—since it is ultimately responsible to its shareholders—constrained to produce and deliver hospital care more cheaply in order to earn a profit. Critics of the for-profit chains claim that they have maximized their revenues by manipulating costs and pricing services aggressively; "skimmed the cream" by choosing to treat the least severely ill and best insured patients; refused to provide, compared to not-for-profits, similar amounts of nonmarket goods, such as charity care, graduate medical education, and medical research; and represented a threat to the autonomy of the medical profession and the physician-patient relationship. Similarly, theory suggests that the consolidation of hospitals, notwithstanding ownership, into multihospital systems would also permit the realization of productive efficiencies, derived from better access to capital and deployment of managerial talent, purchasing discounts, the diversification of revenue streams, and other economies of scale and scope.

What factors have prompted the growth in investor-owned and multihospital systems? Beginning with the inception of Medicare and Medicaid in 1966 and continuing through the early 1980s, the rapidly increasing flow of dollars into the health care sector, presenting clear profit-making opportunities, was greatly responsible for the growth of the investor-owned chains. By any measure, hospital management companies whose stock is publicly traded have demonstrated the ability to profit from the delivery of hospital care. Throughout the late 1970s and early 1980s, the price of stocks in these companies consistently outperformed that of the Standard and Poors 500–Index, as earnings per share continued to grow. Shareholders' equity in the four largest hospital management companies more than doubled, adjusted for inflation, between 1977 and 1984.

Paradoxically, a second impetus for growth in multihospital arrangements, more applicable to the not-for-profit sector, has been the increasing financial pressure faced by hospitals. In this regard, the most important factor which spurs system development appears to be enhanced access to capital, especially of the debt-financed variety, since systems enjoy lower costs of capital than freestanding hospitals. To a lesser extent, the promise of other pecuniary benefits, such as those arising from the putative economies of scale discussed above, also seems to precipitate system formation.

A fairly clear pattern of differences in goals and strategies exists between investor-owned chain hospitals and freestanding voluntaries, which are still the most prevalent type. Before turning to the evidence, it is useful to review how, depending on the perspective of the entity that incurs them, the definition of hospital costs can vary.

Hospitals incur costs in purchasing labor, supplies, and capital in order to produce their services, and we are concerned with these costs in gauging the efficiency of an ownership or organizational type. Further, these average costs of production, at least as recorded by customary accounting conventions and subject to reimbursement disallowances, are the prices or charges paid by *cost-based* insurers and represent a cost incurred by these payers. While Medicare allowable patient care costs may not be equivalent to true economic costs, the cost incurred by providers and cost-based payers is generally similar.

Hospital prices, which are typically higher than the costs of production, are the costs incurred by commercial insurers, some Blue Cross Plans, and self-paying patients. A hospital's gross revenues are usually assumed to be a good indication of the prices charged to and costs incurred by charge-based payers. Finally, a third measure of costs from the perspective of purchasers is a hospital's net revenues, or those monies actually collected, and they may be viewed as the total costs incurred by the community of payers.

Contrary to classical economic theory, the postulated ability of for-profit hospitals to produce comparable services at a lower cost than similar not-for-profit hospitals has not been borne out by the evidence, at least not during periods of cost-based reimbursement and attenuated price sensitivity on the part of charge-based payers. Moreover, the prices for hospital

care paid by charge-based payers and self-paying patients have
been 15 to 20 percent higher in investor-owned hospitals,
especially those that are members of for-profit systems. Taken
together, these findings led the Institute of Medicine's Committee on the Implications of For-Profit Enterprise in Health
Care to conclude, after extensive research, that

*the rise in investor ownership of hospitals has increased health care costs to payers
under both the original cost-based reimbursement approach used by Medicare
and some other third-party payers and the charge-based reimbursement methods
still used by a large number of third-party payers.*

Moreover, and similarly inconsistent with traditional theory,
the economic efficiencies of purchasing, operation, and distribution that should be achieved through the consolidation of
single hospitals into multihospital systems have not been
demonstrated as of the most recent research. Finally and most
ominous, while definitive proof is still lacking, there are suspi-
cions that for-profit chains are less inclined to treat indigent
and Medicaid patients. In sum, the consolidation and commercialization of the industry may not be such a boon.

The Demand for Hospital Care

Over the past fifteen years, there have been fluctuations in
the utilization rates of short-term hospitals and differences in
the trends among payers, but it has been only recently that a
marked decline has been observed across all major payers.
During the period from 1971 to 1977, the national number of
admissions per capita (seasonally adjusted) to community hospitals showed a consistent upward trend, although the curve
had flattened by 1978. The national increase resumed in 1979,
but the annual per capita increase from 1981 to 1982 again
approached zero. During the same period, from 1971 to 1982,
national average length of stay (seasonally adjusted, for all
ages) declined slightly, from 8.1 days to 7.6 days in 1977, and
then remained essentially constant, at 7.6 days, through the
end of 1982.

The second quarter of 1982 marked the beginning of a

consistent pattern of decline in the national number of admissions and average length of stay. From April 1983 to December 1983, total admissions dropped from 38.1 million annually to 37.4 million, or almost 2 percent. In calendar 1984, the decrease of 4 percent was even more pronounced and continued unabated through 1985. Nearly all of this decline in admissions has occurred in the under age sixty-five population; indeed, admissions from the age sixty-five and over population have only begun to drop since the first quarter of 1984. On the other hand, declines in length of stay are much more pronounced in the age sixty-five and over population than in the group under age sixty-five.

Nationally, the number of *Medicare* admissions to all short-stay hospitals (including those not yet phased in under the Prospective Payment System [PPS]) declined nearly 2 percent per year from federal fiscal 1983 to federal fiscal 1985. During the same period, the average length of stay of the Medicare patients who were admitted dropped to 8.6 days from 9.3 days; for those patients who were paid on the basis of PPS principles, the decline was even greater, to 7.4 days.

The second major trend most likely to shape the future is the decline in hospital utilization, which is the product of a confluence of forces. The most noteworthy change in financing mechanisms has been the federal government's switch to a prospective, DRG–based system of paying hospitals for the care rendered to its Medicare beneficiaries. Initiated in 1983, the Medicare Prospective Payment System offers clear incentives to hospitals to shorten the lengths of stay of the Medicare population, although it may also contain incentives to increase the rates of admission for the same population. Furthermore, there is arguably a "spillover" effect onto the non-Medicare population: to the extent that physicians are changing their practice patterns in response to the incentives inherent in a Medicare patient, their treatment of patients of other payers may also be expected to change. As some have remarked, physicians may not differentiate between a sixty-four-year-old patient and one who is sixty-five.

A second factor responsible for the decline in utilization has been the recent growth in the number of enrollees in health maintenance organizations (HMOs). HMOs and other capitated financing arrangements contain much stronger disincentives to admit patients, and if admitted, stronger incentives to keep them in the hospital for relatively shorter periods, than do other financing arrangements that reimburse providers on the basis of fee-for-service. Nationally, HMOs have now attracted more than 15 million enrollees, and their membership growth suggests that they will soon be more than a regional phenomenon. Recent studies conclude that HMOs effect decreases in hospital admissions of up to 40 percent. Preferred provider organizations, while they retain the characteristics of reimbursement on a fee-for-service basis, may have also contributed to declines in admissions and lengths of stay. In return for guaranteed volumes of patients at discounted prices, contracting providers usually must agree to a stringent utilization review process.

Third, the proliferation of treatment settings that can serve as substitutes for inpatient hospitalization—mainly those delivering ambulatory or outpatient care, but also home health and other institutional settings—may have diverted patients away from inpatient settings or siphoned them out of hospitals earlier. Freestanding emergency and surgical centers, in delivering single-day treatments, may force hospitals to compete for similar patients, resulting in a lowering of the hospital's average length of stay.

Fourth, the increasing burden of cost sharing that insured patients have been asked to shoulder has probably also been responsible for the decline in admissions. Private and public insurers have raised deductible and coinsurance levels, and employers have offered financial incentives to employees selecting less comprehensive plans, or those with higher out-of-pocket requirements. Results from several RAND studies suggest that a change from 100 percent insurance coverage to coverage requiring 25 percent coinsurance decreases the probability of hospital admissions by 3 percent.

Greater emphasis on utilization review, both prior and subsequent to a hospital stay, on the part of hospitals, insurers, and employers may also be responsible for the declines in admissions and lengths of stay. Many insurance plans or selective-contracting arrangements now require preadmission testing, second-opinion surgery, and/or postdischarge planning. Similarly, many businesses, as the ultimate payers of hospitalization insurance premiums, have stepped up their claims review efforts directed at detecting and reducing unnecessary admissions and days of care.

Fifth, the declines in admissions and lengths of stay may also be due in part to changes in clinical practice patterns and changes resulting from the introduction of new technologies. By documenting the enormous variation in surgical procedure rates among local areas resulting from differences in medical practice patterns, research may have encouraged physicians to question the necessity of recommending hospitalization and diminished the number of "high outliers." Greater impetus for a reevaluation of traditional practice styles is being provided by the incentives inherent in PPS, and detecting and monitoring practice differences are made much easier today with the advances in hospital management information systems. Likewise, some new technologies and devices have been responsible for shortening lengths of stay; the use of lasers, for example, has been successful in reducing recovery periods for certain types of eye surgery.

Regional variation in under age sixty-five admissions may also be attributable to the unevenness of the nation's economic recovery. In many manufacturing and retail sectors, such as construction, mining, and agriculture, wage and salary earners still show unemployment rates above that of the national average. Higher rates of unemployment are associated with the loss of employer-provided hospitalization insurance, as well as less disposable income available for hospital care.

A final hypothesis advanced to explain part of the decline in admission rates is a general improvement in the health of the nation. The incidence of coronary disease, cerebrovascular disease, pneumonia and influenza, and diabetes mellitus, for example, has been declining for a number of years. Coupled with this trend is perhaps a greater recent awareness on the part of most individuals of the effect of life style on health: people are devoting more attention to the benefits of exercise regimens and to the harms of smoking, alcohol consumption, and similar habits.

Going to the hospital no longer seems chic, and the decline in the use of hospitals was the leading factor in slowing the rate of hospital cost inflation in 1984 to the lowest level since 1963. While this trend should be applauded if it represents the beginning of an effort to eliminate unnecessary utilization or its transfer to less costly settings, it also raises several vexing issues.

First, the decline in hospital utilization has exacerbated the problem of excess capacity in the industry. In 1984 community hospitals delivered about 256 million days of inpatient care. If we assume, as did most planning agencies, that the desired industry occupancy rate is 80 percent (which is more comparable to most other industries), then the number of days delivered in 1984 could have been produced by an industry with slightly over 877,000 beds. Compared to the supply required, we had an excess of 140,000 hospital beds in 1984, or nearly 800 average-sized hospitals. In Maryland, a state-sponsored study concluded that 15,000, or one-third, of the state's beds were unnecessary and recommended closing fourteen institutions.

Because hospitals are often the largest employers in communities, if not their most cherished and protected resources, communities are loathe to see their hospitals close. Worse, as many hospitals begin to limp through the remainder of the 1980s less than half-full of patients, a large proportion of their costs will remain in the health care system. The costs of debt service on buildings and equipment, insurance, heating, and plant maintenance will be incurred regardless of the occupancy rate of a hospital. Even most labor costs are semifixed in the short run.

Declines in hospital utilization have also hastened the consolidation and diversification of the hospital industry. The number of new acquisitions by the for-profit chains has dwindled as the chains have redirected their efforts toward diversification and vertical integration through the purchase of "upstream" and "downstream" providers of care. Humana has developed Humana MedFirst, the largest chain of freestanding ambulatory surgical centers, which serves in part to feed patients to Humana's hospitals. Almost 300 nursing homes supplied National Medical Enterprises with 20 percent of its revenue in 1985; 18 percent of Beverly Enterprises, the largest nursing home chain in the United States, is owned by Hospital Corporation of America. The management companies have recently begun to acquire large teaching hospitals which, besides enhancing public relations as the prestigious flagships of their chains, also ensure that additional groups of patients are captured by their systems. In 1985 Hospital Corporation of America tried unsuccessfully to merge with American Hospital Supply Corporation, the largest seller of medical supplies and equipment. The newest diversification trend to emerge from the chains has been the offering of insurance products, which promises greater margins in addition to new patients.

Perhaps the greatest concern raised by the new incentives to reduce hospital utilization is the potentially deleterious effect on the quality of care delivered. Reimbursement systems like PPS, which pay the same amount whether the length of stay is two days or twelve days, raise the specter of premature discharge. Early experience with Medicaid HMOs in California and recent evidence from a Medicare HMO in Florida indicate that similar financial considerations tempt prepaid plans to skimp on the provision of medically necessary services and thus jeopardize quality of care. Finally, several researchers have demonstrated that a smaller volume of surgical operations is associated with a higher death rate.

The Supply and Distribution of Physicians

In 1979 the Graduate Medical Education National Advisory Committee (GMENAC), created three years earlier by Congress to advise the secretary of HEW on physician manpower issues, was able to summarize its findings in a single paragraph:

There will be too many physicians in 1990. There will be substantial imbalances *in some specialties. There will continue to be a marked* unevenness *in the geographic distribution of physicians. The country may be training* too many *nonphysician providers for 1990. The factors influencing specialty choice are* complex. *The actual cost of graduate medical education is* unknown. *Economic motivation in specialty and geographic choice is* uncertain. *(Emphasis in original)*

From 1965 to 1983, the total number of physicians in the United States increased from 292,000 to nearly 520,000, or 78 percent, during a period when the U.S. population increased only 21 percent. As a result of the nearly fourfold discrepancy in growth rates, the ratio of physicians per 100,000 persons has jumped from 150 to 222. The United States now has one of the highest physician-to-population ratios in the world, and, if current projections are accurate, the ratio is expected to increase to 250 per 100,000 population by 1990.

Of the 483,000 active physicians in 1983, more than 80 percent were engaged in the direct care of patients, as opposed to other professional activities such as medical education, administration, and research. Roughly 75 percent of all active patient care physicians worked in office-based practices, while the remaining 113,000 were hospital-based. For those with a hospital-based practice, 73,000 (three out of five) were interns and residents.

The burgeoning supply of physicians can be traced to several factors. First, throughout the 1950s and 1960s there was a widespread perception that the nation faced a serious shortage of physicians. The American Medical Association succeeded in blocking congressional action until 1963, when the Health Professions Educational Assistance Act was passed. The 1963 act, together with successive reenactments and additional amendments, provided for federal subsidies for physician training primarily through construction and operating grants to medical schools.

Second, the Immigration Act of 1965 facilitated the flow of foreign-trained physicians into the United States. Although there had always been a small stream of physicians immigrating to the United States, during the decade from 1966 to 1976 (when Health Professions Educational Assistance of 1976 effectively ended the importation), approximately one-third of the permanent increase in physician supply was attributable to foreign-born and foreign-trained physicians. Finally, the income expectations that can be realized by a physician are substantial. Even after taking into account the burden of educational debt and the years of forgone income, lifetime net earnings are near the highest of all occupations.

Increasing Specialization and Geographic Maldistribution

At the same time the United States is faced with an expanding supply (to some, an oversupply) of physicians, the distribution of physicians by specialty and by geography remains amazingly uneven. Virtually every physician now participating in a residency training program expects ultimately to be board certified as a specialist. Once the largest specialty group, general and family practice registered a 10 percent decline from 1965 to 1983; as a result, of those physicians in office-based practice, the proportion of family and general practitioners dropped from 30 percent in 1965 to 16 percent in 1983.

The relatively large categories of obstetrics and gynecology, psychiatry, general surgery, and all other specialties increased at about the same rate as the overall increase in physicians, while the numbers of internists and pediatricians have outpaced the overall rate. Growth in the number of some narrower specialties and subspecialties is even more dramatic: the numbers of diagnostic radiologists, gastroenterologists, neurologists, pulmonary disease specialists, and plastic surgeons have all doubled since 1965.

Geographic maldistribution is equally notable. Among the states, there is a threefold difference between the extremes in physician population ratios, from 122 per 100,000 population in Mississippi to 308 per 100,000 in Massachusetts. Within states, the unevenness of distribution is even more pronounced: among counties in Maryland, for example, there is nearly a tenfold difference among counties, from 30 per

100,000 to 312 per 100,000. Even though within areas of high physician-population ratios there are often located major tertiary hospitals that serve many patients residing outside the areas, the variability in geographic distribution cannot explain the wide variations in patient visits, rates of hospitalization, and surgical operations performed.

The Coming Physician Surplus

Current projections of a future physician oversupply are even more pessimistic than those of GMENAC. As a result, the third major trend likely to shape the health care financing and delivery system of the future is, as Eli Ginzberg of Columbia University has referred to it, the coming physician surplus.

Will an expanding supply of physicians be self-correcting? Conventional economic theory would argue that as an excess of physicians is produced, the price for physicians' services and their real net income will fall, and that eventually such reductions in real income will discourage new physician entrants and otherwise serve to reduce supply.

A contrary view that is abhorrent to conventional economics but espoused by many is that physicians have considerable control over the demand for their services. The theoretical and empirical existence of physician-induced demand is still widely debated. However, for many reasons, the market for physicians' services is not self-equilibrating in the usual sense of price balancing supply and demand.

Most research has concluded that, historically, growth in the supply of physicians has resulted in disproportionate increases in health care expenditures. While some of the increase in total expenditures is due to greater direct outlays for physician services, a larger part is attributable to increases in payments for hospital care, the demand for which is being greatly influenced by physician decision making. Such an incentive to increase hospitalization exists because most estimates consistently suggest that at least 40 percent of physicians' gross revenues is derived from work performed in hospital settings. Thus, if certain other elements of the status quo remain unchanged—most importantly, if physicians continue to make most of the allocative decisions in the delivery system, if the emphasis on treatment in acute care inpatient settings persists, and if payment mechanisms continue to insulate physicians from the financial risks associated with their decisions—then growth in the supply of physicians will probably translate into corresponding growth in health care spending. Moreover, much of this spending may be for medical treatments and interventions of a marginally beneficial or even harmful nature in already oversupplied geographic areas.

A competing view is that many beneficial outcomes may flow from the expanding physician supply. The most important predictions hinge on increasing price and quality competition among physicians and among hospitals, physicians, and other nonphysician providers. There is already preliminary evidence of declines in the number of hours worked per week by physicians, decreases in the number of patient visits per physician, reductions in the rate of price inflation for physician services relative to other prices, and a flattening in the increase of the average real income of physicians. Admissions to medical schools have begun to level off, and the ratio of applicants to admissions has declined to 2.1 to 1 from a 1975 peak of 2.8 to 1.

In the future, physicians—especially newer graduates—will probably be much more receptive to salaried employment and/or group practice as a result of the job and income security they promise. Consequently, increases in the number of physicians should facilitate the growth of capitated and pre-paid financing arrangements and speed the demise of solo practice and perhaps even single-specialty group practice. However, as physicians band together they may be a powerful, licensure-protected bargaining force to be contended with by hospitals, insurers, and patients. Competition among physicians in neighboring fields or specialties—such as between family practice and pediatrics, internal medicine and cardiology, neurology and neurosurgery, and general surgery and cardiovascular surgery—will intensify. Whether this will attenuate the value now attached to subspecialty certification or

foster even more and narrower subspecialty fields remains to
be seen. Increases in the number of HMOs, growth in proposed financing schemes based on the concept of primary care
gatekeepers, and increases in the importance of a source of
referrals will all elevate the status of the primary care physician, and may serve to reduce the future shortage.

Physicians' future relationships with hospitals will be mixed,
but likely more strained. A growing physician supply may
serve to exacerbate physician-hospital competition and may
actually decrease hospital utilization by fostering the development of ambulatory care settings (with the concomitant exo-
dus of substantial diagnostic work and minor surgery from the
hospital) and inducing physicians to join prepaid group practices, HMOs, and similar entrepreneurial arrangements that
reduce hospital admissions. For those physicians who must
admit patients, increasing adoption of DRG–based prospective reimbursement methodologies will shift more and more
power to the hospital's administrators and eliminate its organizational structure as "the physician's workshop." On the
other hand, if the most lucrative practice settings remain inside the hospital, disputes over the awarding of hospital privileges will continue to flourish, despite countervailing pressures: while boards of trustees and administrators will seek to
enlarge the size of their hospitals' staffs in response to a dimin-
ishing flow of patients requiring hospitalization, existing medical staffs, in light of the same trends, will likely resist potential
encroachments on their income levels.

The Financing of Health Care Services

Ultimately, individuals pay for all health care expenditures:
while health care is financed by a mix of public and private
payers, the original sources of funds are the consumers, workers, and taxpayers, with the dollars merely taking different
routes on their way to providers. That is, in addition to payments made by patients directly, government payers serve to
rechannel tax revenues, and private insurers transfer the premium payments made to them by employers and employees.

Chief among these third-party payers are two major public programs—Medicare and Medicaid—and two groups of private insurers—Blue Cross/Blue Shield and commercial insurance companies.

Physicians and hospitals provided health care long before the third-party system of financing evolved. Virtually no health insurance existed prior to the Depression; almost 90 percent of health care expenditures were paid directly by patients. Within the space of thirty-five years, however, insurance was invented and the historical ratio of those without insurance to those insured had become inverted.

Blue Cross and Blue Shield

In 1929 a group of 1,250 school teachers in Dallas, Texas contracted with Baylor University Hospital to provide them with up to twenty-one days of semiprivate hospitalization annually in return for a monthly premium of fifty cents. Their pioneering arrangement was the forerunner of what later became known as the Blue Cross Plans.

From their inception, Blue Cross Plans were characterized by several features that would shape their roles as purchasers in the 1980s. First, most plans were originally provider-based and entailed service agreements with the community's participating providers, which were often virtually all of the hospitals in the area, instead of indemnification contracts with insureds. Physicians and hospital representatives often dominated the plans' boards of directors and saw the plans, like most participants, as a means of ensuring the financial solvency of the community's providers. In addition to laying the groundwork for future provider-insurer alignments, Blue Cross initiated the practice of reimbursing hospitals on a retrospective, cost-plus basis. Second, the plans generally calculated a single, community-wide rate for premiums, and thus were conditioned upon a sizable pool of insureds. Partly as a result of this, individual plans—which were not-for-profit undertakings—staked out large territories encompassing many hospitals and tended not to compete with neighboring plans.

Not surprisingly, within a decade after the Baylor University plan, the American Hospital Association began actively promoting the Blue Cross concept, and membership swelled to 6 million individuals by 1940. At about the same time, a group of physicians in California established the first Blue Shield Plan, designed to complement the hospitalization benefits of Blue Cross by providing insurance for physicians' services. Growth in the number of Blue Cross and Blue Shield Plans and their membership rolls accelerated through the late 1950s. Today there are eighty-two autonomous plans, typically covering a single state, and in most jurisdictions the historically separate Blue Cross and Blue Shield organizations have merged. The Blues provide hospitalization insurance for nearly one-third of the U.S. population and insurance for physician services for about 25 percent of all individuals.

Commercial Insurers

Nearly all of the remaining private health insurance in the United States is provided by a collection of over 800 companies, of which about half are organized on a for-profit basis and the rest as mutual funds. The twenty largest companies, including such giants as Prudential, Travellers, CIGNA, Equitable, and Metropolitan, control over half of the share of the commercial market.

Commercial insurers were initially reluctant to offer health insurance benefits. Because, compared to Blue Cross, the commercials more frequently underwrote experience-rated policies (based on the insureds' ages and health status) for smaller groups, it was difficult to calculate actuarial rates that would ensure a profit. Even today, health insurance products for the larger commercial insurers often generate losses, which are subsidized by nonhealth lines such as life and disability insurance, retirement pensions, and annuities.

Growth in commercial (and voluntary) health insurance accelerated during and after World War II. While a freeze on wages was imposed by the War Labor Board, fringe benefits were essentially exempt from the price controls. Shortly after the war, the Supreme Court ruled that the newly enacted National Labor Relations Act envisioned fringe benefits, including health insurance, as proper issues for collective bargaining, and the proliferation of commercial insurance, especially plans with first-dollar coverage, ballooned.

Medicare

Inaugurated on July 1, 1966, the Medicare program provides a number of health care benefits to the elderly (those age sixty-five and older) who were covered by the Social Security System. Amendments made in 1972 to Title XVIII of the Social Security Act (which contains the Medicare provisions) extend benefits to the disabled, to those elderly not meeting the criteria for the regular Social Security program but willing to pay the premiums, and to those with chronic renal disease.

The Medicare program has two complementary but distinct parts: (1) hospital insurance (HI), known as Part A (which covers primarily inpatient hospitalization, but also covers care rendered in certain longer-term skilled nursing facilities or in the patient's home); and (2) supplemental medical insurance (SMI), known as Part B (which covers physicians' services, hospital outpatient services, and also home health services).

The reimbursement method adopted initially by the Medicare program was borrowed from Blue Cross, and it delegated to Blue Cross and commercial insurers (the fiscal intermediaries) the tasks of paying and auditing hospitals and physicians. Medicare paid hospitals retrospectively on the basis of the costs incurred by covered beneficiaries at participating providers and paid physicians their reasonable, customary, and prevailing fees. Despite the rising costs of health care experienced by Blue Cross through the 1950s, the inherently inflationary nature of such a payment system was, if not unforeseen, at least agreed to as the compromise for the federal government's entry into the market as the largest purchaser. Detailed regulations and formulas specify the costs that are allowable to the program and the type of cost apportionment methods that may be used.

Medicaid

The Medicaid program (Title XIX of the Social Security Act), which was also established in 1966, is a joint federal-state program whose designated beneficiary group is the poor. Because each state administers its own program (including the definition of eligibility requirements and covered services), there are effectively fifty different Medicaid programs; the federal role is primarily one of matching state funds (according to each state's per capita income), although the federal government does establish minimum standards for eligibility and benefits.

At a minimum, those eligible for Medicaid include: (1) those receiving cash assistance through one of the existing welfare programs established under the Social Security Act (through, most commonly, the Aid to Families with Dependent Children [AFDC] program or, for the poor, aged, blind, or disabled, through the Supplemental Security Income program); (2) poor children up to age five; and (3) pregnant women who are poor and who would qualify for AFDC were their children born. However, because states have much discretion in defining eligibility standards for welfare, eligibility for Medicaid varies widely across states: some states set their standards below the federal poverty level, while others have expanded eligibility to other optional categorically or medically needy groups. Estimates of the ratio of Medicaid recipients to individuals living below the federal poverty level range from 97 percent in California to 25 percent in Texas.

Under Medicaid, seven categories of basic health care services are required to be covered: (1) inpatient and outpatient hospital care; (2) other laboratory and X-ray services; (3) physicians' services; (4) skilled nursing facility (SNF) care; (5) early and periodic screening, diagnostic, and testing (EPSDT) services for recipients under age twenty-one; (6) home health services; and (7) family planning services.

Medicaid is financed through general tax revenues from the states and from federal income taxes; the federal matching share is at least 50 percent in each state, and ranges to a high of 77 percent in Mississippi. Like Medicare, the Medicaid program also paid providers on a cost-based, fee-for-service basis: after the addition of Titles XVIII and XIX to the Social Security Act, the volume of health care services reimbursed on a cost or cost-plus basis nearly doubled.

Distribution of National Health Care Expenditures

In 1985 more than seven out of every eight health care dollars were devoted to buying personal health care services; the remaining dollar was spent on prepayment, administration, government public health activities, research, and the construction of medical facilities. Expenditures for hospital care and physicians' services comprised the largest portions of personal health care expenditures: hospital care alone accounted for about 41 percent of all expenditures in 1985, while 19 percent was spent on physicians' services. Counting the 8 percent spent on nursing homes, roughly half of all expenditures went for care delivered in an institutional setting.

As more dollars were spent on health care from 1950 to 1985, the distribution of spending changed somewhat. The percentages of the health care dollar spent on hospital care and on nursing home care increased noticeably during this period, while all other components declined. From 1950 to 1985 the portion spent for hospital care increased from 36 to 46 percent, and the share for nursing home care increased from 2 percent to 9 percent.

Sources of Funds for National Health Care Expenditures

Public payers—federal, state, and local governments—paid for slightly more than 40 percent of health care expenditures in 1985, while private health insurance supplied an additional 31 percent. Direct out-of-pocket payments by patients accounted for 27 percent, or nearly all of the remainder.

The mix between private and public sources of funding for total health care expenditures has changed significantly from 1950 to 1985. Private funds paid for almost 80 percent of national health care expenditures in 1950. By 1965 the comparable figure was 74 percent; by 1980 it had declined to 56 percent. Nearly all of the corresponding growth of the public share was accounted for by the growth in federal governmental funds, which increased from 13 percent of total expenditures in 1950 to 29 percent in 1985. Over the period from 1950 to 1980, the share of funds supplied by state and local governments (about 14 percent) remained essentially constant.

The Payers' Revolution

More than anything else, the financing of health care services has been marked by a burgeoning purchasers' revolution. As the fourth major trend, the emerging buyers' market for health care promises to generate ripple effects throughout the delivery system.

"M-Day" was April 1, 1983, when Congress passed legislation enacting the Medicare Prospective Payment System (PPS), which went into effect six months later. Taking cues from the efficacy of similar state regulatory programs in effect in New Jersey and Maryland, the federal government fixed per-case payment rates for each of 468 diagnosis related groups (DRGs) into which patients are classified. Besides spelling the demise of cost-based reimbursement, PPS represents a 180-degree reversal of the historical incentives facing hospitals. More importantly, PPS embodies the federal government's recognition that, as a purchaser of 40 percent of all hospital care, it can dictate the price and terms of the transaction. More ominously, as the size of the recent inflation adjustment updating factors granted to hospitals indicates, the Medicare payment system is beginning to yield to budget deficit reduction pressures.

Given the option in 1981 of paying only the costs that are reasonable and adequate for an efficient and economically operated facility, most state Medicaid programs have adopted similar prospective methodologies. As of June 1985, only fourteen states continued to use the old Medicare retrospective cost-based principles as the standard for their Medicaid programs. In thirty-four states, some form of prospective methodology is in place, including seven DRG–based systems modeled after PPS. Effective as of July 1982, the Medicaid program in California (Medi-Cal) was empowered to act as a "prudent buyer" by contracting only with selected hospitals for inpatient services for Medi-Cal recipients. Reimbursement under a successfully negotiated Medi-Cal contract is on the basis of fixed per diem prices, and hospitals rushed to sign contracts with rates as low as 75 percent of their prior year's Medi-Cal per diems.

Commercial insurers have been essentially foreclosed from emulating the unilaterally and prospectively set prices established by Medicare. Although collectively they typically represent 25 percent of a hospital's revenues, it is rare that any individual company commands more than a 5 percent share. (Prudential, the single largest commercial insurer, has about a 4 percent share nationwide.) Federal antitrust laws currently prohibit collective or concerted negotiation by a group of companies, and no single company represents a sufficient volume of patients to threaten a hospital in attempting to negotiate prospectively determined charges.

Instead, commercial insurers—as well as Blue Cross and self-insured employers—have concentrated on reducing their insureds' use of health care. Vigorous utilization review and increased cost sharing by beneficiaries have been the two primary vehicles used by the private third-party payers to contain costs through discouraging unnecessary utilization. Hewitt Associates, an employee benefits consulting firm, documents that between 1982 and 1984 the percentages of firms requiring preadmission utilization review, concurrent review, and/or retrospective review; mandating or paying the entire cost for a second surgical opinion; and restricting care for specified conditions to an outpatient setting have increased dramatically. In 1984 26 percent of the 1,200 companies surveyed had

preadmission review programs compared with 2 percent of the
companies in 1982. In the same year, 79 percent of the companies used detailed claims utilization reports, 76 percent performed audits of paid claims, and 63 percent reviewed the
basis for the "usual and customary" amounts claimed.

Similarly, the number of plans requiring front-end deductibles has doubled, while coinsurance requirements continue to
grow. The same Hewitt Associates survey found that 52 percent of the companies surveyed included deductibles in employee health plans in 1984, compared with 17 percent in
1982; in 1984 only 50 percent of companies provided full
reimbursement of room and board costs in hospitals, compared with 75 percent in 1983; and full reimbursement for
surgery declined from 45 percent in 1979 to 27 percent in
1984.

Employers, as the penultimate payers of health care costs,
have long been plagued by inflation. To the surprise of many,
if not Lee Iacocca, 10 percent of the cost of an American made
automobile went for health care. After much hand wringing,
the business community took its cue from the get tough stance
adopted by Medicare. The most remarkable trend has been
the increase in the self-funding of insurance; currently over
half of all businesses have taken this route. Under the Employee Retirement Income Security Act of 1974 (ERISA), self-
funding permits employers to escape the regulations imposed
by state insurance laws, including premium taxes, minimum
reserve requirements, and mandatory covered benefits, and by
self-funding, employers can avoid the administrative costs levied by a third-party insurer.

Nontraditional Financing and/or Delivery Systems

Two of the most commonly encountered acronyms in the
health care field—HMO and PPO—are also among the most
recent phenomena to appear on the industry's landscape. Further, they represent the most radical departures from traditional financing schemes (indeed, to some they are the hall-
marks of the long-lost competitive marketplace) and are

among the most difficult to classify in a single niche, since they assume diverse and variegated structures and functions, often combining the elements of financing and delivery within a single entity.

Health Maintenance Organizations

Probably the key feature of an HMO or prepaid health plan is the combination of the functions of insurance and delivery within one organization, with the organization being financially at risk for the unanticipated utilization of health care services. Generically, in return for fixed annual or monthly payment (independent of the enrollees' use of services), HMOs assume contractual responsibility for providing a stated (usually fairly comprehensive) range of health care services.

As a result of an HMO's assumption of the financial risk of utilization, providers are faced with diametrically opposed incentives compared to their counterparts paid on a fee-for-service basis. Put differently, traditional financing arrangements offer incentives to hospitals and physicians to increase utilization in order to maximize income; HMOs, on the other hand, create incentives to reduce the demand for medical care services. In addition to discouraging the inappropriate use of hospital and physician services, HMOs encourage the use of less costly alternatives to hospitalization, such as primary and home health care, as well as emphasize wellness and prevention. Why has the HMO concept enjoyed such recent popularity? Not unexpectedly, providers have for a long time shunned the concept of prepaid health care and stifled its growth by lobbying for legislation protecting the patients' right to choose any physician or hospital. However, beginning in 1973 with the enactment of the Health Maintenance Organization Act, the federal government bought into the concept by establishing a program of financial assistance aimed at promoting federally qualified HMO development. Between 1973 and 1983 the government pumped $145 million in grants and $219 million in loans into 115 HMOs, and the private sector responded with an additional investment of $348 million. While direct financial support from the federal government terminated in 1981, federal and state policy makers have continued to promote capitated financing approaches, especially those covering Medicare beneficiaries and Medicaid recipients.

While HMOs are by no means a recent phenomenon (their history can be traced back to the late 1920s), their rate of growth clearly is. As recently as 1980, HMOs commanded an enrollment that was less than 4 percent of the population, up slightly from a comparable figure of 2 percent in 1970. In every year since 1981, growth in enrollment has accelerated, and by 1985 over 21 million people in the United States were enrolled in prepaid plans, or 7.9 percent of the population. Between 1982 and 1985 the number of investor-owned HMOs increased at an annualized rate of 70 percent; by December 1985 244 (or 52 percent) of the nation's 472 operational HMOs were organized as for-profit entities. Thirteen multistate HMO companies now offer shares that are publicly traded, and their stocks have displaced those of the hospital management companies as Wall Street's most highly touted.

Preferred Provider Organizations

Although PPOs are still in an early stage of development, they are perhaps the newest and fastest growing alternative to traditional financing systems, and thus likely to become an important and permanent force in the future: the number of Americans enrolled in health insurance plans offering a PPO option has more than tripled between 1983 and 1985. As of June 1986 an estimated 10.3 million Americans were eligible to use PPOs, up from 1.3 million in December 1984.

While preferred provider organizations, as a result of their diversity and flexibility, resist easy generalization, a generic PPO is essentially a defined, limited, and sometimes organized set of providers that contract with employers or insurers to provide a comprehensive set of health care services on a fee-for-service basis, usually at a negotiated, discounted rate. Subscribers are not usually locked into receiving care from one provider, but may choose to receive care inside or outside of the provider panel. Lower deductibles and copayments encourage subscribers to use the preferred providers, and although care rendered from nonpreferred providers is nearly always covered, subscribers are usually required to pay a greater proportion of provider fees or are subject to a penalty. Finally, all PPOs include some form of utilization review (UR), which serves to counter the incentives offered to providers through the retention of fee-for-service payment, if not functioning as the primary cost-containment mechanism.

The widespread appeal and rapid growth of PPOs have resulted from their seeming ability to provide something for everyone. For employers and insurers, PPOs promise to reduce health care costs quickly and without increasing the insureds' cost-sharing burdens, in much the way HMOs do. For providers, PPOs can be used as a means of increasing the volume of patients without accepting the financial risk inherent in prepaid financing. For patients, the choice of a PPO option preserves, to a great extent, the freedom of choice among providers, and may actually reduce their out-of-pocket liabilities compared to the choice of traditional indemnity insurance.

Physicians, hospitals, and physician/hospital joint ventures currently dominate sponsorship, supporting over half of all PPOs. Insurance company and Blue Cross/Blue Shield sponsorship, however, has been growing, currently constituting 20 percent of the total, as compared with 14 percent in 1984. However, because plans sponsored by insurance companies and the Blues are offered to a greater number of eligibles than those sponsored by providers, provider and insurer shares of total eligibles both stand at 40 percent.

As with HMOs, PPO activity is by no means dispersed equally across the United States: while operational PPOs are currently located in thirty-nine states, Puerto Rico, and the District of Columbia, five states—California, Colorado, Florida, Illinois, and Ohio—contain half of the operational arrangements.

At least four groups of factors have spawned the development of alternative financing and delivery systems. Since, from the provider's perspective, perhaps the greatest benefit offered by the sponsorship of or membership in an HMO or PPO is an increased volume of patients, areas characterized by an excess of hospital beds and/or physicians are conducive to the development of these financing arrangements. Relatively high ratios of beds and physicians per capita, especially when coupled with low hospital occupancy rates, declining hospital utilization, and competition among hospitals and among physicians for patients, are the most reliable indicia of an area ripe for PPO or HMO activity.

Second, prior HMO growth in a region probably paves the way for PPO development, for several reasons. While established HMOs may desensitize providers and insurers to the novelty of alternative delivery systems and demonstrate their cost-containment potential, they also represent market share encroachments and the threat of future utilization declines. Consequently, as mentioned above, providers may see a PPO as a workable compromise between capitated and traditional financing systems, promising cost containment while preserving fee-for-service reimbursement.

A third demographic factor, also correlated with HMO growth in an area, is the existence of a relatively young and rapidly growing population. As with those who enroll in HMOs, younger and more recently settled individuals have fewer and less established ties with physicians and hospitals, and are thus more amenable to restrictions placed on their choice of providers.

Finally, a strong business presence in controlling health care costs and in assuming the role and risk of a self-funded insurer is conducive to the growth of HMOs and PPOs. Business coalitions typically heighten provider awareness of employer and insurer interest in cost containment by disseminating comparative data on the relative efficiency of providers (especially when the variation in charges or lengths of stay is particularly pronounced). Moreover, by contributing to employer adoption of utilization review programs and insurance plans with significant employee cost sharing, they lay the groundwork for the eventual evolution of alternative financing and delivery arrangements.

HMOs, since they assume actuarial risk, are typically within the purview of state insurance laws requiring the maintenance of adequate financial reserves, dictating the form and content of provider and subscriber agreements, and governing permissible types of investments. Compared to HMOs, PPOs presently operate in almost a regulatory vacuum. The same freedom of choice and antidiscrimination laws that earlier impeded the growth of HMOs have been eliminated in most states and, in most cases, PPO–enabling legislation has been enacted.

The Demise of Freedom of Choice

Taken together, the dramatic recent growth in HMO and PPO enrollment; the willingness of public and private sector payers, as well as providers, to develop and offer prepaid and prudent-buyer plans; and the demonstrable cost-containment potential of each suggest that the fifth major trend is the continued growth and perhaps future dominance of HMOs and PPOs in the financing and delivery of health care.

Private sector insurers and employers are increasingly offering "triple-option" benefit plans to their insureds: an HMO, a PPO, and traditional indemnity coverage with stringent utilization review. Consumers now face an array of choices among insurance plans, but those offering unlimited choice among providers are typically the most expensive, and as such may be destined for extinction. The demise of the patient's freedom to choose the most expensive provider may prove to be the most significant, if not most cost-saving change wrought by the advent of HMOs and PPOs.

Alain Enthoven of Stanford University constructed a wonderful analogy to illustrate the problem of moral hazard inherent in the predominantly third-party insured system of health care finance, which is essentially the consumer's demand for more of a service if and when he or she does not bear its full

cost, as is the case generally with insurance. However, the last
two sentences of the analogy are particularly illustrative of
how the consumer's historical freedom of choice compounds
the problem of moral hazard:

*Imagine that you and nineteen friends belong to a lunch club. You agree that
you will each pay 5 percent of the total lunch bill for the group. Each member
is free to choose whatever he or she wants. Consider the incentives. Suppose you
go to lunch one day, feeling that a $2 salad would satisfy your desires and be
just fine for your health. You watch your friends order. One orders filet mignon;
another, lobster. You calculate that if you order the $12 filet instead of the $2
salad, it will cost you only $.50 more. There is little economic incentive for you
to choose the less costly meal. If the waiter expects a tip equal to 10 or 15 percent
of the bill, imagine which dishes he will recommend. And if everybody in town
is a member of this or a similar club, there is not much incentive for anybody
to open an economical restaurant that specializes in healthy $2 salads!*

As HMOs and similar at-risk or prepaid financing arrangements flourish, several problems are likely to surface. "Adverse selection" refers to the phenomenon whereby insureds
(if they possess greater knowledge of their health status or
future health care needs than do their insurers) select those
insurance plans under which the potential benefits to the insured are greater than the actuarially determined premiums.
In practice, it typically occurs when high-risk (and thus high-
cost) individuals seek plans with comprehensive benefits and
first-dollar coverage, as is the case with many HMOs. As a
result of open enrollment policies, the shifting composition of
the risk pool, and the impracticability of identifying those
beneficiary characteristics that predict future health care utilization, the setting of capitated rates for an HMO is a difficult
undertaking.

On the other hand, some have argued that HMOs engage
in or are susceptible to the "favorable selection" of healthier,
low-risk individuals. HMOs, for example, may market to employers more likely to attract employees in better health or
establish hours and offer services, such as routine physicals
and preventive dentistry, that are more convenient and ap-
pealing to a younger and healthier population. At the same

time, younger and healthier individuals, with no prior history of disease and thus few established relationships with physicians, are less averse to enrolling in an HMO that will limit their choice of provider.

The problem of adverse selection is compounded in instances in which employees are free to choose among multiple insurance packages or in markets in which several insurers offering plans with varying levels of coverage coexist. For example, if healthier individuals choose HMO coverage because it is less expensive, more convenient, or otherwise more attractive than traditional indemnity insurance, then the residuum of individuals left with or opting for traditional coverage will be less healthy. The greater risks and subsequent claims experience associated with the sicker individuals remaining in the traditional plans will necessitate premium increases for that group, thus widening the gap between HMO coverage and traditional coverage and driving out even more cost conscious individuals who may perceive that they are subsidizing the remaining relatively sicker beneficiaries. This phenomenon, referred to by some as an "adverse selection spiral," suggests that for employers offering multiple choice plans or for insurers competing with plans that offer different levels of coverage, the segmentation of the market into many small, experience-rated risk pools (with very little concomitant risk spreading) and the demise of extremely comprehensive insurance coverage may be inevitable.

The Economics of Health Care Delivery

While the market for health care services deviates radically from the competitive ideal, it still abides by the laws of economics. The anomalies and imperfections present in the financing and delivery system that have been responsible for its dysfunctional or malfunctional nature have also contributed substantially to the soaring costs of health care.

Perhaps the most visible of the peculiarities is the widespread prevalence of third-party insurance. Actually, since the need for hospitalization and the costs of that care are uncertain, and since consumers are believed to be risk averse, the availability of some amount of insurance will increase welfare by reducing uncertainty. However, once the need for hospitalization has occurred, the consumer will be charged less than the full costs of the resources. In such a situation, the consumer has the incentive for excess consumption, producing the phenomenon referred to earlier of moral hazard.

Moreover, in the absence of varying coinsurance levels, the consumer has the risk-free opportunity to choose among different levels of hospital care (each one entailing different amounts of resource expenditures). As Mancur Olson of the University of Maryland has astutely argued, the inherent freedom of choice among providers granted consumers in this situation is a major contributor to cost inflation.

Further, the U.S. tax system provides a major subsidy to the purchase of hospitalization insurance, since the employers' contributions for their employees' insurance are tax deductible business expenses for employers but not taxable income to employees. The subsidy encourages individuals to purchase "too much" insurance, in the sense that coinsurance payments and deductibles are lower than they otherwise would have been. Similar reasoning suggests that Medicare and Medicaid copayments are too low.

Finally, even without the problems of moral hazard, unrestrained freedom of choice, and tax subsidization, the structural nature of the hospitalization insurance market and its potential for anticompetitive behavior represent another deficiency in the hospital market. Although the close relationship, based on history, between Blue Cross and hospitals has waned, most Blue Cross Plans still reimburse hospitals at lower rates than do commercial insurers, and in a number of states have a variety of tax and regulatory advantages. Further, in many states Blue Cross possesses substantial market power as a result of its size, hospital linkages, and regulatory advantages.

A second major distortion is the consumer's lack of information, not only of his or her own medical care needs, but of the value, quality, and effectiveness of services provided by physi-

cians and hospitals. Medical societies, through the private regulation of the "ethical" practices of physicians, have prevented
advertising and suppressed the dissemination of information
on price and quality. Furthermore, physicians act as purchasing agents on behalf of consumers of hospital care, typically
selling complementary services at the same time. Thus unlike
most producers, physicians may greatly influence the demand
for their services. Finally, uncertainty plays a role from the
physician's standpoint as well. Despite extensive training and
knowledge, the lack of accepted standards of medical practice
may induce many physicians to practice defensive medicine or
continue to provide services as long as their marginal benefits
are greater than zero.

Third, more than four-fifths of the hospitals in the United
States are organized as not-for-profit entities, and thus motivated by different financial incentives than an investor-owned
concern. In nearly every industry besides that which produces
hospital care, the classic model of economic production and
distribution is the private, for-profit firm. In atomistic markets
with informed purchasers and low barriers to entry, for-profit
firms maximize social welfare by producing, at an equilibrium
state, exactly the quantity and mix of goods and services that
consumers want to buy. Goods and services are also produced
in the least costly manner, since existing firms and new entrants are ready to shift resources into the market if excess
profits are observed.

However, for most people there seems to be something
intuitively wrong about making money from the delivery of
health care. Thus despite the growth of investor-owned
chains, not-for-profit hospitals continue to play the dominant
role in the delivery of hospital care. Surprisingly, however,
there is little agreement on the theoretical basis for the existence of not-for-profit hospitals or other firms.

The most accepted theory is that not-for-profits exist in
industries where consumers, due to a lack or asymmetry of
information compared to sellers, are unable to determine the
quality and quantity of the services they may need to purchase.
The complexity of hospital services, their nonstandard charac-

ter, and the circumstances under which they are delivered all suggest that it is difficult for the patient or third-party payer to ascertain the quality and necessity of services. Interestingly, however, physician services, nursing home care, and most other health care goods and services seem to be an exception to this theory of market failure. Economic theories of behavior of private not-for-profit hospitals usually ascribe to them objective functions other than that of maximizing profits, such as maximizing quality; attempting to recover costs; maximizing output, in terms of number of patients served or volume and mix of services provided; or serving as "physicians' workshops" and as such maximizing physician income.

However, most agree that a large part of the increase in hospital costs was due to the lack, in the historical methods by which hospitals were paid, of any incentives or inducements for hospitals to control costs or operate more efficiently. Until the early 1980s, Medicare, Medicaid, and most Blue Cross Plans reimbursed hospitals on the basis of the costs that the hospitals actually incurred. Further, under retrospective cost-based reimbursement, all capital investment is nearly risk free. In recognition of the inherently inflationary nature of retrospective reimbursement, the key attribute of Medicare's new payment system has been to alter the historical method by replacing it with an alternative *prospective* methodology.

While some argue that the definition includes additional elements, prospective reimbursement is a generic term given to those methods of paying hospitals under which the rates of payment are set in advance for a prospective period of time, and hospitals are paid such amounts regardless of the costs actually incurred during such a period. Generically, prospective reimbursement systems move the locus of pricing power from individual hospitals to an external authority that establishes fixed-dollar limits for payments to hospitals. Prospective methodologies sever the direct link that exists in retrospective reimbursement between the cost of services provided by a hospital and the revenues received by that hospital. That is, the *sine qua non* of prospective reimbursement is that the hospital is at risk for the costs it incurs. Under a prospective system, if a hospital's costs exceed the established payment rates of revenue caps, the hospital will face a real dollar loss. By the same token, most systems permit hospitals to retain, as profit, any difference between incurred costs that are less than the prospective payment amounts.

Health Care Expenditures in the National Economy

The United States has witnessed, in the past three decades, persistent and substantial increases in the costs of health care. Adjectives such as "rampant," "explosive," and "staggering," chosen by researchers to describe the phenomenon in the introductory paragraphs of many articles, do not overstate the dimensions of the problem, nor its implications. Few phenomena admit to their intractability as completely as rates of growth in health care expenditures. Before concluding the chapter, it is illuminating to review once again, as Donald Cohodes has phrased it, the numbers which have by now become a painful litany.

National expenditures for health care services have increased at an average annual rate of 10.4 percent during the thirty-five-year period from 1950 to 1985. In 1950 national health care expenditures were $12.7 billion; by 1965 they had increased to $41.9 billion, and were $425 billion in 1985. Put differently, in 1950 the United States spent about 1 billion dollars per month for health care; by 1985 it was spending more than 1 billion dollars a day.

In every year from 1950 to 1985 except three (1973, 1978, and 1984), the inflation in national spending for health care outpaced that of the rest of the economy. More than half of the increase in national expenditures represented real growth: over the period from 1950 to 1985, the annualized growth in real national health care expenditures was 5.9 percent.

As a result of the persistent real rate of increase in health care outlays, a continually growing share of the gross national product (GNP—a measure of the total production of the U.S. economy) was devoted to health care. The share of the GNP spent on health care increased from 4.4 percent in 1950 to 6.6

percent in 1965; by 1980 the United States more than doubled the share by devoting 10.7 percent of the GNP to the health care sector. Such a shift of wealth implies that other goods and services—housing, food, national defense—were consuming a decreasing proportion of the gross national product.

Conclusion

In the course of describing the most prominent features of the current financing and delivery landscape, I have argued that five trends will be among the most forceful in shaping the future terrain. Hospitals will continue to band together in systems, and for-profit enterprises will spread vertically, if not horizontally, across the hospital industry. At the same time, the burgeoning excess capacity of hospitals and supply of physicians—brought about by different forces—will splinter the historical cohesiveness that characterized the providers' side of the market. The purchasers of health care, long accustomed to a passive role, have become the sleeping giants that have awakened, and the shift of power to them has been facilitated by a dearth of patients to treat. Finally, and in large part a result of all of the above trends, radical new financing arrangements have emerged which, by restricting the patient's unfettered freedom of choice and the provider's incentive to provide services as long as their marginal benefit is not negative, promise to exorcise several of the remaining demons that plague the health care market.

As is hopefully clear, the spillover effects of the latter two trends—the payers' revolution and the future dominance of alternative financing and delivery systems—should serve to sustain and reinforce the former three trends. The market leverage increasingly being wielded by health care purchasers is likely to accelerate the affiliations among hospitals and the agglomeration of hospitals and physicians into bargaining units able to match the payers' power. The predicted growth in HMOs and PPOs, taken together with the success of direct utilization controls, suggests that the declines in hospital and physician utilization are not going to bottom out in the near future. The coming surplus of physicians and hospital beds may be more aptly characterized as simply a shortage of patients. In the ensuing scramble for revenue-generating utilization in the face of an uncertain future, providers will be even more receptive to sharing and consolidating their resources, diversifying into nontraditional lines of business, and selling health care services for a profit.

More importantly, the evolution of the health care financing and delivery system of the 1980s promises to turn the spotlight on, if not force the resolution of, a critical issue not yet discussed in this chapter. Close to 33 million Americans lacked hospitalization insurance in 1982, and perhaps another 16 million had inadequate coverage. Of these two populations, roughly one-half of the uninsured and one-third of the underinsured were also below 150 percent of the 1982 poverty level, making questionable their ability to pay for hospital care. Between 1980 and 1982 the number of inadequately insured poor—the group presumably most dependent on free hospital care—grew nearly 21 percent, a rate that suggests their ranks are even more swollen today.

Many believe that the newly emerging competitive and market oriented financing and delivery system will be more efficient and less costly than the one it is gradually replacing, and such beliefs may prove to be true. However, one of the fundamental attributes of a competitive marketplace is its failure to provide nonmarket goods, or those services for which no payment is received. As the current era of prudent purchasing and prospective payment unravels the historical cross-subsidies which once paid for such goods, one can foresee several alternatives: hospitals will strain even harder to weed inefficiencies out of their operations, or sacrifice their margins, or refuse to provide services for which they receive no payment. Charity care, graduate medical education, technology development, and research are some of the archetypal nonmarket goods whose provision will be jeopardized if the present system continues along its current path of evolution. Where the compromises will be struck between competition and cooperation, between efficiency and equity, between cost containment and quality, and between the financial solvency and social responsibility of providers, insurers, and government remains to be seen.

2

Public Opinion and
Health Care Costs

ROBERT J. BLENDON AND
DREW E. ALTMAN

Introduction

R ecent press reports have proclaimed victory—or at least
light at the end of the tunnel—in the nation's battle to
control its health care costs. Battered by DRGs, HMOs, PPOs,
PROs, and other cost-cutting weapons, the problem of health
care costs is said to be succumbing to the weight of a rapidly
changing health care system. However, despite the recent re-

ROBERT J. BLENDON is senior vice president of The Robert Wood
Johnson Foundation in Princeton, New Jersey. He has served on the
faculties of the Woodrow Wilson School of Public and International
Affairs at Princeton University and the Johns Hopkins University
School of Hygiene and Public Health.
DREW E. ALTMAN is commissioner of the New Jersey Department
of Human Services and former vice president of The Robert Wood
Johnson Foundation. He has been a research fellow in the Interdisci-
plinary Programs in Health at the Harvard School of Public Health,
and has served with the Health Care Financing Administration in the
Department of Health and Human Services.
   The views expressed in this article are those of the authors, and no
official endorsement by The Robert Wood Johnson Foundation is
intended or should be inferred.

ports of the cost crisis demise, all the available evidence points otherwise—health care costs continue to remain a major national problem.

(1) Independent forecasters suggest that if current trends continue, the nation will expend a staggering $2 trillion, or 14 percent of its gross national product, for health care in the year 2000.

(2) In July of 1986 the federal government announced that the medical care component of the consumer price index (CPI) once again was rising at a dramatically faster rate than the overall consumer price index. During the first six months of 1986, the medical component of the CPI rose at an annual rate of 7.5 percent, while the overall index rose by 1.7 percent.

(3) Health policy journal articles now report that the recent sharp reduction in the nation's health care spending relates primarily to the United States' overall success in containing inflation and renewed economic growth, not to major changes in the health care system. Real growth rates in spending for health care continue with little change, rising at historically high rates. In 1984 the real rate of increase in health spending was 4.5 percent. This figure is average for the decade and does not approach the lowest rates, achieved in the years 1973–1974 and 1979–1980 of 2.5 and 2 percent respectively.

(4) A recent analysis of trends in the nation's overall health expenditures shows that the savings from the dramatic reduction in the use of hospitals have been almost completely offset by the sharp rise in outlays for out-of-hospital health services —physician's fees, nursing homes, home care, drugs, etc.

In short, despite some press accounts and political claims to the contrary, the underlying health care cost problem is still very much with us. In addition, a $200 billion federal deficit, an uncertain economy, and the serious problem of 37 million Americans without health insurance all provide a real stimulus for continuing concern with this problem by the nation's private and public decision makers.

Public Opinion on Health Care

But before anything more can be done with this issue, we must answer this question: why, despite so much earlier attention to this problem, have we been unable as a nation to agree on a coherent strategy or solution for it? We believe that the answer lies in the fact that the general public is much less inclined to take major steps to resolve this problem than are the leaders of government and business, the major payers of today's health care bills. Although public opinion is only one of many factors that influence the nation's decision making, in an area such as health care, where any major cost-saving strategy will affect the medical care of millions of people, public opinion sets important practical and political boundaries within which decision makers can operate. Thus the public's views on health care costs have been crucial in preventing any single strategy from being adopted.

In a 1984 paper presented in the *New England Journal of Medicine,* we assessed the implication of public opinion for the nation's efforts to control health care costs, analyzing fifteen national opinion polls conducted between 1981 and 1984. In this chapter we update that analysis by reviewing twenty more recent polls, taking into particular account the implications of the current concern with the federal deficit. We also assess in more depth the implications of public opinion for specific cost control measures the country might take. We begin with a summary of the major themes drawn from the polls.

Data from Polls and Surveys

Reality 1. There are many other things on the public's mind besides health care costs. Today the public sees rising costs as the nation's number one problem in health care. However, it does not rank this issue very high on a list of the most important problems now facing the nation.

In 1986 surveys showed that rising health costs did not

appear among the ten most important problems facing this country, as seen by the public. Unemployment, threat of nuclear war, the federal deficit, and others all ranked higher. Thus efforts to resolve the complex problem of health care costs take place in an environment in which the public's attention and energies are largely focused on other national problems. In the parlance of the pollsters, this is not a high-salience issue.

Reality 2. Most Americans are concerned about their own, not business's or the government's health cost problem. Americans are disturbed by the sharply rising prices of their health care, particularly the increasing cost of a stay in the hospital or a visit to a physician. However, contrary to the views of many national leaders and economists, most Americans are not troubled by the growing share of the nation's economy that is devoted to health care. In fact, most believe that our society currently spends *too little* rather than too much on these services.

In 1984 surveys showed that two out of three Americans saw the high cost of medical care as the major problem facing the nation's health care system. Most of those polled (78 percent) recognized that health care costs have been rising at a faster rate than general inflation, and most (68 percent) believe that this trend has made the costs of their own medical care unreasonable.

However, Americans are not particularly concerned by the increasing share of the nation's resources devoted to health care. In 1984 only 14 percent of the public thought that our society was spending too much for health care, and 53 percent thought we were not spending enough. Even with 81 percent of the public seeing our escalating federal deficit as a serious problem for the country, 54 percent of Americans believe that federal spending for health care should be *increased,* 71 percent still favor some form of national health insurance, and 89 percent favor the enactment of a catastrophic health insurance program for the elderly.

Although these poll results may seem contradictory, they

are consistent with the public's general belief that inflation has made many important family needs, including housing, new automobiles, food, and medical care, prohibitively expensive. Americans believe that their vision of constant material improvement is threatened not only by the cost of a six-day stay at the hospital, but also by the high price of a new home or automobile or a pound of meat. It is the unit price people see on their bills and pay that troubles the public most, not the proportion of national resources spent for housing, automobiles, meat, or medical care.

Reality 3. People are happier with the status quo than one might think. Most Americans state that the country's present health care arrangements are not satisfactory. Surveys show that almost three-quarters of the American public believe that the U.S. health care system requires fundamental change. One in four of the general population and one in three of the nation's elderly say that our health care system has so much wrong with it today that "we need to completely rebuild it." Barely one in five Americans thinks our country's health care arrangements "work pretty well." Sixty-seven percent say that doctors are too interested in making money, 73 percent that physician fees are not usually reasonable, and 62 percent that physicians do not spend enough time with their patients.

However, in sharpest possible contrast to the public's view of physicians in general, Americans like their own doctors. Seventy-two percent say that their own physician is not too interested in making money, 77 percent that he or she spends enough time with them, and 71 percent that their own physician's fees are usually reasonable.

With regard to their own most recent illnesses, 72 percent of those who were hospitalized in the previous year, 78 percent of those who have seen a physician recently, and 63 percent of those who have needed emergency treatment say that they were completely satisfied with the medical care they actually received. The only major complaint (expressed by about 40 percent of those receiving care) was with high out-of-pocket costs that were not paid by an individual's health insurance plan. Similarly, in a 1985 study, 95 percent of Americans with a regular physician said they were satisfied with the doctor, and 93 percent of those recently hospitalized rated the care they received as good to excellent.

Reality 4. "You caused this problem, not me." Most Americans do not see themselves as having any responsibility for creating the problem of health care costs. Surveys show that only about 25 percent of Americans think that they have a great deal of personal responsibility for the nation's rising health care costs. Most believe that the high costs of health care are due to factors other than their own behavior.

Reality 5. "I trust my doctor at least more than you." With regard to the various proposals that have been advanced for slowing the rise in the nation's health care costs, the views of practicing physicians are often more influential with the public than the opinions of the groups proposing change, such as government officials, business, and labor leaders.

Surveys show that three out of four people believe physicians bear a major responsibility for the nation's rising health care costs, and two out of three say they are beginning to lose faith in doctors. However, physicians still maintain a unique credibility with the public.

Survey results indicate that Americans continue to place more confidence in the leadership of American medicine than in almost any other leadership group. Unpublished data from Louis Harris and Associates reveal that, although the public's confidence in medicine has fallen dramatically since the mid-1960s (from 73 to 39 percent), in 1985 it still ranked substantially higher than public confidence in the leadership of the nation's major companies (17 percent), organized labor (10 percent), the Congress (16 percent), and the executive branch (19 percent).

Likewise, in 1985 58 percent of the American people ranked physicians high or very high on "honesty and ethical standards," whereas less than 25 percent gave similar high marks to the major groups proposing change—senators and members of Congress (22 percent), business executives (23 percent), and labor union leaders (13 percent). To bring this home most forcibly, labor union families rank physicians higher, in terms of integrity, than labor union leaders (55 and 16 percent respectively). All in all, three of four Americans still believe "most doctors are generally dedicated to helping people."

Moreover, the public is more trusting of information from the medical community (79 percent) than from either organized labor (46 percent) or major companies (43 percent). This strong credibility is reflected in public responsiveness to the major concerns of physicians about various cost-containment proposals.

Reality 6. Cut the deficit, but don't cut funds for health. Though the majority of Americans see the deficit as a major threat to the nation, they do not see cutting federal health outlays as the most desirable way to reduce it. Instead Americans would rather see a sharp cut in the nation's defense outlays (71 percent) as an alternative to reducing federal health expenditures.

In 1985–86 polls showed that 58 percent of Americans characterized the deficit as a very serious national problem and one of the most important problems facing the country. In addition, 61 percent agreed that it is very important to cut the deficit in half by 1988. However, as shown in Figures 1 and 2, at the same time, 89 percent of Americans opposed as a deficit-reducing measure cutting Medicare spending; 79 percent, Medicaid; 82 percent, federal health programs for women and children; 61 percent, taxing health insurance premiums paid by employers; and 74 percent, reducing support for biomedical research. In fact, public support is so strong for continuing federal health care expenditures in this Gramm-Rudman era that 66 percent of Americans said that, if necessary, they would support a small earmarked federal sales tax with the money going for health care.

The apparent unwillingness of Americans to make sacrifices in their health care for the purpose of reducing the deficit

FIGURE 1. America's View of Deficit Reduction Measures

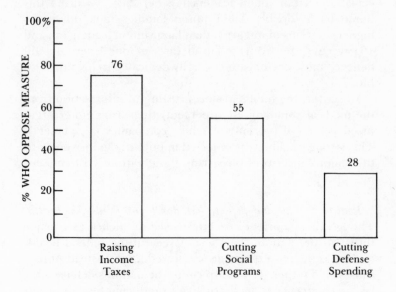

appears to relate to two factors. The first is the public's continuing belief that the nation is spending "too little" in health. The second is that the public does not place the same priority on solving the deficit "crisis" as on our earlier serious problem of sharply rising inflation. Unlike the early 1980s, when 73 percent of Americans thought inflation was the single most important national problem and that governmental expenditures had to be reduced in response, today only 16 percent see the deficit as the nation's *single* most important concern. Thus we do not see the public response of 1980, when 66 percent of Americans said "controlling inflation was worth a substantial cut in federal expenditures for the programs they most liked."

Today what most Americans would support in an effort to reduce the deficit would be a "freeze" on federal health expenditures.

FIGURE 2. America's View of Deficit Reduction Measures

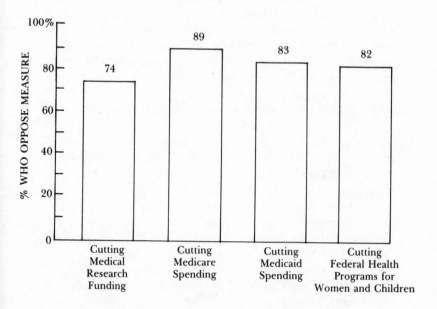

Solutions

Broad Implications

Most Americans are reasonably satisfied with their medical care arrangements and do not want to change them to reduce national health spending. As a result, despite the concern with rising health costs, we are extremely unlikely to see a consensus reached on any single "solution" to the health cost problem that would require significant change in how Americans get their health care.

Further findings from the polls underscore this resistance to cost-containment strategies that would require substantial changes in how people currently get their medical care. Only 8 percent of Americans give a high priority to enactment of either "socialized" medicine or a national health service; only 33 percent would agree to go to physicians and doctors from a list provided by insurance companies, with no extra charges; only 21 percent wish to limit the use of new, expensive medical equipment and techniques; only 37 percent would be interested in paying a higher health insurance deductible; only 28 percent favor a tax on employer-paid health insurance; only 18 percent would be willing to wait longer than usual for an appointment with a physician; only 21 percent would be willing to give up the right to sue for malpractice; and only 40 percent would like to save money by giving up their personal doctor and being treated by a group of physicians, e.g., at a clinic.

The dichotomy between the public's desire for a reorganization of the nation's health care system on the one hand and the desire to maintain their present personal health care arrangements on the other can best be seen in this last survey question. The majority of the Americans polled are not in favor of giving up their own personal physicians for care delivered by lower-cost physician groups. In fact, studies show that the major reason many working Americans choose not to join HMOs is their reluctance to break ties with their family physicians. Thus we see in 1984 only 8 percent of Americans expressing a great deal of interest in joining an HMO, with another 32 percent expressing some interest in possible enrollment. However, the public is quite enthusiastic (66 percent) about requiring low-income people to use less costly clinics or HMOs. The message seems to be: "reorganize the nation's health care for others, but don't change my own health care arrangements."

In contrast to these approaches, two broad categories of cost-containment strategies are most acceptable to the public: (1) those seen as increasing the range of choices people have available or as not disrupting existing health care arrangements; or (2) those that look to the public as if they might actually improve the quality of their care while also possibly saving money.

The favorite obvious option available in the first category is to change the way hospitals and doctors are paid and to reduce levels of payment. Because this option is not viewed by the average American as directly threatening his or her medical arrangements, changing payment for health care institutions or professionals is the major short-term cost-containment strategy most acceptable to the public. For example, 60 percent of Americans find government price controls on doctors and hospitals relatively acceptable. Seventy percent favor a requirement that hospitals budget prospectively using a DRG system. Seventy-seven and 84 percent respectively favor a requirement that physicians and hospitals publish their fees. And, despite strong public support for services for the elderly, 55 percent favor freezing Medicare payments to doctors and hospitals.

In terms of saving money through new arrangements that might improve the quality of their health care, Americans see the reduction of unnecessary institutionalization as a positive objective. People are fearful of going to a hospital or nursing home. Thus 75 percent support the requirement of a second opinion for surgery, 56 percent find it acceptable to encourage performance of tests and minor surgery in outpatient clinics and doctors' offices, and 46 percent strongly favor home treatment for serious chronic illness. Similarly, 80 percent believe that the family of an unconscious, terminally ill patient should be able to have the physician remove life-support systems. All these potentially cost-saving measures are seen by the public as improving the quality of life. They also correspond to the public's view that medical care costs can be reduced without reducing the quality of health care (86 percent).

Of particular interest is the fact that Americans are the most resistant to major cost-containment proposals when they are directed at the health care needs of the elderly. Today, 56 percent of Americans think we spend *too little* on health services for the elderly. When questioned about the looming financial problems facing Medicare, 54 percent oppose raising the Part B monthly premium paid by those covered by Medicare for doctors' fees, 64 percent oppose increasing the deductible under Medicare, and 54 percent of Americans oppose freezing the rates Medicare pays the hospitals. In addition, two out of three elderly Americans say that they are currently not interested in joining an HMO.

Specific Choices

Generally, the suggested solutions to the problem of rising health care costs can be categorized as either short term or long term. The long-term approaches are of two types: biomedical breakthroughs and major positive changes in life style. Not surprisingly, both are acceptable to the general public. Polls show that the public rates medical research as the highest priority for national research support. In addition, more than half of those polled believe we should give more emphasis to the prevention of disease. Unfortunately, however, neither of these long-term approaches is likely to have a large impact on health costs in the next decade.

The short-term solutions that have been proposed to slow the increase in health care costs include: (1) regulation—reimbursement, utilization, and capital-investment controls; (2) reducing the future supply of physicians, now growing at three times the rate of the general population; (3) competition—the restructuring of health insurance benefits and the development of alternative health plans, such as HMOs and preferred provider organizations; (4) curtailment of services to the poor, through major reductions in public sector support of health services for low-income citizens and the unemployed; (5) rationing of high-cost equipment and procedures; and (6) nationalization of the industry—the British and Swedish solution to the problem.

Polls tell us that the last two options are not seen by most Americans as desirable for the United States. Although there is support (74 percent) for regionalizing "big ticket" technological equipment, such as nuclear-magnetic-resonance and computerized axial tomography (CAT) scanners, only 21 percent of Americans are in favor of rationing costly new technological approaches. In fact, 90 percent of Americans favor the continued development of highly expensive heart, kidney, and

other organ transplantation, and 64 percent favor moving
ahead with the development of new vaccines by means of
genetic engineering. Ninety-two percent of Americans show
no strong interest in either "socialized medicine" or a British-
style health system.

On the other hand, there is support for the first three short-
term solutions—regulation, reducing the supply of physicians,
and competition—though they are grounded in different
premises. Such support is limited, however, and does not suggest a blanket endorsement of these strategies. For example,
58 percent of the public support the idea of paying hospitals
a fixed, prospectively set payment for their services. However,
the majority of Americans are opposed to a comprehensive
federal regulatory system to control health care costs or to
limitations on the use of expensive medical procedures.

In addition, some Americans will accept higher out-of-
pocket payments as part of their insurance coverage or are
willing to receive care from less costly groups of physicians,
but the majority are opposed to or uncomfortable with these
alternatives. Most Americans are willing to use less costly physician groups on a voluntary, but not a mandatory, basis. Similarly, joining an HMO would be more acceptable if their current physician were part of the plan.

Likewise, there appears to be little public opposition to reducing the numbers of young physicians graduating from
medical school in the future. In 1984 only 26 percent of
Americans thought there were not enough physicians in their
community. On the other hand, 12 percent thought there were
too many, and 59 percent thought the numbers were about
right.

This leaves one final short-term solution: curtailment of
public programs supporting health care for the poor—an approach that may prove extraordinarily expensive over the long
haul in both human and economic terms. Surveys suggest
some reason for concern that we might move in this direction.
Though polls show public support for the Medicaid program,
in practice, eligibility of Medicaid is closely linked to the nation's welfare programs. In striking contrast to medical care,

welfare is an area in which Americans are highly ambivalent, with 59 percent believing that "welfare benefits make poor people dependent and encourage them to stay poor."

Conclusion

For those heavily in favor of competition or regulation, or for others who seek still more sweeping changes in our health care system, the polls offer more bad news than good. No single solution, much less a sweeping change, would appear politically feasible. Nor does public opinion support a clear direction for the smaller changes that may be necessary. While there is support for certain elements of both the competitive and regulatory approaches, public opposition comes with the degree of change in individual personal medical care arrangements, not the philosophy inherent in these two approaches.

There should be nothing surprising about these survey findings. And they do not necessarily imply that the health cost problem need go unchecked. Instead of picking any one way to go, they suggest that the nation must proceed along several different lines. Many supporters of competitive or regulatory policies may have a difficult time reconciling themselves to a state like Massachusetts, which boasts both an all-payer rate-setting system and the third highest HMO penetration in the nation. But in this instance, if not in matters political, it may be a state like Massachusetts with its "many routes to Rome" philosophy that offers the greatest promise of long-term public support for cost-containment measures. In summary, it is clear that the advocates of sweeping solutions for the nation's health care cost problem are right about the need for action, but the public seems to have a very different sense than the "experts" about what action should be taken at this particular time.

Bibliography

ABC National News Survey. Storrs, Ct.: Roper Center, University of Connecticut. July 8, 1984; January 16, 1985; October 28, 1985; January 26, 1986.

Associated Press Survey. Storrs, Ct.: Roper Center, University of Connecticut. November 19, 1984.

Blendon, R.J., "Health Policy Choices for the 1990s," *Issues in Science and Technology*, 2, no. 4 (1986), 65–73.

Blendon, R.J., and D.E. Altman, "Public Attitudes About Health Care Costs: A Lesson in National Schizophrenia," *New England Journal of Medicine*, 311 (1984), 613–616.

Freshnock, L.J., *Physician and Public Attitudes on Health Care Issues*. Chicago: American Medical Association, 1984.

Lipset, M.L., and B.J. Wattenberg, eds., "Opinion Roundup," *Public Opinion*, 2, no. 1 (1979), 27–28.

———, "Opinion Roundup," *Public Opinion*, 2, no. 5 (1979), 30–31.

———, "Opinion Roundup," *Public Opinion*, 8, no. 1 (1985), 19–26.

———, "Opinion Roundup," *Public Opinion*, 8, no. 3 (1985), 26–27.

Louis Harris and Associates Survey. Storrs, Ct.: Roper Center, University of Connecticut. September 9, 1984; January 2, 1985; January 27, 1985; February 12, 1985; November 4, 1985; January 7, 1986; February 3, 1986.

———, *Shaping a Compromise: Americans' Attitudes toward Reducing the Deficit and Simplifying Taxes*. New York: Sentry Life Insurance Company, 1985.

———, "A Report Card on HMOs: 1980-84." Menlo Park, Ca.: Kaiser Foundation, 1985.

Merrill, J.C., and R.J. Wasserman, "Growth in National Expenditures: Additional Analyses," *Health Affairs*, 5, no. 4 (1986), 91–97.

Pollack, M.A., and U. Cohan, "Why Health Care Costs are Having a Relapse," *Business Week*, May 12, 1986, p. 34.

Public Policy Analysis Group Survey. Storrs, Ct.: Roper Center, University of Connecticut. January 14, 1985.

Shriver, J., ed., "Most Important Problem," *Gallup Report*, 219 (1983), 4–6.

———, "Federal Budget Deficit," *Gallup Report*, 237 (1985), 2–7.

———, "Honesty and Ethical Standards," *Gallup Report*, 238 (1985), 2–28.

———, "Most Important Problem," *Gallup Report*, 243 (1985), 11–14.

Tyson, K.W., and J.C. Merrill, "Health Care Institutions: Survival in a Changing Environment," *Journal of Medical Education*, 59 (1984), 773–781.

USA Today—Gordon Black Survey. Storrs, Ct.: Roper Center, University of Connecticut. November 29, 1984.

3

The Loss of Innocence: Health Care under Siege

DONALD R. COHODES

Introduction

Ironically, the assassin's bullet that shattered one set of dreams set in motion the hopes and aspirations of millions of others. The Democratic electoral landslide of 1964, propelled by the nation's loss of President John F. Kennedy, led to the swift proposal and passage of a series of reforms now known as the Great Society Programs. Medicare and Medicaid, the health care entitlement programs for the elderly and the poor, which were partially by-products of a long, incremental battle over national health insurance, were swept along with the Democratic tidal wave. Enactment was swift and served as

DONALD R. COHODES is the executive director of policy for Blue Cross and Blue Shield Association in Chicago. He also serves as a senior program consultant for The Robert Wood Johnson Foundation, and is an associate in the School of Hygiene and Public Health with the Johns Hopkins Medical Institutions. Dr. Cohodes has written extensively on issues regarding the financing, planning, and payment of health care, and he is currently editor of *Inquiry*, the Blue Cross and Blue Shield Association's Journal of Health Care Organization, Provision, and Financing.

a partial tribute to the vision of America's lost leader. To many, Medicare and Medicaid became the symbol of hope, the assurance that the government was the agent of the people and that in their moments of greatest vulnerability the elderly and the poor would have some recourse.

As originally envisioned, Medicare and Medicaid were to be low-cost programs easily financed from the tax revenues flowing in from a growing economy. Only hindsight is always twenty-twenty; none of the actuaries in the government anticipated the magnitude of demand that was unleashed by the introduction of Medicare and Medicaid. What was once thought to be an easily managed undertaking grew and grew until the demands placed on the federal government could no longer be ignored. A recession-plagued economy in the 1970s, coupled with tremendously escalating costs, served as the clarion call for cost containment.

Medicare was a legitimate target for congressional oversight, while Medicaid presented a more complex situation due to its federal-state revenue-sharing characteristics. In the late 1970s and early 1980s, the first significant warning signs about Medicare's fiscal solvency emerged. Past Medicare "crises" had been resolved by simply increasing the payroll tax to support the new expenditures. This one was not going to be resolved so simply. Predictions were that the trust fund itself would be bankrupt by the end of the decade. On the heels of a similar Social Security crisis, it suggested to some that large portions of America's welfare state were collapsing. The momentum triggered by the perception of the risk to the set of social contracts binding the American people to their government led to the single largest change in Medicare since its inception in 1965. Medicare would no longer be sacrosanct; it, too, would be subject to the heavy hand of budget restraint. Medicare's payment system conversion from retrospective cost-based to prospective per-case payment, based on diagnostic related groups, was simply a harbinger of the change in attitude and policy yet to come. The conversion of Medicare from a "hands-off" to a "hands-on" program set in motion a series of forces that will fundamentally change the financing and delivery of health care for the remainder of the twentieth century and, perhaps, beyond.

The Medicare trust fund crisis alone did not trigger this destruction of the old health care financing paradigm. Medicaid and private sector initiatives also provided further impetus. Medicaid is a classic federal matching funds program. By meeting certain minimum program benefit and eligibility criteria, states could spend "fifty-cent dollars," using the federal matching funds to purchase care on behalf of the poor. Like Medicare, Medicaid was caught in the tentacles of cost containment. Budget pressure at the state level caused the Medicare scenario to be replayed or expanded on a micro level, time and time again. Medicaid parsimony accompanied Medicare cutbacks, leaving those who provided care to the poor and the elderly wondering whether the funds to finance these programs would still be there in the future.

This retreat from collective responsibility can be viewed as an incremental repudiation of the Great Society Programs. The policies of the federal and state governments in the mid-1980s seem directed at returning to an idealized version of individual self-responsibility as the guiding force in health care. Government's role was to be the payer of last resort, with the test of eligibility for "last resortdom" applied as vigorously as possible. In essence what appears to be occurring in the mid- to late 1980s is a return to the values and policies of the pre-Medicare and Medicaid era. This withdrawal from responsibility is hidden under many guises. Medicare payment reform is both a reform and a euphemism for minimizing federal fiscal responsibility. "Benefit redesign" is a code word for unenlightened cutbacks, and individual responsibility can be translated into a strategy to shift the burden of payment from government to individuals.

Budget realities cannot be denied or ignored. The large federal deficits of the 1980s and the anticipated deficits in the 1990s will continue to bring incessant pressure on the scope and generosity of the federal government's welfare programs. The withdrawal from governmental leadership sets the stage for the private sector to play a far more significant role in the financing and delivery of health care than has been witnessed since the advent of Medicare.

Down with the Old, Up with the New

If the financing and delivery of health care itself were not so complicated, the emergence of the alphabet soup of acronyms that characterize the health care marketplace would be somewhat more palatable. It is easy to get lost in the menu of DRGs (diagnostic related groups, a payment mechanism used by Medicare and a few others), HMOs (health maintenance organizations), PPOs (preferred provider organizations), SHMOs (social health maintenance organizations), HCFA (the Health Care Financing Administration, the federal agency in charge of the Medicare program), and on and on. As in all professions, health care professionals have created their own language and shorthand to talk to one another. In doing so, they have added an unnecessary layer of mystery to the whole process of financing and delivering health care. When the uninitiated try to assess what is happening, they are quickly dissuaded from going any further by the awesome barrier of language.

Before the alphabet invasion of the 1970s and 1980s, it was relatively easy to understand the health care industry. The industry was composed of doctors, hospitals, nursing homes, health care suppliers, drug companies, and insurers. Everything was relatively neat and clean. With the exception of a few hybrid health maintenance organizations, there was a separation between the financing and delivery of health care. Payment to health care providers (e.g., doctors and hospitals) was made on a retrospective cost-plus basis. The delivery of health care was viewed as outside business management principles. Managers of health care institutions had few incentives to elevate cost containment to a high priority. Quality of care was the king, supported by a powerful ethos of doing everything possible to prolong life, no matter the cost. Physicians behaved and practiced with great autonomy. Oversight of their behavior was infrequently suggested, even inconceivable. As part of management-labor negotiations, business entered into agreements with labor to provide them with relatively rich benefit packages to ensure their access to the health care system. The tax system encouraged this practice, and a private insurance system geared toward first-dollar coverage became commonplace.

While there are, of course, real differences, the structural characteristics of the health care marketplace of the 1960s remain strikingly similar to the ones observed in the mid-1980s. Health care is distinguishable from most other products in a number of important ways. First, medical care services are not purchased because of any inherent demand for them; the demand for medical care is a derived demand—derived from the "demand" for good health. Perhaps most striking here is the recognition that health care is only one determinant of health status and, for many people, not even the most important. Nutrition, exercise, the environment, work site risks, and personal habits are but a few of the many other factors that influence health status. The need for health care is not readily predictable; as a result, the associated expenditure track is irregular and uneven. Often the need is immediate, allowing little time for shopping around or seeking advice. Many consumers are unaware of their medical care needs; they simply do not have the knowledge to diagnose them and "demand" the required services. Finally, medical care is not an exact science; it is a discipline characterized by uncertainty. There is not one right way to treat a patient presenting himself with chest pains; there are many ways.

The Nontraditional Market for Health Care Services

As a result of these institutional peculiarities, the market for health care has historically functioned in nontraditional ways. Due to the consumer's uncertainty about the health care services he or she requires, the physician assumes a dual role. Once the consumer has decided to seek care and has selected a physician, the physician diagnoses problems and decides on the course and place of treatment. The individual has the most discretion before seeing the physician. Once a physician's assistance is sought, physician preferences come to the fore. The physician then becomes the agent for the consumer. But as agents, physicians provide more than advice; they also provide medical services. Unlike most producers, physicians can control a portion of the demand for their services. The more services they provide, the more fees they collect. It is this aspect of the doctor-patient relationship that makes fee-for-service pricing of physician services a serious concern to those who would like to see a more competitive medical care market. The problem is compounded by the uncertainty of medical science. The physician may not know exactly what a patient needs. The absence of clear-cut accepted standards of medical practice (and the attendant fear of malpractice suits) leads many physicians to practice "preventive medicine," the provision of services that may be neither warranted nor efficient but are provided to create a case history of completeness. When the physician makes decisions for the consumer, containing cost is only one of the factors considered, and certainly not the guiding one.

Due to the risk and uncertainty of incurring health care expenses, consumers purchase insurance to regularize their anticipated expenses. The predominant form of insurance purchased is characterized by direct third-party payments of some or all medical care expenses. Most individuals obtain insurance coverage through their place of employment. Many observers of the health care arena believe that the low level of consumer payment for services is a significant factor affecting consumer and provider decision making. As in any purchase decision, paying more directly out-of-pocket reduces the demand for services. In health care this creates a classic dilemma; the hesitation to use health services introduced by the presence of significant deductibles and copayments does introduce some cost consciousness into the health care purchase decision, but it does so at a price. Delay in receiving care or perceived barriers to access may result in a more complex medical episode when the patients ultimately present themselves to a physician or to an emergency room.

The third distinguishing characteristic of the health care marketplace is the retrospective cost basis of reimbursement. Not only are payments made by a third party, but payments are generally based on incurred costs. The more cost generated by physicians and hospitals, the greater the revenue reward. While a great deal of rhetoric has been observed decrying this payment practice, in the mid-1980s retrospective cost-based payment remains the principal provider payment method used by private insurers.

Together, the aforementioned factors undermine virtually all normal incentives for market efficiency. Consumers trust providers to make consumption decisions; and since they often pay little directly for medical services, consumers have few incentives to economize. Providers are generally paid by a third party; and since they are reimbursed for their fees and incurred cost, providers have little incentive to economize. Insurers spread the costs among all subscribers, who in the end pay for this inefficiency in the indirect costs of their premiums. Historically, no one in this triangular flow of dollars had sufficient incentives to make economizing choices; indeed, the predominant incentives were for more and more spending.

These societal and institutional attitudes—that cost should not be a factor in medical decisions, that health has no price, that quality is of paramount concern—are unique to the medical care marketplace. They created strong pressures to follow the axiom of "when in doubt, do more." The institutional and financing arrangements in the market offered little resistance to cost increases and little incentive for efficient resource allocation.

This world of benign innocence came to a shuddering halt in 1983 with congressional passage of a new Medicare payment system for inpatient hospital services. The DRG system is a payment method that prospectively pays hospitals a fixed amount or price for each case type. Patients are assigned to one of 468 DRGs for payment purposes. The DRG system is to be phased in over a four-year period. Payment will reflect a blend of hospital-specific and national rates, moving from greater reliance on hospital-specific to national rates as the transition unfolds.

The DRGs hit the health care system with a force that exceeded all expectations. The psychic impact on American medicine went beyond the incentives embedded in the payment reform. The DRGs' incentives were to admit more patients, but to discharge them sooner. The DRGs served as a catalyst, a rallying cry, for reform. In the words of one physician, the day the DRGs passed was "the day the music stopped." The passage of the DRGs occurred in the midst of a private sector orgy of introspection. Benefit redesign, utilization management, and the introduction of copayments and deductibles were increasingly surfacing as cost-containment mechanisms. Business was developing a voracious appetite for data and information on what it was spending for health care and the value it was receiving for its investment. A whole new industry devoted to the management of health care benefits emerged.

The Arrival of Utilization Management

The focus on utilization management has found wide acceptance from management and labor alike. Utilization management translates into the vigorous administration of an existing benefit package. The strategy behind utilization management is simple: keep the patient out of the hospital. To that end a large array of utilization services is part of the benefit packages purchased by many corporations. The label that has become affixed to such programs is managed care. Managed care encompasses such diverse activities as preadmission review for all elective admissions, mandatory second surgical opinions, concurrent review (continued stay review while in a hospital), discharge planning, case management (individual benefit oversight), and alternative benefit coverage (ambulatory surgery, home health care, and skilled nursing facility care). In the 1980s utilization control as embodied in managed care has grown in attractiveness. It is viewed by many as a necessary first step in the health care cost-containment

battle. Utilization control is not as controversial a change in
benefit design as the introduction of deductibles or copayments. Utilization management is viewed as a prudent and
more effective administration of an existing benefit package.
Copayments and deductibles represent an actual shifting of
dollar responsibility and contain the seeds for labor-manage-
ment controversy.

Interest in utilization control or managed care had its gene-
sis in the pre-Medicare era and then blossomed in the early
1970s, stemming from a series of initiatives introduced by
Blue Cross Plans and commercial insurers. Business was
warming to the notion of utilization management when the
DRG system was passed by Congress. The greater accountability engendered by Medicare payment reform linked up
with the interests of business in cost control to create irresist-
ible system pressure for change. Businesses' efforts to redesign their benefit offerings were opportune. The move to
greater cost accountability and the shedding of the patina of
organizational paternalism coincided with an acknowledged
physician surplus and a rapid growth in the number of health
maintenance organizations.

Here Come the Doctors

The growth in the supply of physicians witnessed in the
1970s and the early 1980s, stimulated by federal subsidies,
created an altogether new and receptive health care marketplace. The old tried and true laws of economics indeed did
have some applicability in the health care sector. If there are
enough suppliers, competition will eventually emerge. The
change has occurred grudgingly, but it has occurred nonetheless. Unheard of events were witnessed in selected market
areas in the 1980s. New physicians could obtain patients only
by stealing them from existing practices or siphoning off patients from hospital emergency rooms. "Doc-in-the-boxes"
and "McDoctors" started up around the country. Discounting
of fees became prevalent, and many physicians joined a variety
of prepaid group practice settings, effectively creating de facto

employment arrangements and willfully subverting their own claims of unfettered autonomy. Housecalls returned and physicians began to spend more time with their patients. Perhaps the most significant change was a subtle shift in society's view of the physician. Sullied by coarse marketplace behavior, physicians have found their elevated status in society under attack. The endless onslaught of medical professional liability claims and the failure to act internally to discipline marginal physicians continue to reduce the physician of the 1980s to the ranks of mere mortals. As information about medical practice emerges, medicine is revealed not as an inviolate science, but as a discipline still searching for answers. Our growing knowledge of nutrition, environment, and behavior and the proliferating array of new self-diagnostic and self-treatment kits further demystify the physician's place in society.

In practical terms we have a shortage of patients, not a surplus of physicians. Demand for health care will not suddenly fade away. The aging of the population, new technological innovations, and the ability of the medical profession to endlessly subdivide specialty care will fuel the fires of demand. Nonetheless, the growing supply of physicians, whose ranks are annually enlarged by another 15,000-plus new members, is more than able to meet the anticipated and existing demand pressure. The shortage of patients has a tangible and dramatic impact on the psyche and pocketbook of the average physician. Average physician income has stabilized in the 1980s, and future income gains are unlikely. Adding to this sense of growing powerlessness in the face of market demand is the appetite of business, insurers, and government for information detailing the intimate facts of a physician's practice style. The bounds of physician discretions have been pierced, and there is no return. No longer will the physician's judgment prevail without question. Doctors are and will be asked how their behavior compares to their peers' and, if it is found to be different, why that is so. New methodologies and techniques have emerged that begin to shed light on the murky concept of quality. With the advent of these techniques, physicians can no longer find release from scrutiny by saying that their patients are sicker than those of their peers or that they can produce better outcomes. The concept of accountability is one of the battle cries of the 1980s. The consequences of the loss of the physician's special elevated role in society are being witnessed in the 1980s. The 1990s will see further erosion of the remaining vestiges of professional dominance. Most physicians will become employees of large prepaid group practice arrangements, stripped of many of the privileges that are now viewed as inalienable rights.

From Coast to Coast, HMOs and PPOs Are on the March

If one were to believe the predictions of a number of Wall Street health care gurus, the health care system of the 1990s will be dominated by health maintenance organizations. HMOs are the most visible symbol of a new wave of delivery systems that are likely to become household words by the early 1990s. HMOs are prepaid health care organizations that combine health care financing and delivery. For a predetermined price, HMOs assume the risk of providing care for those who enroll. If the HMO is efficient or fortunate in patient enrollment, it makes money. If an HMO is inefficient or the victim of adverse selection, e.g., the enrollment of a sicker-than-average population, it will lose money. HMOs have been successful for many reasons—their ability to keep people out of the hospital (HMO hospital use rates are 40 percent less than traditional fee-for-service providers'), the selection and training of physicians with a conservative practice style, an emphasis on health promotion, and an ability to attract better risks in the marketplace.

HMOs are not new entities. In one form or another they have been around for over fifty years. Public acceptance of HMOs was enhanced by federal legislation in the early 1970s, which established a mechanism for certifying "federally qualified" HMOs. Still, public acceptance of HMOs has come slowly. The 1980s were witness to a turning point in HMO market share and in consumer acceptance. In 1985, 7.9 percent of all Americans were enrolled in HMOs. HMO growth has been occurring at more than 20 percent per year. Enthusiasts forecast that there is no end in sight and that soon HMOs will supplant fee-for-service medicine as the dominant form of health care delivery.

Although HMO growth has been rapid in the 1980s, it is inevitable that new HMOs will share in the common experience of most new enterprises—namely, business failure. Twenty-five HMOs were fighting for survival and market share in Chicago in 1986. The market simply cannot sustain that many HMOs. Failure of even a few HMOs will contribute to an underlying discomfort for many consumers. This failure may result from any number of factors: lack of management talent, undercapitalization, inadequate enrollment, or adverse selection. While the future for HMOs is bright, there is good reason to believe they will not dominate the market as some health care seers predict.

The emergence of managed care offerings and preferred provider organizations is the reason HMO growth will not be without limit. PPOs can be placed in the middle of a continuum with unconstrained fee-for-service on one end and HMOs on the other. PPOs represent arrangements where comprehensive insurance benefits are offered to employers through a select panel of providers. These preferred providers agree to deliver services at a discounted price in return for the promise of patient volume. Most PPOs also have sophisticated utilization management components as a standard feature. The speed of PPO growth is even greater than that of HMOs. In 1983 PPOs were a new and little recognized or understood phenomenon. California transformed the idea of selective contracting (another label for PPOs) from a novel idea to a crystalline reality. In 1982 the state of California, in a cost-containment move, converted its Medicaid business into a selective-contracting or PPO setting. Soon thereafter, legislation was passed in California to allow the private sector to follow suit. As with the invasion of so many ideas that emerge from the sun-bleached beaches of America's western frontier, PPOs swept across the continent. In 1986 there were over 400 PPOs in operation, with enrollment approaching 10 percent of the population. Part of the great appeal of PPOs is that, in addition to reducing cost through negotiated provider payment discounts and utilization management, they preserve more freedom of choice of providers than HMOs.

Businesses around the country are likely to follow the lead of large companies such as General Motors and offer their employees three health insurance options: a managed care product, a PPO, and an HMO. The insurance offering most familiar to business today, unfettered fee-for-service, will become an anachronism. Less than 10 percent of the health service market will be served by unconstrained fee-for-service insurance offerings by the mid-1990s. This movement toward greater management of health benefits is inevitable and irreversible. The three-headed hydra—managed care, PPO, and HMO—is here to stay. New labels may be affixed to variations on a theme, but the basic approaches will encompass the overwhelming majority of Americans well before the turn of the century.

The success of managed care and PPO arrangements will, by necessity, stand as the single largest impediment to HMO growth and dominance. The advantage which HMOs bring to the market is their ability to constrain inpatient expenditures for their patient populations. Managed care and PPO arrangements can now do the same. What was once an advantage of more than 50 percent in hospital usage has been cut by more than half by the practice style of managed care and PPO physicians. If HMOs are unable to offer employers large premium savings, alternative offerings with enhanced freedom-of-choice will undoubtedly find greater favor. HMOs are likely to secure between one-quarter and one-third of the market for health services delivery with the balance of the market committed to managed care and PPO offerings.

Hidden under the surface of this fundamental movement to managed arrangements is one of the unseen driving forces of change—the advance of medical technology and technique. The refinement of anesthesia and surgical technique is a partial explanation for the movement of service provision from inpatient to outpatient settings. The diagnostic revolution in imaging techniques accompanied by a creative array of new acronyms—CT scanning, MRI, and PET (computerized tomography, magnetic resonance imaging, and positron emission tomography), to name a few—has facilitated the easy transition of the hospital from a house of hope and primary care to an institution devoted to treating only the most seriously ill in our society. The decline of the hospital from its central eminence is well under way in the 1980s. Hospitals, of course, will always be with us. Only they may not be thought of as hospitals as much as they will be viewed as health care service centers offering cradle-to-grave services. It would surprise few observers of the hospital industry to learn that one of the next diversification strategies being considered by some institutions is the ultimate form of discharge planning—mortuary services. Technology has been the silent partner contributing to this reduction in the hospital's place in a community. As the force of the medical-technological imperative unfolds, as much as 60 percent of a typical hospital's former inpatient business will be served in settings outside of the core hospital's doors.

Competition and the Poor

The movements from cost to price, from unconstrained behavior to intensive scrutiny, from paternalism to self-responsibility reflect some of the seminal changes driving health care from a public good to a private good. These changes are being brought about by the twin forces of government and the private sector. The Reagan administration has aided and abetted the private sector initiatives. Under the Reagan administration the federal government has retreated from regulatory approaches to health care problems and instead has embarked on a course of marketplace reform.

Competition in health care based on price yields certain returns, but it also creates an enormous social problem. Competition is the conscious decision to place efficiency considerations above those of equity. Those who can afford to pay have leverage in a competitive arena; those who cannot are at risk.

In 1986 there were an estimated 37 million Americans without health insurance and another 7 to 10 million with partial coverage for a portion of a year. Half of these Americans are under age twenty-five, a third are children, and many are employed. From all signs, the number of the uninsured is growing year by year. Growth in the economy is occurring most rapidly in those sectors (e.g., the service sector) which historically do not provide health insurance to their employees, while growth is the slowest in sectors such as manufacturing which have provided health insurance benefits to their employees. Tightened state eligibility standards for Medicaid contribute to the growing number of poor and near-poor lacking health insurance protection. Between 1975 and 1985 the percentage of Americans below the poverty line covered by Medicaid fell from 63 percent to 46 percent. The "uncompensated care" problem is a national disgrace long hidden by the historic shell game of robbing Peter to pay Paul. Self-accommodation practices of providers in the pre–DRG era of the late 1970s and early 1980s yielded a largely invisible system of cross-subsidization from those who could pay to those who could not or did not. Hospitals are the focal point of the uncompensated care problem. On average, nearly 5 percent of all hospital business is classified as "uncompensated care." This is equivalent to the average operating margins earned by hospitals in the 1980s. Averages, though, are but one way to hide distributional inequalities. The burden of providing care to the medically indigent falls most heavily on the urban public and teaching hospitals. For these institutions it is not uncommon to discover uncompensated care case loads exceeding 10 percent.

"Uncompensated care" is one of those wonderful misnomers that has entered the lexicon of healthspeak. Care is indeed compensated, but not by those who receive it. Historically, those who paid for care paid for more than their care alone. A portion of every hospital bill was allocated to finance the cost of uncompensated care. There is not even a good working definition of uncompensated care. In general, uncompensated care is thought to consist of two portions: bad debt—the cost of care for those who can pay, but do not; and charity care—the cost of care for those who simply lack the ability to pay. Depending on accounting practices, one provider's bad debt is another's charity care. Collection practices in the hospital industry will never serve as a model for other industries. The caring ethic makes hospital administrators hesitate to vigorously pursue those who have some resources but fail to pay.

There is a great deal of discussion over just how much care is rendered to the medically indigent by providers. In 1984 hospitals estimated they rendered nearly $8 billion of care to the medically indigent. There is a certain artificiality to this estimate. The $8 billion number is reported in funny money—it is measured as foregone hospital charges, not as incurred costs. The number is also a gross number, failing to reflect the revenue offsets that are specifically provided for indigent care by other third-party payers. Regardless of the exact dollar amount, it is clear that hospitals do provide the bulk of health care services to the medically indigent seeking care.

The uncompensated care issue is a problem noted more for words than action. The health care industry is engaged in the delicate undertaking of studying the problem, leading to a condition commonly known as "analysis paralysis." The historical response of health professionals to a problem is to study its etiology and to describe in great detail the dimensions and characteristics of the phenomenon. Uncompensated care is now the recipient of that type of attention. Studies of various color and stripe have been commissioned from all corners of the health care world. The results will inform, but they will bring us no closer to a solution. When a problem has a surface intractability, it is far safer and easier to study it than to do something about it. Expending further funds to identify the parameters of the uncompensated care problem is largely a waste of resources. We know the problem is large and it will not go away soon. We also know some of the salient characteristics of the population most at risk; they are: young, poor, employed in settings without health insurance, in poorer health than the general public, and high-volume users of hospital emergency rooms.

Three Strategies to Address the Uncompensated Care Problem

There are three basic approaches that offer relief for the uncompensated care population: expanding the availability of health insurance, reducing the cost of delivering care (stretching the health care dollar), and generating a new revenue stream to finance the cost of care no one wants to pay. In one form or another, or in combination, all of these strategies have been invoked to address the problem of medical indigency. Each of these three approaches has multiple components.

The expansion of health insurance can come from two quite different sources. While politically unlikely, government could expand the eligibility requirements of Medicare and Medicaid, or new entitlement programs could be introduced for certain population subgroups. The ill-fated Mondale platform of 1984 contained a health plank that would have created a special insurance program for children lacking health insurance. In President Ronald Reagan's second term of office his secretary of Health and Human Services, Dr. Otis Bowen, proposed the addition of a new Medicare program, a Part C of Medicare to extend coverage for the elderly for catastrophic inpatient expenses. At the state level, eligibility for Medicaid benefits could be expanded by simply raising the income threshold.

The private market analogue to the expansion of government entitlements is the development and marketing of insurance offerings for the employed, but uninsured, population. This market, thought of as the small group market, has traditionally been unattractive to insurers. Marketing and administrative costs are high, and insurers frequently lose money on the small group business due to a phenomenon known as adverse selection. Adverse selection occurs when individuals behave rationally in purchasing insurance. Those who anticipate incurring substantial health care expenditures during a given year purchase health insurance, while those in better health elect to forgo purchasing insurance. The result is an insurance pool consisting of above-average risks with an associated above-average expenditure experience that exceeds the premium revenue generated. This process spirals as insurers raise the price of their coverage to offset the higher cost profile of the high-risk population, effectively driving marginal purchasers out of the market and leaving an even poorer set of risks. Nonetheless, in spite of adverse selection and other problems, the expansion of private insurance coverage to the employed uninsured could reduce substantially the magnitude of the uncompensated care population. In a number of communities across the country, private sector coalitions have worked to develop innovative approaches to expand private insurance coverage to the employed uninsured.

In the mid-1980s, a coalition of business, labor, health care providers, and insurers in Tulsa rediscovered the concept of community rating. In effect, big business has agreed to accept a surcharge on its health insurance premiums to subsidize an insurance offering to the small group market. The hope is to encourage small business to purchase health insurance for its employees and, in the process, reduce the amount of uncompensated care rendered in Tulsa. Big business in Tulsa believes this is a win-win program. Insured Tulsa businesses already are paying for the cost of care for the medically indigent through their payments to providers (the payment to providers consists of three basic elements: the actual costs of care, a profit margin, and a subsidy factor for the medically indigent). By making insurance affordable to small businesses and drawing them into the market, the size of big businesses' payments to providers should stabilize or decline. While big businesses' insurance premiums will reflect an explicit surcharge to subsidize the price of insurance for small employers, this surcharge should be more than offset by the reduction in the hospital daily room rate due to a reduced bad debt and charity care case load.

Historically, the majority of care for the medically indigent has been rendered in inpatient settings. Physicians also provide substantial amounts of free care. Still, it is somehow ironic that the site of care most frequently used by the medically indigent is the most costly site of care, the hospital. The sec-

ond strategy to overcome the uncompensated care problem
focuses on cost management of the services rendered to this
population. This strategy operates on the principle of providing service at the lowest cost. Generally, it necessitates enrolling the current uninsured population in a managed health care
plan. In the managed care plan, physicians serve as gatekeepers to the health care system, directing the patient to the least
costly setting and creating incentives to minimize expensive
inpatient services. Emphasis under these schemes focuses on
early diagnosis, treatment, and preventive services. Primary
care is the care of choice. If the medically indigent received
their care through managed care insurance arrangements, the
direct cost of treating them could be reduced substantially,
perhaps by as much as 25 percent.

The third tactical approach is to find a new sugar daddy to
underwrite the cost of care for the medically indigent. Uncompensated care is one of those marvelous issues that can always
be portrayed as the other guy's responsibility. The financing
proposals for generating new revenue are basically variations
of taxation schemes. The proposals on the table run the gamut
from sin taxes (alcohol, tobacco, etc.) to payroll and income
taxes to provider use taxes (hospital admission taxes). Most of
the proposals find advocates in parties who are now carrying
the burden and who are trying to spread the responsibility to
others. In the total scheme of health care, a $425 billion enter-
prise in 1985, an $8 to $10 billion uncompensated care problem should not seem so insurmountable. The problem is a
classic political one of a disequilibrium between costs and
benefits. Those who will benefit from financing are relatively
powerless in our society, while those asked to bear the costs
have concrete economic and political power. As much as
Americans have a natural affinity to champion the underdog,
financial realities do intrude and, on the margin, additional
costs matter greatly.

The inequity of uncompensated care is an open wound fes-
tering beneath the surface of the rhetoric of competition in the
new health care market. Competition in health care will not
succeed unless a mechanism is established to finance care for

society's less fortunate. Grappling with the turmoil of change in the 1980s has made all of the major participants in the health care market hesitant and cautious. Everyone is waiting for the other fellow to take the first step. America's politicians and health care leaders seem able to live with the reality of 37 million uninsured Americans. If 37 million is not the threshold for a call to action, perhaps the magic number will be 50 million. It is difficult to imagine that 20 percent of the U.S. population could lack health insurance without some concentrated political energy spent to rectify the issue.

The New Health Care

In the words of Jack Kent Cooke, owner of the Washington Redskins, when asked why he fired his football coach George Allen, "I gave him an unlimited budget and he exceeded it." By the mid-1980s, in business's and government's eyes, the health care system had exceeded its unlimited budget. The health care inflation numbers are still the leaders of the pack. The perceived decline in health care cost inflation may be illusionary. The dip below double-digit inflation in the mid-1980s is widely viewed as testimony to the decline of inflationary forces in health care. Medical inflation has not been this low since Medicare and Medicaid picked up steam in 1966. Yet all is not as it seems. Medical care price inflation is still running at more than twice the general consumer price index. The lower levels of inflation observed in the health care sector are largely attributable to the overall decline in inflation. Sector-specific inflation is not under control. The historical pattern of medical care inflation racing along at twice the consumer price index remains unbroken.

It is hard to believe that the efforts in the first half of the 1980s were fruitless. The movement to the three-option form of health care delivery and financing was surely a movement of lasting import and will have a dramatic impact on the cost of health care. In 1986 less than a third of all Americans were enrolled in a managed health care plan, be it a managed fee-for-service product, an HMO, or a PPO. As the remaining population converts to managed arrangements, some, but not all, of the demons of cost inflation will be exorcised.

Business Takes Up the Fight

Perhaps the single most important force driving change in health care is the awakening of the sleeping giant of business. Benign neglect has given way to demands for accountability. Business is extraordinarily interested in health care benefit management, both for its active employees and for its retirees. Unfunded liabilities for retiree health benefits have been the sticking point in more than one merger discussion. With greater frequency, business now self-funds its health benefit offerings to its employees, avoiding premium taxes, state insurance mandates, and reserve requirements, while reaping the benefits of cash management. ERISA, the Employee Retirement Income Security Act of 1974, allowed businesses to treat their health benefit offerings as cash management programs if they were self-funded. ERISA explicitly excluded self-funded plans from state insurance regulation. Estimates vary, but by 1985 more than 60 percent of businesses in America with more than 5,000 employees self-funded their health benefits programs, and a significant percentage of firms of smaller size also have followed suit. Companies contract with insurers for administrative services, claims processing, and stop-loss coverage. This movement to self-funding complicates and frustrates government initiatives to regulate insurance and to finance care for the medically indigent. State governments' attempts to extend the comprehensiveness of employer insurance offerings through the requirement of mandated benefits (e.g., mental health benefits) may have the opposite effect. The marginal purchaser of health insurance may find the increased cost of mandated benefits too much to bear and will then have an incentive to self-insure. The net effect of government's attempt to enrich the benefit package may be a dilution in comprehensiveness as firms move from regulatory scrutiny to the laissez-faire environment of self-funding.

In the 1980s business demonstrated that it was no longer

willing to write blank checks for health care. This heightened
interest in understanding and valuing the purchased product
dovetails nicely with a Medicare product oriented, per-case
payment system. For many businesses, health benefit costs
were equal to corporate net revenues and in some instances
served to further contribute to the labor cost disparities with
their international competitors. Business expressed its new
awareness of the financial consequences of unconstrained
health care inflation by calling its insurance carriers to task.

Health Insurers: Becoming More than Money Changers

Insurers come in all types and categories. Just as there is
Baskin and Robbins with thirty-one flavors of ice cream to
choose from, there is a huge number of insurers (more than
800 private insurance companies) competing in the marketplace. The dominant health benefits provider in America is the
collection of Blue Cross and Blue Shield Plans. There are
eighty-two Blue Cross and Blue Shield Plans providing hospitalization coverage for almost one-third of the population and
coverage for physician services for 25 percent of the population. The next closest competitor has no more than a 5 percent
share of the market. The Blue Cross and Blue Shield Plans and
their competitors, which include both insurers and third-party
administrators, have been scrambling to respond to the demands of business. Product development is at an all-time high.
Every insurer wants to be able to offer an employer a full range
of product offerings and cost-containment services. Insurers
are busily establishing relationships with providers to be able
to deliver PPO and HMO products. Most Blue Cross and Blue
Shield Plans have a competitive advantage in these endeavors.
Their advantage derives not so much from market share as it
does from the nature of their longstanding relationships with
providers.

Historically, Blue Cross and Blue Shield Plans have entered
into participating agreements and negotiated arrangements
with providers. The Blues have the knowledge and experience
in working with providers, in establishing the nitty-gritty basis

for payment, and in introducing utilization review methods. It should not be surprising then to discover that Blue Cross and Blue Shield Plans have the nation's largest network of HMOs and PPOs and faster-than-average rates of growth for these lines of business. Contrary to some beliefs, health care is a product packaged and delivered in local markets. Blue Cross and Blue Shield Plans are well positioned to offer employers the broadest panel of select providers and a wide range of cost-containment features. Commercial insurers are by no means standing idly by. They are formidable competitors who are rapidly developing networks of providers, effectively eroding one of the Blues' greatest competitive advantages. Still, it takes time, knowledge, and experience to negotiate effective relationships with providers. For the remainder of the 1980s, Blue Cross and Blue Shield Plan enrollment gains in their PPO, HMO, and managed care product offerings are likely to exceed the industry norm.

One of the phenomena witnessed in the 1980s is likely to continue to unfold in the 1990s. Insurance companies are picking their partners and entering into joint ventures with hospitals and physicians. Some of these ventures are readily visible on the rapidly changing HMO and PPO landscapes, others are more subtle. Financing ties in accessing capital, in underwriting risk, and in undertaking joint investments in related as well as unrelated health activities are all actions being explored. The natural evolution of joint ventures is readily visible in the 1980s. Insurance companies are moving into the delivery business through HMOs and PPOs. Delivery systems such as the large investor-owned, multihospital chains (Hospital Corporation of America and Humana) have begun to develop insurance offerings. It will be intriguing to observe how these hybrid entities perform. In health care, insurance companies make money by keeping people out of hospitals and by reducing the amount of care required. Hospitals make money by doing just the opposite. Higher occupancy and greater intensity normally translate into greater profitability. These countervailing incentives may make joint delivery and financing ventures rather risky undertakings.

Payment to Hospitals: From Caterpillars to Butterflies

Insurers are busily engaged in changing the way in which they pay providers. With hindsight, the 1980s will be viewed as a transitional decade. Payment reform will be one of the achievements of this era. Medicare payment reform was the signal fire on the horizon. Per-case payment, the mechanism for transferring risk from payer to provider, was an idea that caused a seismic shock on the health care Richter scale. All payment changes in the future will use per-case DRGs as the baseline for performance. Retrospective cost reimbursement will linger on through the early 1990s, but it will be a dinosaur in the face of major climatic change.

Payment changes are terribly important. Providers respond to financial incentives, and how they are paid does indeed affect their behavior. In the hospital arena, the transfer of risk from payer to provider is well under way. The incentives embodied in such payment schemes generally pressure institutions to examine the internal hospital "production process." Hospital length of stay declined steadily from 1982 through 1986; the same was true for occupancy levels and the population's hospital use rate. While the payment system alone has not caused all of these changes, it is one of the engines driving the decline in hospital usage. The change is dramatic. Under a prospective per-case payment system, hospitals are rewarded for quickly treating and discharging a patient—just the opposite of the incentives embedded in the historical retrospective cost reimbursement system. The change has had a ripple effect on hospital management practices and on the state of the art of information systems.

Under per-case payment, hospitals need to know how much it costs them to deliver care for, say, a typical heart attack patient. The Medicare DRG payment system pays hospitals a fixed price for each of 468 different DRGs. In order to prosper under such a payment system, hospitals must know what it will cost to deliver a particular bundle of services that comprise a DRG. Basic cost analysis as well as the information systems to answer the questions raised by the payment system have been developed and are in use in hospitals throughout the country. Companies have shot up and are prospering, providing hospitals with the information they need to survive under changing payment rules.

Prospective per-case payment is not the only payment change under way. Risk transfer is the underlying concept driving payment reform. Reform generally means payment will move from an after-the-fact basis to a before-the-fact basis. The unit of payment may be per diem, per admission, per case, or per capita, but it will be prospectively administered. Depending on the unit of payment, the provider will be faced with different incentives: per diem—to increase the number of days; per admission and per case—to increase the number of admissions and reduce their length of stay; and per capita—to reduce admissions and length of stay. Equally as important as the unit of payment is its level. The relationship between actual costs and payment level is critical to hospital profitability. Both the unit and the level of payment are being probed in the health care marketplace of the 1980s. Competitive bidding for patients from business, with insurers as the administrative agents, is yielding a prospective payment unit and a competitive payment level.

Physician Payment

In 1986 physicians were trying to hold off the payment reform Visigoths. Of the $425 billion spent on health care in 1985, 19 percent constituted expenditures for physician services. The direct costs of physician services are only the tip of the iceberg. While payment for services constitutes but 20 percent of the total, influence over another 50 to 60 percent of health care expenses is under the physician's sway. The federal government is acutely aware of the role of physician costs in the Medicare program. Part B of Medicare, a program to pay for physician services, financed by a mixture of general revenues and premiums, has been the fastest growing part of the nondefense budget in the 1980s. Despite the introduction of a payment freeze in 1985, Part B costs increased by 12 percent due to growing enrollment in Medicare, increased services per enrollee, and inflation.

In 1985 there was one physician for every 450 Americans. By 1995 there will be one physician for every 380 people. Not surprisingly, solo practice is rapidly declining. In the mid-1980s, about one-third of all physicians were practicing in groups of three or more, with the trend line for this type of arrangement following a steep upward slope.

Most physicians are paid by Medicare and private payers on a controlled charge basis. Standards for reasonableness vis-à-vis peers and their own historical profile are used as payment benchmarks. The payment system values procedures more than the rendering of cognitive services. Payment reform is moving from the reliance on historical charge profiles to fee schedules or risk arrangements. Fee schedules are simply a huge price list for medical services: perform service "x" and a physician receives payment "y" from a patient's insurance company. Risk arrangements refer to capitation payment, where for a fixed fee paid in advance of service, a physician agrees to treat a patient for whatever medical condition he or she may have. Capitation arrangements are more prevalent for those physicians whose practices have a significant HMO component. Of course, payment reform for physicians, like payment reform for hospitals, brings with it a concomitant need for utilization oversight. If physicians are paid a fixed fee per service, the payment method creates incentives to increase the number of services or to unbundle the traditional package of services into discrete components. Utilization management is thus a vital component of any payment scheme.

Of concern to insurers who are offering a benefit package to business is provider willingness to participate in their offering and to accept the insurer's payment as payment in full for service. These "participating agreements" characterize the payment practices of Medicare and most Blue Shield Plans. If the payment level is set too low, physician participation is less than full-hearted. Medicare's participating physician rate was under 30 percent in 1986. Typically, Blue Shield Plans obtain participation rates of more than 75 percent of the physicians in a given service area. If a physician elects not to participate, he or she then must collect the payment from his or her patients. Medicare and Blue Shield will pay the patient the amount they would have paid the physician. By electing to see a nonparticipating physician, the patient is assuming the risk of any balance billing in excess of the payment amount received from the insurer. Establishing participating agreements is a difficult undertaking, but one that can benefit both the physician and the subscriber. With a participating agreement, patients can rest assured, once they satisfy their policy's deductible and copayment requirements (if any), that payment to the physician will be accepted as payment in full for services. Physicians benefit by avoiding the cost of collection, through simplified administration, improved cash flow, and more cordial patient relationships.

Payment Reform and Quality of Care

Payment reform has as a secondary objective the maintenance of quality of care. There is a broad perception that the range of acceptable quality for a given service is wide. Physician variability in practice style is well documented. Length of stay differences between the East and West coasts have been witnessed for years. East Coast physicians typically keep patients 30 to 40 percent longer than their West Coast counterparts. A whole analytic method, called small-area variation, has evolved to depict variation within defined geographic areas. Medicine is not performed on a cookbook basis. Third-party payers and the government are deeply concerned over the impact of their payment practices on the perceived and actual quality of care. As hospitals responded to the incentives of the Medicare DRG system, claims that patients were discharged "sicker and quicker" were aired. As of 1986 there was only anecdotal information suggesting this may be happening. Medicare's response to such charges has been fascinating. The Department of Health and Human Services issued a patient's bill of rights, and the professional review organizations

(PROs, the government's watchdog for medical appropriateness and quality) under contract to the federal government were asked to increase their vigilance. Private payers remain watchful. Both private payers and the government have complaint-activated systems. Payment reform will move inexorably forward until the complaint level necessitates relief. Intuitively, it seems that the continued squeeze of payment dollars to providers will have an impact on the quantity of services rendered and the level of amenity accompanying service provision. Quality of care seems not to have been seriously compromised yet, but the specter of that occurring is not far from the minds of health care payers and providers.

If there is an issue lurking on the horizon for the 1990s and beyond, it is quality of care. The rush to embrace the ethic of cost containment has triggered a vision of the health care system that will endlessly yield to the onslaught of programmatic restraint. There is a threshold, once crossed, which leads to diminished quality. Professional ethics are the greatest weapon in the battle against poor quality. These, though, are being eroded as physicians are removed from their elevated place on the professional pedestal, leaving the risk of diminished quality a growing one.

Hospital Fiscal Status

Payment and organizational delivery changes are having a profound impact on the financial position of providers. Average hospital occupancy levels are approaching historic lows. Excess capacity, once the nightmare of health planners, is now a reality in every major health care marketplace. It will get worse before it gets better. Hospitals are adapting to the fiscal pressures, but many are under financial duress. Hospital financial distress is realized and materializes in a variety of areas: service reduction, poor or limited access to capital, a change in institutional mission, reduced access to care, diminished quality of care, or ultimately, closure. An insidious early warning sign is "patient dumping." Patient dumping occurs when an institution refuses to accept a patient or, after accepting and discovering an absence of insurance, transfers the patient to an institution willing to take him or her.

Hospitals of last resort typically are public general or public teaching hospitals. Lives have been lost and cases complicated by the unwillingness of the institutions that house our nation's care givers to accept patients without financial resources. It is an unconscionable practice and a growing one. Fiscal solvency for some institutions means that social responsibility must be sacrificed on the balanced-budget altar. A serious and troublesome trade-off is emerging. In order to render care to some of the medically needy, others must be denied care or shuttled off to hospitals willing to take them. While perhaps good for business, the practice of patient dumping effectively dislodges the hospital from its special place in a community. The justification for retention of hospitals' tax exempt status will become far more tenuous if the practice of patient dumping becomes widespread.

Hospitals' Access to Capital

The result of a reduced inflow of funds in the hospital sector will be witnessed in two related areas: access to capital and industry concentration. Capital is the lifeblood of the hospital industry. In 1986 fewer than a fifth of all hospitals were considered sufficiently good credit risks to be able to sell their bonds as anything other than junk bonds. As the 1980s draw to a conclusion, many hospitals will be unable to gain access to the capital market because of the populations they serve and their locations. Without adequate capital investment, hospitals cannot replace or modernize outdated facilities; respond to changing demand conditions by providing new programs, plant, amenities, or services; or change the nature of the hospital "product" through the addition of new technology or equipment.

Hospitals finance most of their capital needs through the issuance of tax exempt revenue bonds. Historically, the reimbursement system rewarded hospitals for financing their renovation through debt. Regardless of the prevailing interest rates, all interest and depreciation expenses were treated as allowable costs, creating a cost pass-through for tax exempt financing and an incentive to borrow. In 1984 capital costs constituted more than 7 percent of all Medicare payments to community hospitals.

As was the case for payment reform for health services, payment for capital costs is a topic of considerable interest to Congress. When Congress passed the legislation creating the DRG Medicare payment system, it specifically excluded graduate medical education and capital costs from the system reform. In 1986 Congress still had not incorporated capital costs into the DRG payment amount. The Reagan administration's intent was to pay hospitals one all-inclusive amount for capital and operating costs—a capital-inclusive DRG as it were. The incentives are obvious; pay hospitals one fixed price per diagnosis and leave it up to the hospital to manage its own affairs.

Many hospitals are in no position to access the capital markets regardless of how Medicare or private payers pay for capital costs. Due to their locations in inner cities, the poor paying and uninsured populations they serve, and their lack of nonoperating revenues to subsidize their inpatient revenue shortfalls, many hospitals face a difficult choice: deplete their depreciation funds to pay for operations, or dramatically curtail services for the populations who have no other health care recourse. One of the dilemmas posed by the near failure of the least credit worthy hospitals is the absence of adequate substitutes. Inefficiency is not the reason for the potential market exit of these hospitals. Rather, it is an inadvertent conspiracy of mission, location, inadequate payment, and aging physical plant that may yet trigger the death knell.

In the competitive model, hospitals that cannot survive should exit from the market. The disruption in the health care market from the exit of these war-weary institutions in the battle against medical indigency goes beyond the direct services they provide. Should these institutions fail, their inadequate paying patient population will not vanish from the portals of hospital emergency rooms. A portion will migrate to other institutions and begin the process of fiscal erosion anew.

While competition may value the strongest, in health care, supporting the weakest also may be a way for the strong to remain strong.

Hospital Self-Defense: Joint Ventures

One strategy for hospitals to better position themselves to compete and to access the capital market is joint ownership or cooperative ventures. It is almost eerie. If one were to substitute the label of hospital management company for HMO, the rhetoric of 1986 would bear a striking resemblance to that witnessed in 1978 when predictions were being made for a health care system dominated by investor-owned, multihospital systems. Investor-owned dominance did not come to pass, just as HMO dominance is unlikely to occur. Still, investor-owned hospital management companies do offer their owned institutions a tremendous advantage over their not-for-profit counterparts, namely, greater access to capital. The ability to raise equity through stock offerings is a singular advantage that investor-owned hospitals possess. When philanthropy and government grants flowed to not-for-profit hospitals, this advantage was partially offset. With the decline and unlikely resurgence of these sources of revenues in the 1980s, not-for-profit hospitals cannot modernize or rebuild with the ease of most investor-owned facilities.

In increasing numbers, the not-for-profit hospitals have tried to respond to the challenge of the investor-owned, multihospital system by developing their own systems and by forming voluntary cooperatives. These linkages have helped hospitals improve their credit worthiness, but they have not been sufficient to overcome the disadvantages of a poor payer mix, unfavorable location, or less-than-stellar management. A not-for-profit hospital system composed of weak hospitals does little to advantage its members. When the strong link together, as is the tendency, the gap between fiscally solvent and financially tenuous hospitals grows.

Neither the investor-owned nor the not-for-profit multihospital system has completely weathered the turmoil of the "day the music stopped." Utilization declines have made the hospital inpatient business far less attractive than it once was. Both not-for-profit and investor-owned companies are responding by diversifying their portfolios, moving into related and unrelated lines of business, and reducing their dependence on inpatient revenues as a source of corporate profitability. The new health care has reduced the formerly glamorous hospital management company stocks of Wall Street to the ranks of average return investments. It is debatable whether the growth experienced in the 1970s will ever resurface.

The hospital industry in America is a mature industry entering a period of decline. As occupancy levels continue to move downward, due to the enrollment of an increasing percentage of the nation's population in managed care arrangements, some degree of hospital failure and consolidation will occur. Already one can observe hospitals reducing bed capacity, mothballing beds, cutting back on staffing, diversifying into health-related outpatient activities, and plotting a course for survival in an environment promising fewer inpatient days. Many communities will rally to the defense of their hospitals and engage in heroic efforts to prevent their demise. Still, hospitals will fail and industry capacity is likely to be 15 percent to 20 percent less in 1995 than it was in 1985. Hospitals will remain at the hub of the health care system, but their centrality will be challenged by a growing and, at times, confusing array of outpatient and group practice arrangements.

The Turmoil Yet to Come

The new health care of the 1990s promises an end to paternalism and a resurgence of individual choice. Government will continue its retreat from collective responsibility. To the extent it can, Congress will rewrite the Great Society Programs and view the passage of Medicare and Medicaid as an albatross enacted by a guilt-ridden nation. This retreat will be reflected through direct and indirect actions. Medicare programmatic redesign will occupy the federal legislative agenda, while at every possible opportunity the private sector will be encouraged to substitute the invisible hand of Adam Smith's market-place for the prescriptive actions of government. The credo of "the government that governs least governs best" drove the health policy actions of the Reagan administration. The financial demands placed on the private sector will grow, and many of the parties to the financing and delivery of health care will find themselves confronting new challenges and decisions.

The churning in the financing and delivery of health care will not run its course until after the start of the last decade of the twentieth century. Some observers of the health care marketplace predict it will be dominated by a small number of megacorporations—large, national, broad-based companies, involved in all aspects of services delivery and financing.

National megacorporations offer two singular advantages in the health insurance market: economies of scale in administration and centralized marketing for companies with multisite locations. Neither seems sufficiently compelling to warrant the predictions of a health care market dominated by a few companies in the 1990s.

The reasons are complex, but one does stand out. Health care is very much a local commodity. The financing and delivery of health care depend on relations between insurers and local providers of care. National economies of scale are not available when 90 percent of an employer's health insurance costs are incurred as local medical expenses. Constructing a national provider network is not an impossible task, just an exceedingly difficult one. Local delivery systems have a competitive advantage in any given market against a national "megacorporation." Not only do local delivery mechanisms have established provider networks, they also are not burdened by the administrative overhead costs of sustaining a national headquarters.

The health care system of the late 1980s and 1990s will place greater demands on consumers to buy right and to spend their health care dollars wisely. The decision to select a health plan from an employer will be complicated by a growing menu of choices. Choosing the wrong plan could have significant financial out-of-pocket consequences for an individual. Freedom of choice of provider will remain an important attribute of any benefit offering. Insurance plans that overly limit the choice of provider are likely to be less successful than those offering a broad panel of primary care physicians. Consumers can be expected to have a greater stake in effective cost control, and health plan selection may be made on that basis.

Business to the Front

Business will be at the focal point of health care change in the 1980s and the 1990s. The shedding of passive interest has been accompanied by an aggressive posture of benefit design and payment scrutiny. Business will need to tread a careful line, as the potential for irresponsible behavior is great. The key question for business is the trade-off between economic self-interest and social responsibility. What is the appropriate balance between government and the private sector? How strong an advocate should business become in the health policy arena? Does business have a stake in assuring an adequate level of funding for the Medicaid program? What responsibilities fall on big business to encourage or cajole small business to provide insurance protection for its employees? How will employers use health related information in hiring decisions? And, what is business's responsibility in prefunding potential postretirement health benefit obligations?

Presently, business is in the business of paying for the cost of care that no one else wants to pay for—the costs of uncompensated care. Business does not pay for these costs in a visible manner; rather, the costs of indigent care are embedded in the charge structure—the price—presented by a health care provider. As business moves to pay only for the cost of care for its employees, the effect on the delivered volume of uncompensated care will be dramatic. If business withdraws its subsidy, who will pay for care? If it is to be government, then a business stance in opposition to efforts to increase Medicaid eligibility or to expand government support programs is difficult to justify. If government is to be the insurer of last resort, then it must have the financial capacity to pay for the care for the indigent. In simple terms, this means increased taxes. Business will need to choose whether it will continue to pay the additional hospital charges for the medically indigent or whether it will finance and support government initiatives to address the problem. Should business decline on both counts, legislative and judicial alternatives are likely to follow.

One of the substantial causes of uncompensated care is the lack of health insurance coverage for employees of smaller firms. Big business should have an overriding interest in reducing the magnitude of this problem. There is much that big business could do to encourage its vendors to provide health insurance for its employees. Large companies could institute a purchasing policy of only buying goods and services from suppliers who offer their employees health insurance, or business could follow the example of Tulsa and help to subsidize the cost of health insurance for smaller enterprises. As leaders in our society, executives of major corporations have an opportunity to step forward and actively bring about change.

The dilemma between self-interest and social responsibility is also present in the mundane activities of hiring and firing. How will information on a potential employee's health status be used in such decisions? Will a smoker, an alcoholic, a test-positive AIDS carrier be hired? How will these decisions be made? Can an employer legally exclude people with such characteristics from employment eligibility? If employers are willing to hire people with these characteristics, will they also be willing to provide health insurance? Is there a role for government in providing protection from catastrophic illness? Who will pay for it?

As managed care options become the dominant mode of health care delivery, business will have to make a more difficult decision on behalf of its employees. Which HMOs and PPOs should be included, which excluded, and why? How will quality be judged? What is the liability of a business providing managed care offerings to its employees when the management of care leads to an unsatisfactory outcome triggering legal action? Will the cost of litigation exceed the cost savings from managed care offerings?

The unfunded liabilities for retirees' health benefits is a ticking time bomb. Estimates of the size of this liability vary, but $100 billion in 1986 would not be out of line. A rule change in 1985 required that health benefit liabilities be reported on corporate financial statements. The delicate balance between private sector responsibilities and the role of government is brought into question by the magnitude of the unfunded liabilities. If business wishes to minimize its obligations for these liabilities, then business should have more than a passing interest in any legislation designed to ensure that Medicare is sufficient to meet the needs of the elderly. Federal legislative involvement in pension reform in the 1970s was triggered by the underfunding of pension liabilities. The same could happen in the 1990s with unfunded retiree health benefit obligations.

Temptation in the Health Insurance Market

The potential for irresponsible behavior is great for insurers as well as for business. The temptation for insurers is to avoid the poorer risks in the marketplace. This practice of "cream-skimming" undermines the notion of an insurance risk pool. By enrolling better-than-average risks into insurance offerings, insurers can earn substantial profits. HMOs, and to some extent PPOs, begin with the advantage of holding appeal for below-average risks in the population. Federal requirements necessitate that an employer who offers a traditional health insurance plan must make an equal contribution to an HMO benefit offering. Given the population characteristics of HMO enrollees, it should not be surprising to learn that HMO stocks are some of the more attractive investment opportunities on Wall Street. Combined with their ability to constrain hospital use, favorable selection in enrollees makes it possible for HMOs to earn substantial profits. Many of the new market entrant HMOs achieve their initial success from the effects of favorable selection.

Health insurance companies come in two basic models: Blue Cross and Blue Shield Plans and commercial carriers. Blue

Cross and Blue Shield Plans have traditionally accepted enrollment from all through a process of open enrollment, though this practice is changing in the face of competitive pressure. The risk pool for Blue Cross and Blue Shield Plans is a broadly based one. Less than 2 percent of the policies written by Blue Cross and Blue Shield Plans have medical underwriting conditions. Blue Cross and Blue Shield Plans provide insurance for nearly 80 million people; among them are 11 million Americans who do not belong to groups and who represent higher risks than group members.

Commercial insurers, too, are in the business of providing insurance to those at risk. In fact, in the aggregate, commercial health insurers provide coverage to a greater number of individuals in the nongroup market than do Blue Cross Plans. However, many commercial insurers have avoided portions of the nongroup market because of the higher-than-average enrollment risks. Thus while commercial insurers may offer nongroup coverage, for many individuals it may not be affordable and for others it may not be available. Most commercial nongroup policies require evidence of a person's medical condition as a consideration in the rating and pricing of a policy.

State insurance regulation provides oversight of both Blue Cross and Blue Shield Plans and commercial insurers. There are, however, significant differences in the level of oversight. Commercial insurers must file their rate changes; Blue Cross and Blue Shield Plans, due to their enabling legislation, are subject to a formal public hearing and a review and approval process. As a consequence, there is a disparity in regulatory oversight among Blue Cross and Blue Shield Plans, commercial insurers, and self-insured plans.

Lessons from Government

The experience with the federal government in health care in the 1980s has yielded lessons and challenges for the rest of the century. The first lesson, learned painfully by all of the major participants in the health care arena, is that the government is an unfaithful and unreliable partner. Congress has little institutional memory for last year's crisis. Old agreements are readily and eagerly toppled in the face of new and unexpected demands. This is not done maliciously. Rather, the mix of budget realities facing Congress in any given session dictates constant revisions of formerly inviolate agreements. The Medicare payment reform stands as an illustration of this behavior. Originally, DRG payment was to be adjusted annually by an index that would reflect the "marketbasket" cost increases of inputs plus a 1 percent adjustment for new technology. Over a three-year period, the inflation adjustment effectively moved from marketbasket-plus-1-percent to marketbasket-minus-2-percent. The history of Medicare payment suggests that we have not seen the end of the "revisiting" of the original payment arrangements.

The second painful lesson is that government is unlikely to introduce or expand existing entitlement programs for the poor or the near-poor. Perhaps there will be expansions on the margin, but significant change is not likely to happen by 1990. Even if the political will were present, the financial capacity to undertake any new initiatives is lacking. Those who call for government action to solve the uncompensated care problem need to answer this question: are they willing to pay more in taxes? On the heels of a 1986 tax reform program, with a central tenet of reducing effective tax rates, the likelihood of new taxes to finance care for the indigent is indeed small.

The third lesson is a corollary of the second. To the extent possible, the federal government will reduce the number of eligible program participants in Medicare. The euphemism will be "income related benefits," but the translation will be "means testing." The fight to convert Medicare from an entitlement program to a welfare program will be heated and divisive. The outcome, while uncertain, seems headed toward limiting Medicare benefits to those most in need.

The fourth lesson is that the government is in the business of risk transfer, wherever and whenever it can. Future Medicare payment reform will continue the path paved by DRGs and transfer more of the risk of providing care from the government to another party. In health care this means individual voucher payment proposals for Medicare, capitation payment, encouragement of HMOs, reduction in the role of the government as primary payer, and on and on.

Government's role in health care will be reduced from that witnessed in the 1960s and 1970s. The activism that stimulated hospital construction and the growth in the supply of physicians has been supplanted by a prudent purchaser mentality. The desire to purchase care on behalf of entitlement recipients is governed by a least-cost principle. The longstanding practice of awarding business to the lowest-cost supplier is a practice fraught with difficulty in health care. Cost, quality, and assured access, the iron triangle of health care, are rarely compatible. While low cost need not equate with poor quality and limited access, the burden of proof is on the government to demonstrate that adequate quality is being maintained.

Doctors at the Crossroads

In the new world of health care finance, providers are placed in the critical role as agents of change. Providers are being asked to do more for less, to somehow stretch the limited health care dollars in new and imaginative ways. Financing changes have introduced a new and uncomfortable tension to physician practices. The conflict among training, ethics, and payment is played out daily. Physicians are taught to do all they possibly can to prolong life and to defeat the ravages of disease. The reimbursement system of the 1960s and 1970s reinforced this caring ethic. In the 1980s and beyond, there will be financial penalties for keeping a patient an extra day, for administering the extra test, and for delivering the marginal service.

Physician discretion and practice autonomy have been violated, and a return to the days of unexamined behavior will not occur. The human dilemma of maintaining an ethical mode of practice in the face of compelling contrary financial incentives places physicians uncomfortably in the middle. More and more primary care physicians are being asked to serve as gatekeepers to the health care system. They are asked to make trade-offs between treatment costs and benefits. Physicians are ill-suited by training and inclination to undertake such responsibilities. Nonetheless, they have been placed in a position where they must. The disquiet is readily visible within the potential and existing physician community. Applications to medical schools are down from a ratio of four applicants per admittee to two to one. Many of America's best and brightest are choosing professions other than medicine. The decline in medicine's appeal is nowhere more evident than in the typical primary care physician's office. Anyone who has had a recent conversation with a practicing physician cannot help but note how weary he is of the demands and pressures intruding on his life and how puzzled he is over the changing financing environment. There are so many new organization and payment arrangements. Which to join? What patient volume will be gained? At what price discount? What about liability insurance? The complexity of medical practice has exceeded all expectations. Difficult choices face our nation's physicians. They are the front line of America's health care system; they can be agents of change or intransigent guardians of the status quo. It is up to physicians to stand as the protectors of quality in a world lusting for cost containment.

Whose Responsibility Is It?

One of the striking observations of health care in the 1980s is that while the problems which emerge are national in scope, their discriminating characteristic is their local variation. Looking to the federal government as the answer for local health care problems will be frustrating and fruitless. Where you live in America may prove to be the critical variable in determining the set of services for which you are eligible. Variability in the quantity and quality of health care is likely to become the norm. States with relatively rich Medicaid benefit programs can expect to be the beneficiaries of an inmigration of medically indigent searching for the most comprehensive protection for their families.

The health care problem/solution matrix can and should be overlaid on local settings. Health care problems are local in nature—and it would not upset the laws of physics to imagine that solutions to health care problems could be local as well. The locus for health care policy decisions needs to devolve from the macro to the micro level. Forums to bring together the disparate health care interest groups are one vehicle to begin to establish working programs. Coalitions of business, labor, providers, insurers, and consumers can accomplish a great deal if they set their sights high. In communities around the country, leaders have stepped forward to place a particular set of health care issues high on the public agenda. Government is looked to for support, but the energies and the financing come from the private sector.

Government's withdrawal has helped to create this leadership vacuum. The challenges of finding a way to rationalize excess capacity, of reducing the scope of the indigent care problem, of altering the practice patterns of physicians, of finding a way to humanely meet the needs of our elderly population are compelling and urgent. The problems are far more manageable when viewed through the lenses of local initiatives. The key is the energy imparted to a cause by a local champion. If the major employer in a community makes health care reform one of its priorities, others will follow suit. In the absence of leadership, health care problems will grow in complexity and in cost. Perhaps it is time to rekindle the spirit of achievement once ignited by John Kennedy when he said:

> For those to whom much is given, much is required. And when at some future date the high court of history sits in judgment on each of us, recording whether in our brief span of service we fulfilled our responsibilities . . . our success or failure . . . will be measured by the answer to four questions: First, were we truly men of courage . . . . Second, were we truly men of judgment . . . . Third, were we truly men of integrity . . . . Finally, were we truly men of dedication?

In communities around the country, the jury is still out. It is up to us to make a difference. We can and we should.

4

Risk Bearing in
Health Care Finance

SUSAN FEIGENBAUM

Introduction

The evolution of today's health care system is remarkable both for its technological advances and its impact on the way in which health care is distributed. No longer would household members be the primary care givers, nor would extended families provide support for communal health resources. By the mid–nineteenth century, an increasingly industrialized and urbanized society was already grappling with

SUSAN FEIGENBAUM is chief of the methodology division at the Maryland Health Services Cost Review Commission and associate professor of economics at Claremont McKenna College in California. Dr. Feigenbaum is an associate with the Center for Hospital Management and Finance at Johns Hopkins University, and was awarded a faculty fellowship in health care finance with The Robert Wood Johnson Foundation. She has written several articles on the financing of medical care and research.

Dr. Feigenbaum gratefully acknowledges the seminal works of Paul Starr (1982) and Mark Pauly (1986), which contributed extensive background information for this chapter.

the dilemma of financial responsibility for the sick and disabled, and developing institutions that addressed the issue of who should bear which financial risks of illness and injury.

The existence of company doctors, state mental asylums, public health programs, mutual society sickness funds, and commercial and social insurance programs reflected the wide disparity in views about the appropriate distribution of the financial burden of treatment and prevention. To what extent would employers bear responsibility for treatment costs and income losses of sick or injured employees and their families? Would government support of facilities for the mentally ill and for contagious patients extend to prevention and treatment programs in the general population? Could private, voluntary mutual funds be relied upon to provide more than a nominal cash benefit for illness ("sick pay") or funeral expenses? Would commercial insurance markets evolve to spread not only the financial risks arising from the death of a wage earner but also the direct costs of health care? Should such social insurance programs as workers' compensation be extended to provide mandatory coverage of direct and indirect losses from any illness or disability, whether work related or not? Such concerns were a natural outgrowth of the patchwork of private nonprofit, for-profit, and public institutions that was developing during the late nineteenth and early twentieth centuries in response to society's demand for mechanisms to diminish and share the risks of illness and death.

This chapter offers a historical overview of private initiatives, public policies, and institutions that have evolved to address the need for risk sharing in health care finance. It identifies both economic efficiency and equity considerations that may impact the design of such a risk-sharing system. Finally, this work examines the risk-sharing implications of several public and private health care financing strategies popular in the 1980s.

A Historical Perspective on Risk Sharing

Risk Sharing in the Early Years

By the late nineteenth century, employers—faced with competitive labor markets, increasing accident rates, and the threat of personal liability suits—began to assume some of the costs associated with hazardous workplace conditions. Through the employment of company doctors to treat industrial accidents and the establishment of victim relief funds, employers sought to reduce wage costs (by reducing the wage premium required to attract workers to risky employment) and to discourage lawsuits (by terminating relief benefits upon threat of suit). With the adoption of state workers' compensation laws, employers became subject to a "strict liability" standard with respect to workplace injuries, responsible for all direct costs (medical care) and indirect costs (income loss), irrespective of who was at fault. These laws forced employers to reevaluate the appropriate level of workplace safety by comparing the costs of reducing occupational risks with the probable costs of workers' compensation claims if the risks were not eliminated. It may be argued that employees "paid" for this shift in financial responsibility for injury through lower wages; nonetheless, it is clear that the sheer incidence of injury dropped with the employer (rather than employee) as risk bearer, because of the employer's superior ability to assess workplace hazards and to invest in safety devices that provided collective protection to employees.

Although employers were legally required as early as 1910 to assume the costs of occupational injuries (and of occupational diseases with the enactment of the Occupational Safety and Health Act in 1970), they were under no mandate to protect the overall health of their workers. While company-supported medical services were used extensively to screen for healthy employees and keep them on the job, workers too ill to continue working were sent home (often without pay) and referred to a private physician or hospital. Only a few firms, typically located in isolated areas, provided comprehensive medical services to employees and their dependents through compulsory employee withholding plans and the employment of a salaried company doctor. Representatives of labor continually pressed for cash benefits in lieu of mandatory participation in such employer-provided medical plans, ostensibly to preserve the employee's choice of physician and treatment. It would not be until the 1940s that collective bargaining and preferential tax treatment of employer health insurance premium contributions would stimulate widespread involvement of industry in the financing of medical care.

Since the legal responsibility of employers was limited to occupational injuries, there remained a demand for additional institutions to spread the financial burden of illnesses not directly work related. Voluntary mutual benefit societies, fraternal orders, and employee associations that provided members with life insurance, sick benefits, and, in some cases, medical care by contracted physicians proliferated in the late nineteenth and early twentieth centuries, especially in urban, immigrant communities. Nationwide, however, only about 1 percent of the $97 million in sickness benefits paid by fraternal organizations in 1914 went directly for medical care. The overwhelming emphasis on cash benefits for death and sickness indicates that income stabilization was the paramount concern of members, presumably because wage losses from episodic illness tended to be two to four times greater than treatment costs in the early 1900s. Since cash benefit plans also preserved the freedom to choose one's health care provider, they received wide support from local medical societies, which actively discouraged physicians from taking contract positions.

The focus on cash benefits for sickness and death was likewise adopted by the commercial insurance industry, which profited handsomely from the marketing of "industrial" policies that provided lump-sum payments in the event of terminal illness. Companies that offered such policies dominated the insurance market in the first decades of the twentieth century, accounting for more than $183 million in business during 1911 alone. This success was particularly remarkable given that only 40 percent of premiums were eventually paid out as benefits, the remainder going to insurance agents involved in the weekly collection of premium installments.

Early efforts by the Prudential Insurance Company to offer sickness benefit policies for nonterminal illness met with failure, as the company found itself unable to monitor at low cost the extent to which policyholders feigned conditions or overstated their seriousness to avoid work. In contrast, mutual societies and fraternal organizations were generally successful in preventing exploitation of their programs because of their small membership and the fact that members interacted with each other frequently, both in and out of the workplace. The problems that commercial companies faced in evaluating the validity of policyholder claims would remain largely insurmountable until employers became directly involved in the provision of health care and disability insurance. As employers (and, indirectly, workers) began to shoulder the burden of insurance fraud via higher policy premiums, they faced incentives to monitor excessive claims actions. More importantly, such participation by employers virtually guaranteed the commercial insurance market a large number of relatively healthy policyholders over whom the excesses of a few could be spread.

While government efforts to mitigate the income losses and medical costs arising from work related injury culminated in workers' compensation laws, initiatives to spread the financial risks of nonoccupational illnesses were slow to appear. While European countries were adopting such income stabilization policies as compulsory sickness insurance (Germany in 1883 and England in 1911) and subsidization of mutual society sickness funds (Sweden in 1891, Denmark in 1892, and Switzerland in 1912) for their working classes, local and state governments in the United States limited their attention to the establishment of charity care hospitals, mental asylums, medical dispensaries, and pesthouses for contagious disease. In this

way, the United States established a precedent for shifting the
costs of medical care for certain groups to the state (taxpayers), rather than requiring that every person's financial risk of
both medical care and income loss be borne (with some subsidy, if necessary) by publicly or privately formed sickness
funds.

State and local governments became active not only in the
financing but also in the provision of medical care, subsidizing
private charity care and community health activities only as a
distinctly secondary course of action. The shift in financial
responsibility for medical care for the poor to the state apparently justified denying the poor the right to choose their health
care providers and courses of treatment. By directly participating in the provision of care, bureaucrats controlled the nature
and extent of service utilization, thereby containing public
outlays. Instead of rationing their limited medical resources by
nominal user fees, government dispensaries imposed high
time (waiting) costs on their indigent clientele, thereby discouraging utilization by the poor working class. It would not
be until the 1960s, with the enactment of Medicare and Medicaid, that the relationship between government finance and
provision of medical services would largely be severed,
thereby granting most beneficiaries (veterans and Indians remaining the primary exceptions) their choice of provider
while, at the same time, severely weakening public sector control over utilization and outlays.

Although the public sector assumed only limited financial
responsibility for the direct medical costs of illness and completely ignored such indirect costs as wage losses, it played a
central role in public health activities related to sanitation and
communicable disease control. In addition to providing vaccines for the poor and eventually requiring immunization by
private physicians, public health agencies engaged in screening and diagnostic programs to isolate contagious disease victims. The primary objective of these agencies was to reduce
the health and financial risks of communicable disease for the
community at large, rather than provide treatment for the ill.
In fact, victims typically were isolated from work or school and

were directed to seek care from private providers or public dispensaries.

In summary then, the first decades of the twentieth century in America saw a shift in the financial risks (costs of medical treatment as well as income losses) of workplace injuries to the employer. The public sector assumed the financial responsibility for communicable disease control and for medical treatment of the needy and the mentally ill. Less than one-third of industrial workers enjoyed any form of sickness benefit, and an even smaller percentage of the population participated in sickness funds or medical service plans to ease their losses from unexpected illness or disability. By the time of the Depression, families were beginning to feel the increasing financial burden of vastly improved, but expensive, medical interventions. Moreover, income stabilization policies attracted renewed attention as millions became unemployed.

Risk Sharing in the Post-Depression Period

The Depression provided a strong catalyst for government programs to stabilize personal incomes. The Social Security Act of 1935 guaranteed workers compensation for income losses owing to involuntary unemployment, to be financed through employer payroll taxes; thus the financial risks of the business cycle were explicitly shifted to the employer and only indirectly (and not necessarily fully) borne by the employee via lower wages. The act also mandated worker participation in an old-age assistance fund financed by employer and employee payroll contributions. The Social Security program provided true insurance, rather than simply forced savings, in the form of a guaranteed stream of retirement income, which mitigated the financial risk of long, postemployment life spans. Moreover, because the contributions were generally unrelated to the expected mortality of the worker and, instead, were pegged to wage levels, the program also served as a vehicle for transferring income from higher- to lower-income individuals and from workers with systematically shorter postretirement life spans to those enjoying greater longevity. This divergence between contributions and expected benefit payout also bestowed a tremendous windfall on older persons (particularly at the start of the program), courtesy of younger labor force participants.

Remarkably, the same act that instituted risk-sharing programs for unemployment and old-age assistance failed to adopt a similar system to spread the risk of financial loss from sickness. Instead, it reaffirmed and extended the government's policy of funding public sector medical programs for specific patient subpopulations, including disabled children, infants, and dependent children under sixteen. The rejection of compulsory sickness or health insurance occurred despite irrefutable evidence of the insidious link between sickness, wage losses, and poverty and, particularly after the 1920s, despite increasing pressure on families of all income levels to absorb escalating medical costs.

The real value of hospital and medical care had increased significantly with the introduction of often costly new health technologies and antiseptic measures, resulting in greater outlays for treatment. More aggressive and successful medical and surgical procedures had enhanced the attractiveness of hospital versus home care for the middle and upper classes, providing the hospital with a heretofore absent population of paying patients. By 1934 inpatient stays and attending physician charges accounted for approximately 40 percent of medical outlays, up significantly from 7 percent in 1918. Nearly half of total family medical expenditures were incurred by only 3.5 percent of families, reflecting both the low incidence of hospitalization (one in seventeen in 1929) and the high cost of hospital stays. Given this greater demand for costly medical interventions, Paul Starr describes

the shift in concern from the wage loss of sickness to medical expenses, [which] reflected the objective change in the ratio of the two costs, particularly for the middle class. Estimates at the end of the 1920s showed that medical costs were 20 percent higher than lost earnings due to sickness for families with income under $1,200 a year and nearly 85 percent higher for families with incomes between $1,-200 and $2,500.

Clearly, individuals needed new institutions that would allow them to spread the relatively low expected costs of treatment over time (prepayment) and to share the risk with a group of individuals (insurance).

The severe reduction in personal income caused by the Depression significantly reduced the population's ability to pay for hospital services, despite widespread agreement on their value by members of all income classes. Moreover, these same economic forces threatened philanthropic support for hospitals and fueled an increasing reliance on local, state, and federally subsidized emergency relief efforts and providers. By 1930 voluntary hospitals could generate enough patient revenue and contributions to cover only about 80 percent of their outlays, thereby establishing a dangerous pattern of deficit spending. While many patients simply defaulted on hospital bills as their ability to pay diminished, others deferred or refused recommended hospital services, causing a substantial drop in private hospital utilization. Suddenly, hospitals found themselves unintentional partners in bearing the financial risks of sickness.

The introduction of prepaid plans by hospitals sought to remedy this situation by providing families with a method for budgeting the costs of illness over their healthy, wage-earning periods. Inasmuch as this new payment system guaranteed reimbursement for services rendered, it was also expected to stimulate utilization. The first such plan, designed for school teachers by the Baylor University Hospital in 1929, provided a fixed number of inpatient days per year for a nominal premium. Similar "single-hospital" prepayment plans were quickly adopted by other hospitals in Dallas, creating competition in premiums and services rendered. While such plans were marketed primarily as budgetary devices for a fixed package of future hospital services, it was nevertheless the case that not all individuals used their purchased options fully, nor could they resell or be reimbursed for those services that remained unused. Since all covered persons faced the same prepayment premium regardless of health status or history of utilization, a significant element of risk sharing was introduced by these prepayment programs. The hospital itself would also bear financial risk if it underestimated utilization among its prepaid clientele.

Whether to forestall the growing competition between single-hospital prepayment plans or to increase aggregate demand for such plans, multihospital prepayment systems quickly supplanted their single-facility predecessors. These market-wide plans (later known as Blue Cross Plans) permitted subscribers to obtain their prepaid days of hospitalization from any of the participating hospitals, all of which agreed to provide services and to collect directly from the plan. These arrangements came to be known as "service benefit" plans. They had the potential to reap substantial returns by limiting interhospital competition and by achieving a dominant position (if not a monopoly) in their respective communities. Nevertheless, this potential would be increasingly eroded as hospital participants faced new incentives to promote utilization and costly interventions, perceiving that they would bear only a fraction of the subsequent cost of plan overruns, yet receive guaranteed payment for services rendered. In contrast to the earlier single-facility plan, all participating hospitals now shared in the financial risk of underestimating aggregate demand for the plan's service benefits, while individual hospitals profited only partially and indirectly from controlling such demand. As the number of hospital participants and prepaid subscribers grew (to over 6 million by 1940), so did the potential for costly overutilization.

Commercial insurers observed the initial market success of Blue Cross Plans, but they remained skeptical about the viability of service benefit contracts without dollar limits (e.g., twenty days of hospital care per year), given the inherent incentives for overutilization of services by both patients and providers. It was no surprise, therefore, that in 1934 when commercial insurers did finally offer coverage for sickness, it was in the form of an indemnity policy, which guaranteed lump-sum reimbursement for only a limited set of services, subject to a dollar limit and often a copayment or deductible requirement. In this way, insurers sought to overcome the tendencies toward overutilization created by the presence of a third-party payer and to assure accurate forecasts of their aggregate liability from such policies. Copayments levied a marginal cost on patients for services rendered, thereby restraining demand for, or acquiescence to, costly services or lengthy hospitalization; deductibles imposed an up-front "loading" charge, thereby discouraging expensive and often discretionary treatments. Most importantly, indemnity coverage left patients the residual risk bearers for outlays due to sickness that exceeded the indemnity benefit. By 1940 indemnity coverage for hospitalization had been extended via employer group plans to almost 4 million individuals.

The growth of prepaid hospital service benefit plans and commercial indemnity policies not only reduced the hospital's financial risk of patient default, but had the secondary effect of lessening the rate of default on uncovered physician bills. Despite the overwhelming evidence that the new hospitalization coverage significantly lessened the financial losses of health providers, physicians initially resisted the development of such a provider-controlled plan for their services. While a number of prepaid plans did exist between employer or employee association and physician groups, the American Medical Association sanctioned only indemnity coverage until 1942. Then, realizing that a prepaid physician service benefit plan analogous to the Blue Cross Plans would be viable only if providers accepted a fixed-fee schedule, the AMA reluctantly approved physician participation only in those plans that were sponsored by a state medical society.

These early plans, the forerunners of Blue Shield Plans, suffered from the same inherent instability that plagued their Blue Cross counterparts: providers had an incentive to overutilize expensive services, receiving guaranteed reimbursement and suffering only minimally from resulting plan overruns. The problem was especially severe for Blue Shield given that its large number of participating physicians reduced each provider's loss from overruns and increased the cost of monitoring individual utilization patterns. As reimbursement per service "unit" began to fall precipitously due to cost overruns, many prepaid physician plans converted from service to indemnity benefits, thereby once again leaving physicians to set their own fee schedules and patients to be residual risk bearers for charges beyond the indemnity benefit. Those plans that continued to offer service benefits were often forced to provide indemnity payments to subscribers for services rendered by the growing number of nonparticipating physicians. As physician support waned for all but the simplest indemnity coverage, the spread of Blue Shield Plans slowed, enrolling only 2 million subscribers by 1945.

Insurers focused primarily on employee group health plans, thereby exploiting a low-cost vehicle for collecting premiums —employer withholding. More importantly, the workplace purchase of health insurance as a collective fringe benefit meant that employees were usually limited to a uniform benefit package, irrespective of their health condition, expected future losses, risk preferences, and willingness to pay. The possibility that only high-risk individuals would apply for extensive coverage was thereby greatly diminished; nevertheless, the adoption of a single premium rate for all members of the group allowed such higher-risk and more risk-averse employees to benefit at the expense of lower-risk and more risk-preferring workers. So long as workers could not "vote with their feet" for their preferred package of fringe benefits and wages, the early workplace-based system of uniform benefits and premiums would remain a stable one for the marketing of health insurance.

Two government actions would contribute critically to the explosive growth of employee health plans. The first, adopted in 1942, exempted fringe benefits from wage and price controls, thereby permitting real wages to rise at a time of tight labor markets. The second, incorporated into the Internal Revenue Code of 1954, excluded employer health insurance premium contributions from an employee's taxable income, thereby creating a bias (which increased with an employee's income and, thus, marginal tax rate) toward more insurance in lieu of higher money wages. Exempting fringe benefits from wage and price controls during World War II caused the number of group subscribers to virtually quadruple from its pre-1942 level of 7 million. Still, by the end of the war, only one-fifth of the population participated in an employee group plan, and far fewer had coverage extending beyond hospitalization.

Risk Sharing in the Postwar Era

The postwar rise of collective bargaining and the increasing importance of health benefits in the negotiated package promoted the growth of employee group health plans such that by 1958 almost 80 percent of full-time workers enjoyed some type of health coverage. Both the scope of benefits and the share of the employer's (tax free) contribution were subjects of negotiation, creating incentives for management to control the costs of their employee health plan. Employers monitored employee utilization of services and began to comparison shop for the best premium rates. Indeed, a number of large employers established "self-insured" programs for their employees, thereby assuming the responsibilities of a health insurer. As competition for large employer accounts raged, service-benefit and indemnity policies began to look increasingly alike. To remain competitive, Blue Cross Plans adopted several indemnity policy features including differentiated premium schedules (based on a group's previous utilization experience), restrictions on covered services, and copayments and deductibles to control utilization. On their part, commercial carriers expanded their indemnity plans to cover many routine "prepaid" services previously reimbursed only by service-benefit contracts.

Some employers soon realized that their most effective means of controlling utilization and costs was to adopt the government's early strategy of both financing and providing health care. A new version of company medicine arose as Henry Kaiser, faced with a smaller postwar labor force, opened his employees' comprehensive health facilities to

workers in other industries. By the early 1950s, the Kaiser
direct service plan had enrolled more than 500,000 subscribers. At the same time that many service benefit plans were
shifting to pure insurance (indemnity) coverage and imposing
copayments and deductibles to control utilization, direct service plans were moving in the opposite direction, providing
comprehensive coverage with few exclusions, limits, or copayments. Such prepaid systems of medical care were feasible
where previous service benefit contracts had failed, because
health care provider services were contracted for by the same
organization that bore the financial risks of overutilization. To
lessen these risks, direct service plans typically adopted physician payment schemes that were independent of services rendered, thereby minimizing incentives for overuse of costly
services. Indeed, putting physicians on salary or otherwise
severing the link between physician reimbursement and services rendered the patient could create incentives for un-
derutilization on the part of physicians. Still, subscribers faced
incentives to overuse facilities and providers when no copayment was required. Direct service plans sought to turn this
behavior to their own advantage by encouraging patients to
seek comparatively low-cost preventive or early treatment
rather than deferring care to the point where expensive interventions and hospitalization would become necessary. The
market penetration of these plans (and, later, health maintenance organizations) would be significantly enhanced as employees began to offer their employers a choice of health coverage options. Employees would thereby be allowed to trade
off the freedom of choice in providers offered by traditional
insurance coverage—with its attendant exclusions, limited
coverage, and higher deductibles and copayments—for the
more comprehensive care provided by a closed panel of physicians associated with direct service organizations.

Although employee group health plans were eminently successful in providing health benefits for the full-time permanent work force, reliance on the workplace for coverage meant
that a sizable number of individuals were left without any
mechanism for prepaying or sharing the financial losses of

sickness. Unemployed, transitory, and part-time workers, as well as minimum-wage earners (whose money wages by law could not be reduced in exchange for employer-provided health benefits), faced prohibitively expensive, individually underwritten insurance policies. Likewise, some retired and disabled individuals qualified only for high-risk, high-cost policies. In fact, the very success of employment-based coverage may have imposed significant costs on the residual, uninsured population. Paul Starr contends that "in leaving out millions of Americans, the insurance system actually worsened their position because of the inflationary effect that insurance had on the cost of medical care." Moreover, as risk pools of relatively healthy employees formed in the workplace, the unemployed often found themselves relegated to residual, high-risk groups for underwriting purposes.

The introduction of Medicaid and Medicare in 1966 sought to lessen the financial risks of illness for millions of elderly and indigent individuals. Medicaid offered to share with state governments the burden of providing health care for the poor (and in some states, the medically needy) by reimbursing a percentage of state outlays. Although states with lower per capita incomes received proportionally more federal funds for their Medicaid populations, they were hard pressed to finance the required contributory payments. Thus those states with the greatest need instituted only limited Medicaid programs with stringent eligibility criteria.

In contrast, Medicare was implemented as an extension of Social Security. The Medicare amendments to the Social Security Act established a compulsory contributory hospital insurance plan for the aged (called Part A coverage) and a voluntary physician and outpatient insurance program (called Part B coverage). Its hospitalization plan offered cost-based reimbursement and virtually "first-dollar" coverage beyond the first day of care for a fixed number of hospital days, thereby encouraging both the subscriber and hospital to overutilize services and offering no reward for cost-effective patient management. (It would take nearly a decade of plan overruns before Medicare would attempt to control hospital utilization through the use of Professional Standard Review Organizations [PSROs]; almost another decade of overruns would occur before the Medicare reimbursement system would be totally revamped in favor of diagnosis related group [DRG] payments.) Similar open-ended incentives were—and still are—embedded in Medicare's physician payment system, which reimburses physicians on a fee-for-service basis according to "customary" or "prevailing" area charges (often significantly higher if a procedure was performed in a hospital).

In both Medicare plans, premiums were unrelated to health condition, thereby benefiting high-risk individuals at the expense of healthier subscribers. Moreover, uniform and compulsory hospital coverage denied individuals the freedom to choose how much and what kinds of financial risks from illness they would prefer to bear and how to mitigate such risks (e.g., by private savings or indemnity plans). The plan's heavy reliance on payroll taxes also created substantial windfalls for older workers and the retired at the expense of younger employees.

Whereas Medicare was viewed (albeit improperly) as an actuarially sound benefits program for the aged, Medicaid was branded a tax-supported public assistance program. As a result, political and financial support for Medicaid was substantially more limited than for Medicare. While Medicare eligibility criteria and benefits, for example, were standardized on the federal level, those for Medicaid were set by the states. Moreover, Medicare encouraged physician participation by allowing physicians to charge patients more than Medicare would cover, whereas Medicaid required participating providers to accept its reimbursement as payment in full. Congressional ambivalence toward Medicaid as a means of financing health care for the poor was perhaps best exemplified by its continued flirtation with the direct provision of medical services for the categorically needy. Indeed, only one year after the introduction of Medicaid, public health care centers were being touted as the most viable mechanism for providing health care to the poor. It was clear that despite their public criticism of a two-tiered health care system, political leaders remained uncomfortable with the decision to "mainstream" the poor into the private provider network. Thus the debate would continue over the relative merits of government-provided insurance versus government-provided medical services as the most cost-effective means of helping the poor meet the financial burden of sickness.

By the late 1970s, Medicare and Medicaid outlays were doubling in the span of three years (to more than $25 billion and $18 billion, respectively, in 1978) and tax expenditures for employer-provided health insurance had topped $10 billion. Nevertheless, 28 million Medicare recipients faced increasingly onerous, inflation-bloated first-day deductibles ($572 in 1986) and had no coverage for long-term care; more importantly, only one-third of the poor were covered by Medicaid and more than 26 million individuals remained without any public or private coverage whatsoever. Excluded from Medicaid were most low-wage earners, the recently unemployed, and low-income two-parent families, widows, and single persons without children. Faced with the entire burden of financial loss from illness and escalating medical charges, these individuals increasingly withdrew from the market for medical care except in life-threatening situations. In such instances, the enactment of laws requiring that emergency care be rendered once again left providers (and in some cases, other paying patients) as the residual risk bearers for the financial losses of the uninsured and underinsured population.

In 1986 the scenario remained largely unchanged except that the ranks of the uninsured had swelled to more than 37 million people and an increasingly competitive environment had substantially limited the potential role of health care providers as residual risk bearers. Clearly a commitment to improving access to health care must focus on the development of new institutions that permit individuals to share the financial burden of sickness.

Risk Sharing: Some Economic Considerations

Prepayment Versus Insurance

Faced with both certain ("routine") and uncertain future medical expenditures, individuals may wish to minimize the burden of such outlays through either prepayment or insurance schemes. With prepayment schemes, the cost of a fixed bundle of medical services is spread over time prior to, rather than after, utilization. The provider of care is no longer subject to the financial risk of default on services rendered or the expense of often lengthy collection processes. In return, the subscribers to such "forced savings" plans are guaranteed medical care, irrespective of ability to pay, when they need it. As long as there exist government subsidies for these prepayment schemes in the form of tax deductibility of premiums and exclusion of employers' contributions from taxable income, there will be incentives for individuals to favor prepaid health options over other voluntary savings efforts to pay for future health care.

In reality, prepaid health policies typically offer much more than a simple budgeting mechanism for future medical consumption. Not all subscribers fully exhaust their service options, nor are they permitted to resell or otherwise transfer the remaining benefits; as a result, prepaid plans can offer potentially expensive services at vastly discounted premium rates (the original Blue Cross Plan offered twenty-one days of hospital care for $6 per year). The underwriters of such plans will typically set premiums equal to the expected cost of care rendered the subscriber during the policy year (i.e., service cost weighted by the probability of utilization) plus a fee to cover administrative expenses, profits, and reserve requirements. As the probability of utilization or the cost of the covered service increases, so will the premium charged; thus, policies that cover routine but inexpensive procedures such as vaccinations or rare but expensive treatments such as heart transplants will have higher premiums than those that do not.

When utilization is certain (i.e., its probability of occurrence equal to one), subscribers have in fact engaged strictly in a prepayment arrangement for medical care, paying a premium roughly equal to the cost of the future treatment. When utilization is uncertain, however, subscribers have purchased insurance against the risk of requiring medical services. Health insurance spreads the direct financial costs of illness across participants in its risk pool, usually according to each individual's probability of making an insurance claim. Individual risk preferences dictate the degree to which someone will trade off uncertainty about future financial obligations for a certain current payment. In theory, a risk-neutral person will participate in a risk-sharing arrangement as long as the policy premium is less than or equal to his or her expected future expenses, whereas a risk-averse individual will be willing to pay somewhat more to avoid the chance of incurring large financial losses in the future. According to widely held assumptions concerning risk preferences, people will more often insure against low-probability, high-loss events than against predictable, low-cost events. This prediction is consistent with the observation that in 1983 more than 80 percent of private hospital expenditures were reimbursed by third-party payers whereas less than one-third of dental services were covered by insurance.

Insurable Versus Uninsurable Risks

When there exists a high degree of uncertainty with respect to either the probability or cost of utilization, health insurers will be reluctant to cover specific services or illnesses. For example, it has been argued that Medicare specifically excluded long-term care from its coverage because of the lack of good actuarial information in the mid-1960s about either the incidence or expense of such care. More recently, insurers have contemplated limiting coverage for expenses related to the costly treatment of acquired immune deficiency syndrome (AIDS), given the imprecision with which they can forecast its incidence. Often, as technology changes or experience with specific health conditions grows, previously uninsurable risks will become insurable. The development of antibody tests to identify potential AIDS victims may, if allowed by law, provide insurers with important information on the pattern of incidence of the disease. Likewise, the evolution of the private long-term care industry has yielded important insights into utilization and costs for this kind of care.

It is important that the distinction be drawn between potentially insurable risks and those that are in fact insured against. Just as individuals at age seventy will rarely opt for a term life insurance policy given its high premium cost (based on the odds of payout), they will often choose not to insure against health conditions if the policy premium is too high. Thus, for example, individuals testing positive for AIDS antibodies will face prohibitively high premiums given their greater probability of subsequently developing the disease, uncertainty about the disease's latency period, and the high cost of medical care. Clearly, it would be to those individuals' advantage if insurance coverage were extended to the treatment of AIDS and if (perhaps due to government mandate) they could not be readily identified as at-risk through preenrollment screening. If this occurred, the cost of AIDS claims would have to be spread uniformly over the premiums of all policyholders (as if that risk were evenly distributed), or be allocated according to some discernible characteristic that was correlated with incidence of the disease.

An Efficient System of Risk Bearing

If a system of risk bearing is to meet standards of economic efficiency, each person must bear the full expected cost of his or her future health needs. To do otherwise would discourage individuals from making choices that lessen the incidence or cost of the health risk. If, for example, a worker perceives that the cost of workplace injuries is borne fully by the employer (or, in turn, spread over all employees in the form of lower wages), that worker will have less incentive to engage in such injury-avoidance activities as wearing uncomfortable, but protective, clothing. Likewise, an individual who bears less than the full expected cost of future by-pass surgery will not invest in an optimal amount of "risk avoidance" (prevention) in the form of dietary restrictions and exercise, nor will he or she necessarily seek the least-cost course of treatment. From society's viewpoint, an optimal system of risk bearing would assure that (1) riskiness is reduced in a least-cost fashion to the point where the cost of additional prevention activities outweighs the cost savings resulting from lessening the risk at hand; and (2) the costs arising from the actualization of the risk are minimized.

Having engaged in the optimal amount of risk avoidance, individuals may wish to share the financial burden of the remaining risk through the purchase of insurance. Because a risk-averse person will be willing to pay a premium in excess of the expected cost of future medical claims to avoid highly variable and possibly expensive future outcomes, insurance companies—presumably owned by risk-averse individuals— have evolved to establish risk pools over which to spread these financial risks. As long as the insurer can get enough customers with approximately the same probability of making a claim (the definition of a risk class), and the odds of payout to any one policyholder are independent of that to any other, the company can be reasonably certain of the aggregate payoff it will make to the pool, even though the payoff to any one customer will still remain uncertain. To assure independence in payouts, insurers offering coverage for expensive communicable diseases, for example, might diversify over different geographic areas.

Often the very existence of insurance actually increases the expected claims payout through both a reduction in private prevention activities and larger losses per claim. Once an insurer has set a premium based on an assessment of probability and cost of future medical treatment, the insured party faces no additional cost during the policy period if he or she exceeds this predicted expected claims amount. Thus there is an incentive to engage in activities that increase (rather than decrease) the probability and cost of a claim, thereby causing the expected return from the policy to exceed its premium.

It is not surprising that recent studies have revealed a significant disparity in the utilization of physician, pharmacy, and hospital services for uninsured versus insured individuals. The fact that individuals will increase their demand for often costly covered medical interventions in response to insurance coverage has been termed the moral hazard problem of insurance. In the face of this problem, insurance policies often contain exclusionary clauses that withhold payment in instances where the insured party has clearly biased the "odds" of making a claim (e.g., suicide clauses in life insurance policies). With respect to health insurance, benefits may be severely limited for services presumed to be especially susceptible to the moral hazard phenomenon (e.g., cosmetic surgery), or copayments can be used to impose a cost on the policyholder for increases in the number or size of claims. When future premiums can be adjusted to reflect one's history of utilization (experience rating), individuals may be disciplined by the cost of such future insurance purchases, and the moral hazard problem greatly diminished. In reality, however, the prevalence of uniform employee group coverage and rates severely limits individual-based experience rating, instead spreading the costs of moral hazard over all participants in a plan.

Inasmuch as individuals know more about their health status and expected medical needs than insurers, a second threat to the actuarial soundness of risk-sharing plans can arise through adverse selection—the tendency of high-risk individuals to gravitate toward more extensive coverage as long as they can conceal their greater riskiness and thereby enjoy a premium which is less than their expected expenses. This behavior is aggravated by legal restrictions on the types of information that insurers can use to evaluate riskiness. As insurers subsequently adjust their premiums upward (or benefits downward) to reflect a greater-than-expected payout on their policies, less risky individuals may, if permitted, drop out of the risk pool or opt for significantly more limited, and thus cheaper, coverage.

In reality, it is difficult to assess the degree to which adverse selection plagues the health insurance market. The potential for adverse selection is substantially limited by the prevalence of group plans offering uniform benefits and premiums. Commenting on the insurance industry's seeming lack of concern about whether premiums accurately reflect individual riskiness and thereby minimize incentives for adverse selection, Mark Pauly notes that "insurers seem reluctant even to vary premiums with many of the characteristics they can observe that predict medical expenditures, such as age and family size . . . . This is true of insurance sold directly to individuals, and is even more true for multiple-choice employee groups. Indicators of chronic conditions are even less used." Pauly does suggest, however, that the substantially greater medical expenditures for individuals with Medicare supplemental policies than for those without indicate that adverse selection can indeed affect health insurance markets.

Even when individuals bear the full expected cost of their future medical needs, they may not manage health risks in a socially optimal fashion; that is, they may take risks that impose additional costs on other members of society. Such is the case, for example, when one travels unvaccinated to less developed countries. Individuals will make socially optimal decisions about health risks only if they bear the full expected social costs of such risks or, analogously, enjoy the full expected social benefits of risk-avoidance activities. Where there is a divergence between private and social costs (benefits), there exists an externality that may justify government intervention to influence private risk-taking choices. This externality argument has been used repeatedly (and often improperly) to justify a variety of government health related activities, including public health programs and tax subsidies for insurance.

Equity Considerations in Risk Bearing

Whereas an efficient system of risk bearing requires that one bear the full expected cost of one's future health needs, an equitable system may dictate that such costs be subsidized.

Even with an optimal amount of prevention, individuals will usually face some remaining financial risk of illness or disability that they may be unable to insure against, given their income or health status. In such instances, the actualization of the risky event can often create severe economic hardship and strain available resources. In a market economy where goods and services are distributed according to one's willingness and ability to pay, lack of financial wherewithal can severely limit an individual's options with respect to risk avoidance (prevention is not costless), risk sharing (insurance), and, most importantly, health care.

Low-income individuals are denied a whole host of goods and services by the private market; nevertheless, public attention has focused primarily on their underconsumption of specific merit goods such as health care, food, and housing. Despite the fact that individuals would prefer to be helped by unrestricted grants of income rather than subsidized consumption, grantors (the nonpoor) appear predisposed toward reducing disparities in the consumption of specific goods rather than overall purchasing power. This piecemeal approach to poverty may be aggravated by the presence of powerful industry interest groups that promote subsidies for their specific products and services.

Support for universal access to quality health care, irrespective of ability to pay, has grown to where such access is deemed a right by many. More controversial is the issue of whether society ought to permit variation in the quality or extent of care according to one's ability to pay. Although there is a general inclination to allow such "elective" services as cosmetic surgery to be allocated according to ability to pay, there appears to be less tolerance for differential access to dialysis, for example. Moreover, the altruistic concerns that motivate subsidies for basic medical care may not require that such services be of the same quality as those purchased by the nonpoor. The ongoing debate over public provision of medical care to the categorically needy versus subsidy of private sector health care purchases attests to this tension over the definition and limitations of health care rights.

Just as society may wish to subsidize the risk-avoidance, risk-sharing, or health care choices of low-income individuals, it may also wish to share in the financial burden of individuals who face high expected medical costs owing to uncontrollable factors or chance events. For example, Medicare coverage for end-stage renal disease is available regardless of one's ability to pay. More indirectly, regulations that promote the mainstreaming of the disabled into society via employment and educational guidelines shift some of the expected cost of their health status to others in society. Recent proposals to prohibit health insurance rating on the basis of race or gender have argued that it is unfair to impose a financial burden on individuals because of uncontrollable race or gender related health conditions that increase their expected medical needs. Thus there appears to be some support for a risk-sharing system which distinguishes between risks that cannot be avoided at any cost and those that one chooses not to avoid, however justified on a cost-benefit basis such as described above.

The Efficiency "Cost" of Equitable Risk Bearing

Because individuals engage in an optimal, least-cost strategy of risk management only if they face the full expected cost of such risks, they will have less incentive to engage in risk avoidance if subsidies of controllable risks are introduced in pursuit of a more equitable system of risk sharing. Moreover, when subsidies vary according to type of provider or procedure, one's choice of medical treatment may not result in the least-cost resolution of a given health problem. In short, the achievement of an efficient system of risk bearing can be seriously threatened by the presence of health care subsidies.

Such subsidies can also lead to inefficiencies in the risk-bearing behavior of subsidizers. For example, when insurers are required to charge uniform premiums and offer uniform coverage despite obvious differences in the expected costs of policyholders, adverse selection will occur in the risk pool. Even when such adverse selection can be deterred, cross-subsidies of high-risk individuals by low-risk policyholders can exacerbate the moral hazard problem for low-risk individuals by encouraging them to reduce their prevention activities in order to bring their expected policy payout more in line with their actuarially unfair premium costs.

The feasibility of cross-subsidization in insurance depends crucially on the inability of insured parties to exit the pool. Moreover, insurers must be required to cover both higher- and lower-risk individuals so that competition does not result in a "skimming off" of the more profitable low-risk individuals and an eventual reduction in their premiums. This latter requirement has been increasingly thwarted by the establishment of self-insured employee group plans, which can reduce premiums by restricting the risk pool to a company's relatively healthy work force. Even within employee group plans, cross-subsidization via uniform premiums and coverage can be sustained only so long as workers cannot "sort" themselves across employers according to desired benefits and riskiness; to be sure, the availability of multiple health insurance options within a given workplace may stimulate sorting if workers can enjoy higher wages in lieu of more expensive coverage. In order for Medicare to perpetuate a system where significant discrepancies exist between individual contributions and expected payout, it prevents adverse selection by requiring participation in its Part A coverage; the voluntary nature of Medicare Part B participation, however, makes this latter coverage more vulnerable to the self-selection phenomenon.

Cross-subsidization may also occur in the pricing of health care services and has been particularly well documented in the hospital sector. In 1982 alone, private hospitals were faced with more than $3 billion in charity care and uncollectible bills, most of which were attributed to individuals without public or private insurance. To remain economically viable (nonprofit and for-profit hospitals alike must have sufficient revenues to pay labor and capital a competitive return), hospitals must generate additional philanthropic income or raise their charges to paying patients. Because private contributions to hospitals have not grown sufficiently to cover all uncompensated care (they totalled just $1.2 billion in 1982), the cross-subsidization of patients becomes an increasingly attractive option. As with health insurance, cross-subsidies in health care charges cannot be sustained if providers are permitted to "specialize" in paying customers and thereby offer them lower prices (or otherwise compete on such nonprice dimensions as newness of facility). When demand for specific services is price-sensitive or there exist alternative treatment sites (e.g., the physician's office), the potential for paying patients to opt out of the system will be significant. The fact that most paying patients are covered by private or public insurance clearly reduces their sensitivity to the presence of cross-subsidies. However, as competitive pressures are brought upon private insurers to lower premium costs and public insurance programs attempt to limit expenditures, third-party payers have become increasingly intolerant of cross-subsidization in the health care delivery system.

If adequate subsidies for the health costs of nonpaying patients cannot be generated from philanthropic sources, other insured parties, or paying patients, society must pursue its equity goals through government activity. Indirect action in the form of regulation can be used to bolster cross-subsidization schemes in insurance and health care delivery markets by restricting competition among providers, setting rates, and mandating coverage. Regulation imposes an implicit tax on market participants; its political attractiveness lies in the fact that the burden of the tax—dictated by a host of factors including one's consumption patterns, price sensitivity, and the nature of the cross-subsidy—is largely unclear. It has been argued that the waning of public support for regulations that enforce cross-subsidization is due largely to the government's desire to lower the expenditures of its own paying Medicare and Medicaid populations.

Government can share in the financial burden of health risks through (1) explicit subsidy, (2) favorable tax treatment of insurance and health care expenditures, and (3) the provision of health care or insurance to those deemed deserving of government assistance. In fact, all three approaches have been used extensively to spread financial risk over the tax-paying population. In 1985 more than 190 million Americans benefited from health insurance subsidies resulting from the tax deductibility of premiums and the tax exclusion for employer-paid health premiums; another 27.5 million received assistance through the Medicaid program. Yet another 30 million individuals benefited from Medicare insurance coverage, and an untold number received health services from federal, state, and local government care givers. Finally, a long-standing government commitment to subsidize hospital capital costs— through grants, tax exempt bonds, and government backed debt instruments—has arguably reduced the private cost of hospital care and thereby improved access.

Even when the total amount of government subsidy is held fixed, alternative subsidy schemes will result in substantially different patterns of health services/insurance consumption, as well as in different distributions of the subsidy burden. The tax deductibility of private medical and insurance expenditures, along with the tax exemption for employer premiums, inherently channels subsidies toward upper-income individuals and wage earners (those in higher tax brackets). Pauly reports that for the average U.S. worker, the marginal tax subsidy for health insurance exceeded 35 percent of premiums in 1986, and was significantly greater for high-wage individuals with correspondingly higher marginal tax rates and levels of employer-paid premiums. Perhaps more importantly, Pauly contends that "the effect of a tax subsidy in excess of 10 percent of premiums [the typical loading factor on a group policy] is to make the after-tax price of insurance protection negative for many workers; it becomes cheaper to pay one's medical care bills via insurance than to pay them directly." In effect then, tax subsidies not only promote insurance, but also encourage comprehensive "first-dollar" coverage for even the most routine health care. Moreover, they discourage prevention activities and can exacerbate the moral hazard problem. If the intent of government subsidy is to share the burden of significant health risks only, or to assist only those who are unable to pay, then current tax policy is largely inappropriate.

Direct government subsidy of health care and insurance purchases can more precisely target assistance to the categorically and medically needy or relieve the financial burden of specific health risks (e.g., end-stage renal disease). When the subsidy rate varies across health care options, however, it may bias choices away from the least-cost treatment; for example, the emphasis of Medicaid and Medicare on hospitalization benefits has discouraged the demand for preventive and ambulatory services. The cost effectiveness of health care choices is further threatened when subsidy programs offer cost-based reimbursement, thereby removing any incentive to minimize service costs.

Government-provided health care and government-administered insurance afford the greatest control over total public expenditures, recipient groups, and services covered. At the same time, however, direct provision denies individuals the freedom to choose their health care provider or insurer and, in so doing, can perpetuate an inefficient, bureaucratic government monopoly and discourage least-cost courses of treatment and risk management.

When government resources are insufficient to meet the demand of targeted groups, some mechanism for adjusting or rationing benefits must be developed. In the case of public insurance programs, this has often meant a continual increase in deductibles and copays or eligibility requirements for all recipients and services. Where health care has been directly provided, rationing has been accomplished through lengthy and discouraging waiting times; this, of course, tends to thereby direct services toward those with the lowest opportunity cost of time.

The Risk-Sharing Implications of Financing Options: Some Examples

Community Versus Experience Rating

As Blue Cross Plan service contracts evolved, participants in group plans within the service area were charged the same "community" premium, irrespective of their actual prior utilization. This uniform rating system redistributed the financial burden of health risks from high- to low-risk groups, and, at the same time, significantly lessened the information-gathering and administrative costs of the insurance provider. Inasmuch as premiums were independent of expected health costs, community rating also discouraged individuals from prevention activities and aggravated the moral hazard problem. The viability of cross-subsidizing high-risk individuals through community rating depended crucially on retaining low-risk policyholders in the plan. The initial scarcity of commercial insurance alternatives as well as the cost advantages afforded the Blue Cross Plans by hospital discounts, favorable tax treatment, and lax reserve requirements (policies which lowered the cost of coverage for all risk groups) allowed these early community-rated plans to thrive.

As commercial insurers began to offer health coverage, however, the conditions conducive to community rating began to erode. Just as they set life insurance and liability policy premiums according to claims experience, commercial insurers adjusted group health premiums according to prior utilization. It can be argued that commercial insurers enjoyed a significant cost advantage in administering experience-rated plans, since actuarial information was already being gathered for life insurance rating purposes. Employers of low-risk healthy workers would strongly favor experience over community rating, especially if the cost savings could be partially captured by the employer. Experience rating also gave both employers and employees a greater incentive to promote efficient utilization and risk-avoidance activities. As commercial insurers expanded their market share through the practice of experience rating (by which they were able to "skim" the best risk groups), they put pressure on Blue Cross Plans to abandon community rating.

Certainly, community rating continues to exist, albeit within differently defined "communities." Employee group plans typically levy a uniform premium on their members, irrespective of health status. This cross-subsidization of higher-risk employees will be perpetuated only as long as low-risk employees cannot adversely select against the health plan through their choice of employment or through personalized adjustments in their fringe benefit package (as permitted by so-called cafeteria benefit plans).

Public insurance programs like Medicare have typically solved the adverse selection problem created by uniform premiums and benefits by making participation compulsory; nonetheless, adverse selection would destabilize such voluntary programs as Medicare Part B if the premium charged low-risk individuals, including the cross-subsidy surcharge, were not competitive with private insurance rates. Thus voluntary public insurance programs must be more cost-effective than their private counterparts (enough to offset the cross-subsidy); if not, they will require government subsidy. Similarly, health maintenance organizations (HMOs) which are required by federal law to adopt community rating in order to qualify for government assistance, must be sufficiently cost-effective to remain competitive even in the face of such mandated cross-subsidization.

Capitation and Health Maintenance Organizations

In the early days of prepaid medical plans, participating physicians received a fixed (usually uniform) prepayment per subscriber for services to be rendered in the forthcoming year. As a consequence of this capitation scheme, providers became insurers, because they had to bear the financial risk of divergences from forecast utilization during the contract year. The risk of underestimating demand was great, since the moral hazard problem—the tendency to overutilize covered medical services—was seriously aggravated by the fact that subscribers faced no additional service fee beyond the up-front charge. While capitation biases individuals away from prevention and toward covered medical services, at the same time it encourages providers to minimize the cost and amount of health care delivered (subject to the constraint that they be able to retain subscribers).

The concept of capitation has recently reemerged in health maintenance organizations, a health care delivery system distinguished by the comprehensiveness of its services and its integrated role as health care provider and insurer. The growth in HMOs received strong impetus from the 1973 federal HMO act, which requires employee groups of more than twenty-five members to offer an HMO health option when one is available. Through the use of a closed panel of physicians, HMOs have imposed implicit benefit limits on subscribers in exchange for a broad range of covered health services. The comprehensiveness of HMO services, as reflected by such offerings as mental health, nutrition, and prevention programs, allows subscribers to choose a mix of preventive, ambulatory, and hospital care, free from the bias created by differential coverage. Capitation and the availability of a broad range of services also encourage providers to pursue the most cost-effective course of treatment.

Lower total costs and admission rates of HMOs have been cited as evidence of the improved incentives for risk management facing both patients and providers in HMOs. Whether this trend is the result of more efficient use of preventive and outpatient services or of the incentives of subscribers to seek relatively inexpensive treatment early in the course of a sickness is unclear. More skeptical observers contend that capitated plans have an incentive to reduce costs by skimping on their quality of care (i.e., limiting hospital use irrespective of "need") and imposing lengthy waits for nonemergency procedures, although such behavior would most certainly be constrained by the desire of HMOs to retain subscribers and market share. It has been argued that the apparent cost savings of HMOs may stem largely from "self-selection" of HMOs by young, low-risk individuals who may be attracted to the generous pediatric benefits of HMOs and their reputation for less aggressive medical intervention.

While HMOs are usually distinguished by their capitated subscription system, they are less uniform in their manner of reimbursing their closed panel of physicians. HMO physicians may receive a fixed salary (with or without profit sharing) irrespective of the number of patients they see or procedures they do, a payment per patient or contact, or a fee per service rendered. Thus the degree to which providers are encouraged to manage health risks in a cost-effective fashion will be dictated primarily by their mode of reimbursement. For example, HMO physicians who are remunerated on a fee-for-service basis may require additional monitoring by the HMO's administration to offset the inherent bias toward overutilization of expensive procedures. This ongoing tension between administrator and physician is not unlike that encountered earlier this century between Blue Shield Plans and their participating physicians. In contrast, when physicians participate in a capitated reimbursement system, they may require central monitoring to assure that the quality of care is not compromised, given the incentive to cut costs by reducing services.

Diagnosis Related Group Reimbursement and Medicare

Spurred on by the rapid growth in Medicare expenditures in the 1960s and 1970s, the federal government sought an alternative to the cost-plus reimbursement system in place for nearly two decades. In October 1983, Medicare initiated a phased-in prospective payment system for Part A covered hospital services (Part B physician and outpatient services continued to be reimbursed on a "usual and customary" basis) which utilized diagnosis related groups to determine the price paid per Medicare hospital admission. The price of each of the 468 DRGs is independent of hospital-specific costs and characteristics, but is adjusted to reflect local wage rates, location (urban/suburban), and teaching intensity. In effect, the DRG system has replaced a cost-based reimbursement system, which imposed no financial risk on the hospital, with an indemnity payment per admission. Since hospitals cannot recoup any additional charges from the Medicare patient, this new mode of payment renders the hospital the sole risk bearer should patient costs deviate from the prospective payment. Only in the case of extreme outliers—with costs greater than 1.5 times the DRG payment rate or $12,000—does Medicare provide supplemental reimbursement.

The extent to which hospitals suffer financial losses thus depends on the amount by which their aggregate Medicare patient costs exceed allowable payments. Hospitals can reduce potential losses by pursuing least-cost courses of treatment, reducing lengths of stay, and making full use of lower-cost inpatient and outpatient treatment sites (the latter being reimbursed on a usual and customary basis). In fact, there has already been a documented reduction in the length of hospital stays for Medicare patients less than three years after the inception of DRGs. Because DRG rates approximate the average cost of servicing a particular health problem, however, the DRG system will, by its very nature, cause hospitals to "win" or "lose" on specific cases, depending on their severity and complexity, irrespective of the efficiency with which a patient is managed. Although Medicare contends that its DRG payment will average out across cases in any specific category (i.e., that less severe cases will offset more severe cases), studies have shown that this is unlikely to be true, particularly in small hospitals with insufficient patient volume to validate the law of averages. Thus the DRG system can impose differential financial burdens on hospitals according to their case mix and patient load.

If the least-cost management of patients still leaves the hospital with an expected cost greater than the indemnity payment, it will have an incentive to refuse such patients or reduce the quality of care given (e.g., by premature discharge). Alternatively, the hospital may attempt to shift costs to other paying patient groups. Cross-subsidization of Medicare patients, however, is not viable when the Medicare case load varies (as it often does) across hospitals. In such a situation, hospitals with a lower-cost or volume Medicare patient population will enjoy a competitive advantage in setting lower rates for their non-Medicare clientele, given their lesser need for Medicare cross-subsidies.

Rate Regulation and Mandated Benefits

Just as the federal government was seeking to stem the flow of Medicare funds, states were taking steps to limit their Medicaid commitments. Between 1970 and 1980 state and local expenditures on health care had risen abruptly from $8 billion to more than $24 billion; by 1983 expenditures exceeded $35 billion. Several states instituted hospital rate regulation systems during the latter half of the 1970s in recognition of the impending budgetary crisis in public health finance. The development of an all-payer system (where all payers reimburse hospitals according to the same methodology) in Maryland, for example, signified a shift in responsibility for cost containment from private third-party payers to the state.

Political support for rate regulation was premised on a belief that state health expenditures for the categorically needy could be controlled by limiting inflation in hospital charges. It was also believed that proposals to extend Medicaid coverage to low-income workers could be sidestepped by the adoption of a rate-setting system that built in cross-subsidies for the uninsured and underinsured populations. (It is perhaps telling that rate regulation arose initially in states headed by budget conscious, fiscally conservative Republicans.) Thus adoption of all-payer rate-setting systems—with rates set equal to both the minimum and maximum allowable charge—could provide hospitals with indirect subsidies for uncompensated care and spread financial responsibility for health care services to all primary and third-party payers; moreover, it could prevent undesirable cost shifting between hospital patient and payer groups. In this latter regard, commercial health insurers favored all-payer systems as a vehicle for potentially reducing existing Blue Cross hospital charge differentials.

Hospitals were quick to mobilize support for state rate regulation as a preferable alternative to impending changes in federal reimbursement policies, believing that they could exert greater influence in local policy making and that state regulators would be more sensitive to local needs. The success of rate setting in circumventing federal controls was perhaps most evident when rate-setting states received "waivers" exempting them from the Medicare DRG reimbursement system (subject to the condition that their rate of increase in cost per case mix adjusted Medicare admission be less than the national average).

Perhaps more importantly, state rate setting held the promise of reducing the role (and resulting financial burden) of hospitals as residual risk bearers, by adjusting rates to incorporate losses from uncompensated care. Inner city hospitals with large nonpaying patient populations were particularly supportive of any regulations that would inhibit suburban competitors from attracting paying patients by charging lower rates and thereby destabilizing existing cross-subsidy schemes. In reality, however, many suburban hospitals have retained a competitive advantage even in the presence of rate setting because such hospitals have competed on nonprice dimensions (e.g., newness of facility, proximity, and safety). Furthermore, states such as Maryland have adopted hospital-specific rates derived from base-year historic costs and each hospital's own uncompensated care burden.

By using historic costs and a standard of reasonableness (Maryland has defined reasonableness largely in terms of average, case mix adjusted service costs in the state) rather than actual costs to set rates, rate setting can encourage the least-cost provision of services. Moreover, rates that are neutral with respect to admission (i.e., reimbursement that is uniform for equivalent ambulatory and inpatient procedures) will lessen the bias toward costly hospitalization. However, if regulation focuses only on the unit cost per service, it will reinforce historic incentives for hospitals to maximize revenues by overutilizing expensive services. In fact, these incentives have largely disappeared over time as state rate setters have belatedly imposed aggregate revenue caps on hospitals, adjusted to reflect case mix and admission trends.

On both the federal and state level, the uncompensated care issue has been addressed through the promulgation of regulations that mandate extension of employer-based insurance coverage for individuals involuntarily removed from previous employee group plans. Laid-off workers, nonworking widows and exspouses of covered employees, minor dependents, and those just reaching majority are now protected by federal mandated benefit laws which guarantee them continued participation in employee health plans for as many as three years after a change in insurance status, as long as they pay the full group premium (employee and employer shares) plus a nominal surcharge to compensate employers for additional administrative costs. Clearly, not all previously insured individuals will choose to continue coverage under these terms, since their after-tax cost of participation will be greater than when they were able to purchase coverage with before-tax dollars (i.e., by trading off money wages for tax exempt employer premiums). Thus mandated benefit programs can introduce a substantial element of adverse selection into employee group plans, in that those individuals who purchase the insurance are more likely to use it. This, in turn, will lead to an escalation in premium rates for the entire employee group. Inasmuch as large employers might attempt to circumvent these additional premium costs by opting for self-insured plans (which, under the Employee Retirement Income Security Act of 1974 [ERISA] rules, are exempt from state insurance regulations), federal intervention in the area of mandated benefits becomes crucial to their success.

Sharing the Financial Burden of Health Risks: Future Directions

As competitive pressures mount in the health insurance and health care industries, traditional methods of improving access to risk-sharing and health care systems become increasingly vulnerable. The growing cost consciousness of third-party payers and the public sector substantially precludes the use of cross-subsidization, unless explicitly sanctioned by governmental regulation. Whereas the growing burden of uncompensated care attests to the health care provider's renewed role as residual risk bearer, the long-term solvency of the health care delivery system will demand the evolution of new institutions to spread the burden of health risks.

In 1986 the federal government introduced far-reaching legislation to guarantee health insurance coverage for individuals recently disqualified by employee group plans due to a change in employment status; the predicted impact of these mandated benefit programs has already been discussed. Policy initiatives must now focus on coverage for individuals without access to employer-based plans (e.g., minimum wage and part-time workers) and for those not in the workplace (e.g., the chronically unemployed).

The historical pattern of government intervention in health insurance and health care leads one to predict that public policy will continue to look to cross-subsidy as a means of improving access without imposing an explicit tax burden on the population. Proposals to provide uninsured individuals access to group insurance via state-sponsored insurance pools, of necessity, will require subsidies to be successful. Actuarially fair premiums for such pools would be prohibitive and uneconomical for all but the sickest subscribers. In order to cross-subsidize high-risk individuals who because of preexisting health conditions are unable to obtain private insurance, the government may establish a high-risk pool as it has done for other insurance markets, subsidizing its premiums through a tax on private insurance premiums (rather than through general tax revenues). This approach has, in fact, already been adopted in nine states; however, since employers can escape state-levied premium taxes by establishing self-insured plans, the involvement of the federal government in devising funding for high-risk pools becomes crucial. The cross-subsidization of high-risk individuals via a premium tax would result in a decline in private insurance purchases by all risk groups because of the higher resulting premium (adverse selection); moreover, the possibility that previously covered higher-risk individuals may obtain subsidized coverage through the newly formed pool will also reduce private purchases. Such risk pools would be a natural extension of the Medicare risk-sharing system, which cross-subsidizes high-risk subscribers by setting premiums independent of health status. However, in the case of high-risk pools, private insurance would continue to dominate the market, generating tax revenue to be used to subsidize public high-risk coverage.

The traditional dual strategy of government in improving access to both health insurance and medical care would lead one to predict new public programs to finance health care services for those needing assistance. Again, cross-subsidy schemes rather than general tax revenues would likely be used to fund any such initiatives. The federal government may, for example, consider adopting an approach already taken by several states and form an uncompensated-care pool for hospital care, to be financed by a tax levied on paying patients or insurance premiums. If paying patients (or, more often, their third-party payers) become the relevant tax base, the burden of the tax will be significantly affected by whether the tax is levied on admissions, charges, or inpatient days, since the case mix of third-party payers varies significantly in these respects. The financial soundness of an uncompensated-care pool—a natural extension of the Medicaid program—will require substantial monitoring to ensure that hospitals continue to engage in debt collection activities and that the patient default rate does not increase significantly owing to the presence of such funding. Given the rise in private and public insurance copayments and deductibles, this task may become increasingly onerous.

For the foreseeable future, public policy will continue to grapple with the question of who should bear which financial risks of illness and injury. Debate over the appropriate distribution of the financial burden of catastrophic illness and long-term care promises to continue unabated. As society reconciles its notions of equity with issues of cost and efficiency, new and creative approaches to risk bearing in health care finance will undoubtedly evolve.

Bibliography

Chollet, D., *Employer-Provided Health Benefits*. Washington, D.C.: Employee Benefit Research Institute, 1984.

Fuchs, V.E., *Who Shall Live? Health, Economics and Social Choice*. New York: Basic Books, 1974.

Kasper, J., et al., "Who Are the Uninsured?" Data Preview 1, National Health Care Expenditures Study. National Center for Health Services Research, 1981.

Monheit, A.C., et al., "Unemployment, Health Insurance and Medical Care Utilization," National Center for Health Services Research (unpublished manuscript).

Pauly, M.V., "Taxation, Health Insurance, and Market Failure in the Medical Economy," *Journal of Economic Literature*, June 1986, 629–675.

Starr, P., *The Social Transformation of American Medicine*. New York: Basic Books, 1982.

Van de Gaag, J., et al., eds., *Economics of Health Care*. New York: Prager, 1982.

5

The Changing Role
of the Physician

ROBERT EBERT

Introduction

Largely as a result of the remarkable advances in medical science beginning in the second half of the nineteenth century and the reform of medical education at the start of the twentieth, the medical profession has been able to control the environment in which it has practiced through much of this century. Now there are forces at work that are challenging that control, and these forces will influence who enters medicine, the social status of physicians, the conditions of practice, and the relationship between physicians and patients.

There would be no conference on "health care and its costs" were it not for dual engines of change: scientific discovery and

ROBERT EBERT is special advisor to the president at The Robert Wood Johnson Foundation. He has served as president of the Harvard Medical Center, dean of the Harvard Medical School, and dean of the faculty of medicine and professor of medicine at Harvard University. He also has held several positions in the Department of Medicine at the University of Chicago. Dr. Ebert has published extensively on medical education, national health care, and the U.S. physician.

the attendant technology advances made possible by new scientific knowledge. Even the reform of American medical education was an indirect result of scientific and technological advances, and both contributed greatly to improvement in the social and economic status of the physician. Until recently, the rewards of scientific medicine appeared to be worth the cost to those who paid, but the inflation of these costs year after year at a far greater rate than the consumer price index has had a sobering effect on the principal payers, namely, government and corporate America. The current emphasis on cost containment is the consequence of the inflation.

Cost containment alone would be cause for concern on the part of the medical profession. But there are other things to worry about as well, and after seventy-five years of relative stability, physicians wonder if a true revolution may be in progress. Since the Graduate Medical Education National Advisory Committee (GMENAC) report in 1980, the profession has been aware that there might be a significant surplus of physicians for the first time since the closing of proprietary medical schools at the beginning of the century. The resulting excess of physicians combined with cost containment could lead to a reduction in the per capita income of physicians. That would be bad enough, but what really strikes terror in the hearts of physicians is the possibility that cost containment plus a surplus of physicians, together with the corporatization of medicine, could mean an end to the control exercised by the profession.

The Evolution of the Social Status of the Physician

Even though members of the American public grumble about the medical profession, individual physicians are held in remarkably high esteem, and even some of the sharpest critics of the profession usually make exceptions of their own physicians. Prestige combined with the promise of a high income has made the profession attractive to college students—at least until recently, and medical schools have been able to choose their classes from among the brightest students in the nation. But it was not always so, and it is important to reflect on the lowly beginnings of doctors in this country to understand what they might lose.

Medicine in the Colonies

Although colonial America was profoundly influenced by its British heritage, this influence did not extend to the medical profession. The colonies had no use for the rigid guild system that characterized British medicine, for in the words of William Byrd in 1728, "The New Proprietors [of New Jersey] inveigled many over by this tempting Account of the Country: that it was a Place free from those 3 great scourges of Mankind, Priests, Lawyers and Physicians. Nor did they tell a word of a lie, for the People were too poor to maintain these Learned Gentlemen."

The result was a totally informal system of medical practice, with care provided by both physicians and members of the lay public. Most physicians were educated in an apprenticeship system that had few academic trappings, and the limit to learning was the skill and knowledge of the teacher. Because medical knowledge was primitive, and treatment by physicians trained in the British guild system was often draconian, relying on such extreme measures as purging and bleeding, the colonists were probably better off being attended by relative amateurs in medical practice, since they were less likely to be harmed by the ministrations of doctors than were their British cousins.

Nineteenth-Century Medicine

Toward the end of the eighteenth century, medical faculties were inaugurated at the University of Pennsylvania, King's College (later renamed Columbia University), Harvard, and Dartmouth, but none of these resembled modern medical schools, nor did they become the models for the majority of medical schools that mushroomed during much of the nineteenth century. The founding of a proprietary medical school

in Baltimore in 1815 presaged what was to become the predominant training ground for physicians during most of that
century. These schools were little more than diploma mills
open to anyone with the necessary tuition for a medical curriculum that consisted almost entirely of lectures. There were few
requirements for admission other than the ability to pay and
rudimentary skills in reading and writing. These were the
schools that supplied most of the physicians for the frontier,
and their competition came not from universities but from
schools founded by various medical cults, the most prominent
of which was homeopathy. So-called allopathic medicine
(scientific-based medicine using proven methods of treatment,
literally the opposite of homeopathy and what was to become
the mainstream of American medicine) had to struggle for
predominance, since it had little to offer in the way of diagnosis and treatment that was distinctly superior to what homeopathy and a variety of other medical cults had to offer. Paul Starr
in his book *The Social Transformation of American Medicine* describes in elegant detail the lowly position of most physicians
during much of the nineteenth century.

The Reform of Medical Education

There was of course an elite minority of physicians trained
in Europe and fully aware of the changing nature of medical
practice. This minority was influenced first by the advances in
diagnosis introduced by the French and then by the dramatic
discoveries in the fields of bacteriology, cellular pathology,
and physiology made by scientists in Germany, England, and
France. Scientific medicine based on the discoveries of Louis
Pasteur, Robert Koch, Rüdolph Virchow, and others set the
stage for the victory of allopathic medicine, the disappearance
of medical cults, and the ultimate dissolution of proprietary
medical schools. Those physicians trained in Europe, supple-
mented by equally able physicians trained in the great voluntary hospitals in Boston, New York, and Philadelphia, were
aware of the enormous deficits of American medical education. President Charles W. Eliot of Harvard forced reform of

that medical school, and his battle with the leading figures of Boston medicine practicing at the Massachusetts General Hospital had as much to do with who controlled medical education as it did with curriculum.

But it was the new medical school in Baltimore, Johns Hopkins, rather than Harvard, Columbia, or Penn, that was to become the model for twentieth century medical education in this country. Founded in 1893, the school attracted to its faculty some of the leading figures of American medicine, both preclinical and clinical, established new research laboratories, and became associated with a new teaching hospital, the Johns Hopkins Hospital. The medical school required a baccalaureate degree for admission, and almost immediately became the preeminent school in the nation.

There were reasons other than concern for the medical care of the American public that caused the American Medical Association (AMA) to create a council on medical education in 1904 and, together with the medical elite, to seek reform of medical education. Scientific medicine and high educational standards meant the elimination of rivals, improvement in the social and economic status of physicians, and the ability to fight a movement that threatened the professional independence of physicians, namely, the corporate practice of medicine. (What was meant by corporate practice was the creation of clinics and hospitals by railroads and other companies, using salaried physicians.)

Much of the reform was in progress before the Flexner report in 1910, but Bulletin 10 of the Carnegie Foundation, authored by Abraham Flexner, was the watershed between the informal medical education of the past and professional education for the twentieth century. One by one, all of the proprietary schools closed, new standards were set for admission to medical schools, new state licensing laws spelled out—often in minute detail—both the prerequisites for medical school and the number of hours in required subjects, and the number of medical schools was drastically reduced. Most important of all, medical education was now based on active learning in the preclinical laboratory and on the hospital wards, although to the sorrow of many, reliance on endless hours of lectures was retained.

The reform of medical education in the United States has been praised so often that a darker side to the reform seems to have been forgotten. Whatever their faults, proprietary schools opened the medical profession to all classes of Americans, and they provided physicians for the frontier and rural America. The reduction in the number of medical schools from 155 to 72, the lengthening of the curriculum, the reduction in class size, and, above all, stringent requirements for admission to medical schools changed all that. The Flexner report not only heralded educational reform but a chronic shortage of physicians as well, which was to last much of the twentieth century. It also caused a departure from what had been a democratic, egalitarian view of who could enter the profession to one of elitism.

Admission committees became class conscious, and social position became as important as grades. White Anglo-Saxon Protestants were preferred, particularly if they were the sons of doctors; few women were admitted; there were quotas for Jews; and blacks were relegated to Meharry and Howard, the two national medical schools founded for the purpose of educating black physicians. Hospitals evolved in a similar fashion: Jewish hospitals were founded so that Jewish physicians would have a place to practice, and black hospitals came into being for the same reason. Not until after World War II was there significant change in the unwritten policies of medical school admission committees and the elimination of segregated hospitals. The improved social status of physicians was inaugurated, but at a price.

The Professional Hierarchy before World War II

By the 1930s reforms were established and the social position of physicians was assured. There was of course a hierarchy in medicine with the specialist—particularly the surgical specialist—at the top and the general practitioner at the bottom. But the spread between top and bottom diminished as medical education became standardized. Despite the dependence of the profession on the reform of medical education for its improved social and economic status, medical school professors complained that they were not honored as were their counterparts in Europe. Faculty salaries were low, and few could afford to become full-time clinical professors unless they had independent means or could find wealthy wives.

The leading figures in American medicine during the period before World War II included a handful of full-time clinical faculty; successful specialists, many of whom were part-time members of medical faculties; and physicians who had worked their way to national prominence on AMA councils through local and state medical societies. For a brief period during and immediately after World War I, the medical elite and the AMA displayed an interest in social reform, but that concern was dispelled by the conservatism of the 1920s, never to return. Instead, the energies of organized medicine were directed toward preserving the position of control that the medical profession had struggled so hard to attain.

Post–World War II: Science Is King

World War II was a second important watershed in the evolution of the American medical profession. The favored position of the specialist in the armed services was a lesson learned well by those who had served as physicians in the army and navy during the war, and the practical effectiveness of federally supported research was demonstrated in the development of the atomic bomb. The first lesson changed the nature of medical education to one that emphasized graduate medical education. The other resulted in generous support of medical research and, secondarily, of medical education by the National Institutes of Health. The rationale was simple: if we can harness the energy of the atom, why can't we conquer the killing diseases—specifically heart disease, cancer, and stroke.

Science was now truly king, for the specialty practice of medicine was dependent on the technological advances made possible by medical science. Of course, the medical school-based research establishment was a constant reminder to the physician in training of the importance of science.

If science had become king, the throne room was the academic health center (AHC), a term coined to describe the conglomerate of medical school, primary teaching hospital, other affiliated hospitals, and other health professional schools. These centers trained the specialists, were the laboratories for new medical technologies, and became the paradigm for the intensive care made possible by advances in diagnosis and treatment. Teaching hospitals were the models for the specialty organization of community hospitals, and almost every large hospital (over 500 beds) became affiliated with an AHC.

In 1965 more than 50 percent of the support of American medical schools came from the federal government, largely for research and research training, and much of this funding was justified on the premise that it was directed toward the search for the cause and cure of the major killer diseases. The National Institutes of Health were organized on a categorical disease basis, and Congress funded the NIH handsomely, year after year, in the belief that solutions were just around the corner. They did not worry that a part of the funding was used for the training of subspecialists who would practice rather than do research, since it was assumed that better trained specialists would provide better care. Until the mid-1960s, few worried that general practitioners had become a rare breed and that we might be headed for an oversupply of specialists.

For a period of nearly forty years, the promise of scientific medicine appeared to have come true for the profession. Not only did physicians control their own destinies, but they could do so with the blessing of academic medicine—and who could argue with the presumed objectivity of university-based medicine? It might be expensive, but it was the best in the world —at least for those who could pay. America had become the undisputed leader of medical science and technology, and worldwide renown could only heighten the status of the American physician. No wonder there was little real conflict between academic medicine and the world of clinical practice between 1946 and the present. Despite minor differences, there was a true congruence of interest between town and gown, since both had a heavy investment in maintaining control of the medical care system.

Change in the Nature of Medical Practice

Until World War II, the majority of physicians in practice were general practitioners; the specialties were found in large urban areas or in multispecialty group practices such as the Mayo Clinic. Teaching hospitals associated with university-based medical schools provided another source of specialty diagnosis and treatment.

The Rise of the Specialty Practice of Medicine

With the help of the GI bill, many young physicians who were discharged from the service at the end of World War II sought specialty training in both teaching hospitals and community hospitals. For the first five or six years after the war ended, there was a relative shortage of residency training positions, so all hospitals had their share of qualified applicants.

As the backlog disappeared, however, those community hospitals that were less prestigious and had poorer teaching programs discovered that they could no longer recruit American medical school graduates. But they had become accustomed to the advantages of cheap medical labor (in the 1940s and 1950s medical residents received low salaries, and the better the hospital the lower the salary). To fill their residencies they turned to foreign medical graduates (FMGs), most of whom came from the less developed countries in Latin America and Southeast Asia. Most FMGs had no intention of returning to their countries of origin, but stayed in this country to practice instead. To a significant degree, they filled the less desirable jobs in state hospitals, and they made up in part for the shortage of physicians brought about by the reform of medical education. They did not, however, make up for the growing shortage of general practitioners.

Curiously, the concept of a medical care system in which the majority of physicians are general practitioners who refer their difficult cases to specialty oriented medical centers persisted long after it had become apparent that general practitioners were disappearing and were being replaced by specialists. The majority of academic medical centers had absolutely no interest in the education of general practitioners. Indeed, they competed with one another to train as many specialists and subspecialists as they could, yet somehow held to the naive belief that they would continue to live in a world in which they would remain the referral center for the generalists in the community. Why the chiefs of service thought that their superbly trained young men and women would wish to refer patients they had been trained to care for is beyond me.

The Need for Generalists

What academic medicine failed to see was recognized in the community. Members of Congress began to hear from their constituents that it was almost impossible to find a family physician. During the 1960s and early 1970s, Congress sought to solve the problem of the maldistribution of physicians among the specialties, as well as their geographic maldistribution, by supporting the newly created specialty of family medicine, encouraging the training of so-called primary care physicians, namely, internists, pediatricians, and obstetricians, and by providing financial inducements to increase class size in existing medical schools and to found new schools.

All of this helped but did not solve the fundamental problem of an appropriate balance between general physicians and specialists. Indeed, the most conspicuous result was the more than doubling of the number of medical school graduates and a threatened surplus by 1990. The point I wish to make is that the medical profession, and more specifically academic health centers, having gained control of the system, failed either to recognize the growing problem of maldistribution among the specialties or to do anything about it. It was left to government to try to solve the problem.

Why were academic health centers and the profession so successful in some ways and so ineffectual in others? Perhaps part of the answer lies in the acculturation of the physician.

Interactions between Physicians and the Larger Society

Acculturation of the Physician

Acculturation is defined as "the process of becoming adapted to a new or different culture with more or less advanced patterns." In a very real sense this is what happens to the physician in training. But only a part of the making of a physician is the result of education; equally important is the process of acculturation.

The Medical School Years. Careful studies of twenty-five classes of Harvard medical students found that student values during medical school reflect the current values of the larger society and that these values can change dramatically between one class and the next. Medical education seems to have little to do with these general values, but in the clinical years of medical school, the students begin to be exposed to the special values of the profession. It is here that the teachers are the residents and fellows with whom the students spend their days and often their nights. Thus in one sense the clinical clerkship is a return to the apprenticeship system, but greatly formalized and often with the delegation of a significant degree of responsibility to the students. Part of the acculturation is learning to live with uncertainty and the constant fear that a mistake resulting from ignorance, fatigue, or carelessness can cause great damage or even death. At the beginning, the students are shielded from most of this, but they are acutely aware that soon it will be their turn to make life and death decisions. They see how the residents and fellows seek the security of "objective" tests, but they also discover that there are few absolutes in the practice of medicine and that ultimately they will have to make decisions based on the best information they can gather.

Residency. At the time the young physicians receive their M.D. degrees, their acculturation has only begun. With the first year of residency training it begins in earnest, and each year they are given more and more responsibility for those who follow them. Few laypersons realize the enormous responsibility given residents and fellows in our most prestigious teaching hospitals. They are constantly there, they supervise every aspect of care, and it becomes a matter of pride to do everything that the attending physician might wish and to do it before morning rounds, even though it means staying up all night. It is a difficult, often exhausting experience that draws together those who share the same hardships, for they become the battle scarred veterans who view the world differently from ordinary mortals. Fellowship training is usually less rigorous, but it is here that the technological skills are refined and the final making of the specialist is completed. Not every residency program is as rigorous or as exhausting, and delegation and responsibility vary; but the ideal remains the one described, since it reflects the personal experience of almost every clinical chief in American medical schools.

Respect for Medical Authority. The acculturation I describe above is the post–World War II pattern, which did not exist for the majority of medical school graduates before 1945. In the post-Flexnerian reform period prior to World War II, a minority of physicians went through the rigors just described, and these were usually the ablest students destined for specialty practice, academic medicine, or both. Most graduates, however, went into practice after one year of internship in a community hospital, and few were given the degree of responsibility that prevailed in the major teaching hospitals.

There was an important difference in the quality of the training experience prior to World War II compared with what followed. There was a far greater respect for the authority of the teacher, whether a professor at a major teaching hospital or a general practitioner in a community hospital, in the prewar era. The great clinical teachers were respected because of their personal skill in taking a history or doing a physical examination, and the older practitioners in a community hospital were respected for what they had learned from their years of clinical experience. Those were the days before the clinical trial when case histories were considered respectable contributions to the medical literature.

The rapid expansion of medical knowledge, the introduction of the randomized clinical trial, and above all the logarithmic growth in the number and sophistication of laboratory tests and other medical technologies changed forever a respect for medical authority that characterized the earlier era. Respect for the authority of the teacher gave way to the authority of the most recent randomized clinical trial. Respect for the personal diagnostic skills of clinical teachers gave way to respect for their knowledge of the medical literature and their competence in using the latest medical technology. The generalist teacher was replaced by the specialist, and as I noted in an earlier essay, "Pearls of knowledge became more important than pearls of wisdom."

Medical Mentors. Another change occurred in the quality of acculturation after World War II. Prior to the war, it was common for a young physician who had finished his or her hospital training to become associated with an older physician as a way of starting practice or, in the case of a specialist, of completing the nonhospital part of training. When this was well done and taken seriously by the older physician, it provided a significant mentor relationship for the physician starting practice. When badly done, and the young physician felt exploited, it could cause bitterness. After World War II, this kind of apprenticeship gradually disappeared, and all training was completed in the more formal environment of the hospital. There was less exploitation as a result, but also less opportunity for a mentor relationship.

The Doctor's Dilemma. As a consequence of the acculturation process, young physicians now find themselves a part of two cultures, and it is not always easy to integrate the two. The intensity of the clinical experience both as medical students and as residents and fellows makes them feel closer to their profession than to their fellow citizens outside the profession. They often feel that members of the lay public do not really understand them, and they may even find it difficult to communicate easily with their spouses. Long hours and days away from home during residency can stress any marriage, yet if they delay marriage till after training has been completed, spouses have missed sharing the most important period in their lives. The role of a doctor's spouse in medicine is, if anything, more stressful than the role of the doctor, for it involves decisions about starting a family and caring for children. It is not surprising that divorce rates are high among physicians and that the marriage of doctors to one another is becoming as common as marriages between doctors and nurses were in the past.

Physicians are pulled in three directions. Their patients expect them to devote themselves to their professional duties and be available on call, their families want some of their time, and as educated men and women they are expected to fulfill certain civic duties. It is the last they often resent, for they feel that their contributions to the community are via their profession rather than through other good works. After all, they are expected to work on hospital committees, supervise the clinics, teach, and do a variety of other professional chores that are unreimbursed. Why should they also work in the community?

Physician Values. If there is a common thread that runs through the education and acculturation of physicians, it is the total commitment to the care and responsibility for the *individual* patient. Everything physicians have been taught and learned to value revolves around this one-to-one relationship. Patients expect it, and it is a part of the code of ethics. It is a quality to be valued, but it also poses a problem. Physicians were not trained to think about public health, and when asked about matters of public policy affecting the health care system, they tend to personalize them and ask "how will cost control or diagnosis related groups or competition affect *my* relationship with *my* patients?"

The general values of the physician—humanistic, political, moral, and ethical—are almost entirely formed before entering medical school. Their interest in issues that affect the body politic are, if anything, attenuated during the long years of training. They tend to lose whatever interests they had in matters of public policy other than those that affect them personally, and they quite naturally become more conservative as they consider the huge investment they have made in time, energy, and money in becoming a physician.

They are, for the most part, unsympathetic toward the poor. More likely than not they have spent time during medical school or residency in caring for the poor, and their attitudes in part have been shaped by that experience. Until the mid-1960s and the passage of Medicare and Medicaid, it was a common view among physicians that the poor were obligated to pay for free care by being willing subjects for teaching and research. While that view has changed to some degree, caring for the poor can be difficult, frustrating, and at times seemingly unrewarding compared with caring for middle-class patients who share the physician's values. As a consequence, a two-tiered system of medical care with one for the poor and another for the middle class does not shock physicians. They secretly think it is what the poor deserve and, in any case, they have paid their dues by caring for the poor while in training. Compassion does not seem to be a trait overdeveloped during the acculturation of the physician.

Who Are the Doctors?

Admission to Medical School Based on Merit

After World War II, and consistent with the growing dependence of medicine on science, social discrimination in the choice of medical students was gradually replaced by choice based on merit. The best students were sought, and social position became a factor of minor importance. Even the sons and daughters of physicians were given little preference. Prejudice against women remained for some years, but began to wane when medical faculties realized that a large pool of able women applicants for medical school would enhance the overall quality of medical students.

Recruitment of Minorities

Toward the end of the 1960s and after the assassination of Martin Luther King, medical schools decided that it was time to make a concerted effort to recruit minorities into what had been almost exclusively white medical schools. However, affirmative action meant changing criteria for medical school acceptance, and some faculty members strongly resisted using any standards other than character, accomplishment, grades, and test scores. In fairness, this was not because of opposition to minorities in medicine, but rather because the memory of past admission committees that rejected able students who did not belong to the "right" class or ethnic group was still fresh in the minds of these faculty members, many of whom had been discriminated against in the past.

The recruitment of minorities into medicine has been difficult and only partially successful. Deficiencies in early education are not easily rectified, so that the pool of well prepared minority students who have attended public elementary and high schools in our major cities is not large. Furthermore, medicine is only one career among many open to able minority students. Remedial courses before entry into medical school and special tutorials after admission have helped, but the number of qualified applicants has plateaued in recent years. It does not appear that there will be any significant change in the number of minorities entering medicine in the near future, although the number might fall as tuition rises and the threat of an unacceptable level of indebtedness increases.

Women in Medicine

In contrast, the number of women admitted to medical schools has steadily increased, and about one-third of all medical school graduates today are women (compared with a relatively constant level of 8 percent for the first half of the twentieth century). It is likely that the proportion of women to men entering the medical profession will increase, and it would not surprise me if by the year 2000 the ratio were fifty-fifty.

There are a number of reasons why more women are turning to medicine. First, they are entering the work force, including the professions, in increasing numbers, and it is becoming socially acceptable for a woman to combine a professional career with raising a family. Second, there is no longer any serious prejudice against women in certain specialties of medicine. At an earlier time, most women entered pediatrics, family practice, and psychiatry, but now all specialties, including surgery, are open. Third, as physician incomes continue to fall, fewer men will apply to medical schools and the deficit in the number of qualified men applying will be made up by admitting more women.

Cost of Medical Education

The degree of indebtedness incurred by medical students today has reached a level that worries most medical educators. If the trend toward higher and higher tuition in both colleges and medical schools continues at the same time that physician incomes appear to be falling, there will be little incentive for the poor and members of minority groups to enter medicine. The medical profession could revert once again to a predominantly white middle-class profession, although this time with an equal proportion of women.

Physician Organization

Professional organizations that have been formed by the medical profession have two functions: to set professional standards and to represent the profession or subgroups within the profession both formally and informally. Some do one exclusively, or almost exclusively, and some do the other. The most important do both. In effect, they are the organizations that exercise control over the environment in which physicians practice; therefore, what happens to them will influence to a significant degree how doctors practice in the future.

The American Medical Association

The oldest and best known medical professional organization is the American Medical Association, which, with some historic justification, purports to represent the entire medical profession, even though less than half of all practicing physicians belong to the AMA. Founded in 1846, it struggled to gain respectability and strength in its battle to represent allopathic medicine against other medical sects and to protect physicians against the menace of corporations that wished to employ physicians as salaried workers. Small wonder that in the 1920s and 1930s the main themes of the editor of the *Journal of the American Medical Association* were the dual evils of medical quackery and the corporate practice of medicine. The AMA formed a council on medical education in 1904, which became actively involved in the reform of medical education. The council continues to participate in the accreditation of the nation's medical schools and, as a consequence, plays an important part in setting standards for the profession.

Associated with the AMA are local and state medical societies both of which discipline physicians who are unethical or are proven to be incompetent. Unfortunately, this role has not been carried out in a rigorous manner, and the courts are now more involved in disciplining physicians than is the profession itself.

There is no need to discuss the political role of the AMA, since that is the activity best known to the public. What are less well known are the other functions and services of the AMA, including its many medical publications, the research that it does on public policy, the services it provides to physicians in practice, and its careful demographic study of the profession performed on a yearly basis. It continues to be an enormously important organization, but not as important as it once was, for reasons beyond its control. Science and the technology it spawned created the need for medical specialists, and they in turn formed their own specialty societies.

The Specialties

Today the power of organized medicine is fragmented and diffused. Many specialists look to their own societies for support, attend their own meetings, and have little to do with the AMA, even though they may belong. Thus medicine speaks with more than one voice, and the major societies representing internal medicine, surgery, obstetrics and gynecology, pediatrics, and psychiatry are in many ways more representative of organized medicine than the AMA.

The Association of American Medical Colleges

As a consequence of the importance of medical education and academic health centers since World War II, the Association of American Medical Colleges (AAMC) has grown from a congenial, if not very effective, "dean's club" into a powerful lobby for academic medicine. But it too suffers from the fragmentation that has plagued academic medical centers, so that the Council of Academic Societies of the AAMC, representing the heads of academic departments, does not always speak with the same voice as the Council of Deans or the Council of Teaching Hospitals.

Perhaps there never was an organization that spoke for the entire medical profession even though the AMA attempted to fill that role. Certainly none exists today, and the more specialized medicine becomes the less it will speak with a collective voice.

The Relationships among Physicians and Patients, Hospitals, Insurers, and Government

Doctors and Patients

The doctor-patient relationship has been talked about and written about as everything from a near mystical association to an economic transaction. It is not my intent to review or to analyze the myriad definitions that have been given to what is simultaneously a very straightforward yet complex relationship. It is simple and straightforward when defined as a social contract between a physician and patient based on the assumption of responsibility by the physician for the care of the patient in exchange for a fee. It becomes complex as one examines the relationship in a specialized medical world, one in which payment can be direct or indirect, fee-for-service or prepayment, and a world in which a medical team may be required to provide appropriate care.

What I do wish to examine are some of the complexities created by cross-cultural problems, problems of public versus private medicine, problems caused by the changing relationship between physicians and their middle-class patients, and finally the problems created by the need for special bioethics committees in hospitals—a need generated by the complexities of medical technology.

Cross-Cultural Problems. The usual paradigm for the doctor-patient relationship assumes a common set of values, and most physicians think of this in terms of their relationship to white middle-class patients. But when the attempt is made to use this paradigm to describe the relationship between a white middle-class physician and a patient who is a member of a minority group or who is poor or possibly both, the description is inaccurate. Unless the physician is unusual and has made a deliberate attempt to understand the cultural differences of those who do not share his or her cultural biases, he or she will never form the same kind of relationship with a patient of a different ethnic or cultural background as with one of his or her own kind. This is not to say that the physician will have an ineffectual relationship, only that it will be different. It does mean, however, that there will be inevitable gaps in the physician's understanding of how the patient reacts to illness and a similar gap in the patient's understanding of what the doctor is telling him or her about diagnosis and treatment. If these gaps are large and the illness complex, talking past rather than to each other may seriously interfere with treatment.

It should come as no surprise that in a recent study of the careers of all of the minority students graduating from medical school in 1975, each minority group of physicians took care of a larger proportion of patients from the same minority group than either white physicians or physicians from different minorities. In other words, black graduates of the class of 1975 had a larger proportion of black patients in their practices than did Hispanic physicians, and Hispanic physicians had a larger proportion of Hispanic patients in their practices than did either black or white physicians.

One result of a lack of understanding between a physician and a patient from different cultural or ethnic backgrounds is that physicians tend to become more authoritarian. This is particularly so if the patient is poor. Physicians will make an attempt to understand the cultural differences of more affluent patients, particularly those who come from abroad, but they have little interest in doing the same for those who are poor. As noted earlier, the majority of physicians do not like to treat the poor, and the fragmentation of services for the poor is, in part, caused by this distaste. Care provided in emergency rooms and hospital outpatient departments (OPDs) is neither economical nor effective; yet for many poor people it is the only care available. No doctor-patient relationship of any value can be built if the patient rarely sees the same physician more than two or three times. This is why neighborhood health centers have filled such an important role. Patients receive care that has greater continuity than that provided in the hospital OPD, and many of the physicians who staff these centers are there because they are dedicated to serving the disadvantaged.

Changing Relationships. Although physicians may be able to maintain an authoritarian attitude toward the poor, their relationship to their middle-class patients is changing. Reporters who cover the medical news are so assiduous in their reporting that they are able to write about the most recent randomized clinical trial published in the latest issue of the *New England Journal of Medicine* before the physician subscriber to the *Journal* has received his or her copy. That is, the average middle-class patient has the opportunity to read about or see on television the latest medical advance or the most sensational technological breakthrough before it has assumed an accepted role in the everyday practice of medicine. This leads average laypersons to have great expectations for what modern medicine can accomplish; they share with their physicians a faith in the technology of medicine. This would seem to create an important bond between physician and patient that should enhance their relationship, but there is a problem.

Too often mutual faith in the technology of medicine obscures another important part of the doctor-patient relationship: an understanding of roles. The role of physicians is to understand as much about their patients' background and social and emotional lives as is necessary to provide intelligent care. The patients' role is to understand the importance of telling the physician what they really believe to be their problem and what factors in their private or public lives may contribute to their illnesses. Both physicians and patients need to be honest with themselves and with each other about the uncertainties of medical diagnosis and treatment, and both need to understand the part played by trust in successful therapy, and the difference between curing and healing.

In *Daedalus,* Eric Cassell wrote eloquently about a mechanistic approach to disease that ignores its multifaceted nature. The physician has been trained to think in terms of specific etiologies and specific cures. The tubercle bacillus causes tu-

berculosis, and isoniazid controls the infection. Thyrotoxico-
sis is caused by an excess secretion of thyroid hormone and
can be cured by reducing the production of the hormone. The
difficulty is that many other factors are involved in whether or
not the tubercle bacillus causes a significant infection in a
particular person or the way in which an individual reacts to
an excess secretion of thyroid hormone.

Physicians need to understand their patients, not just the
patients' diseases, particularly at the present time, when it is
customary to ask patients to share in decision making. Not
only should physicians understand the many factors that can
affect the outcome of treatment, but they also must be sensitive to their patients' feelings about shared decision making.
What is appropriate for one patient may be totally inappropriate for another, and physicians must have a comprehensive
understanding of their patients to make the appropriate judgment. Physicians must make most of the decisions, but they
must present all of the options and share the decisions. In the
final analysis, however, both patients and physicians need to
understand that the ultimate responsibility rests with the
physicians for whatever decisions have been reached. Malpractice suits may be a part of a much larger American problem of liability in a contentious society, but it is very likely
that there would be fewer suits against physicians for malpractice if there were a better understanding on the part of both
patients and physicians of the nature of the doctor-patient
relationship.

Bioethics. Not too many years ago, bioethical considerations
were the special province of the physician. There were no
ethics committees in hospitals, informed consent was casual,
and the poor were rarely asked whether or not they wished to
be the experimental subjects in clinical studies that compared
therapeutic regimens. All of this has changed, largely because
the rapid advances in technologies capable of prolonging life
have posed to physicians and to the public decisions that never
had to be made before. When is a patient dead? What rights
does a patient have to death without submitting to all the

interventions possible? Who gets the next heart, kidney, or eye for transplantation? As a consequence, the physician and the patient, or the physician and patient's family, are no longer able to make certain decisions privately. To the extent that patients and experimental subjects are better informed of their rights, these changes have been beneficial, but to the extent that they have intruded on the privacy of patients and their families, they may have been harmful.

In summary, the physicians' relationship to their patients has changed. It is less authoritarian and there is more sharing of decisions with the patients and their families as well as with others who have no personal interest in the patients. The relationship is flawed to the degree that it is based too much on trust in the infallibility of technology and too little on human understanding. Technology may cure, but only the sensitive physician can heal.

Doctors and Hospitals

During much of the nineteenth century, there were four types of civilian general hospitals: voluntary hospitals, usually founded for the care of the sick poor; public hospitals founded for the same reason; company hospitals (e.g., railroad-owned) formed to care for employees; and private hospitals, usually physician-owned. Until the end of the century, those who could afford the best care were treated at home or in private hospitals. Only when it became evident that better care could be provided in a well-equipped hospital was there a move away from privately owned hospitals toward the use of voluntary hospitals by rich and poor alike (although segregated) and the development of the so-called community hospitals. Nor did company hospitals flourish in competition with community hospitals, much to the relief of the medical profession.

The Doctor's Workshop. During the nineteenth century and much of the twentieth century, civilian hospitals (except those owned by companies) were considered the physician's workshop. Physicians decided who would join the staff, who should be admitted, what facilities were needed, and what services should be offered. There were constraints—largely financial—but both trustees and managers tacitly accepted the premise that most decisions would be made by physicians. The system worked reasonably well until the explosive growth in medical knowledge and technology after World War II. What had been relatively modest hospital budgets ballooned at a rapid rate. The need for new facilities required large amounts of capital, and the demand for new and increasingly expensive instruments for diagnosis and treatment seemed insatiable.

The Need to Manage. The philosophy that the hospital was the doctor's workshop and physicians made the rules came into conflict with the need to manage what had become complex and expensive institutions. Trustees began to question whether physicians had the right to exclude other qualified physicians from a hospital staff because the applicants for hospital privileges worked for a staff model health maintenance organization (HMO) and were salaried. Managers started to ask questions about the cost effectiveness of new technologies and whether a particular new technology would replace an older one or would simply be an add-on. Other changes are now taking place in the relationship between physicians and hospitals, and it is likely that more striking changes will occur in the near future. I return to this later.

Doctors and Payers

The costs of medical care are paid for by corporate America as a fringe benefit, by government—federal, state, and local—and by individuals. The mechanisms for payment have been the direct support of public hospitals, Blue Cross and Blue Shield Plans, the private insurance industry, Medicare and Medicaid (using Blue Cross Plans and private insurers to process claims), HMOs, and other prepayment mechanisms, together with stop-loss arrangements with private insurers. I am concerned less with the mechanisms of payment than I am with the attitude of the payers toward physician charges.

Usual and Customary Fees. During much of this century, the
guiding principle of payment in a predominantly fee-for-service system has been the acceptance of usual and customary
fees by the federal government, by industry, and by individuals. Public hospitals that served the poor were different. These
city and county hospitals usually operated with volunteer or
salaried physicians, or both, and a paid house staff. There were
exceptions, but as a general rule cities and counties did not
reimburse physicians on a fee-for-service basis until the advent
of Medicaid, which was jointly funded by federal and state
governments.

Physicians opposed the legislation authorizing Medicare,
seeing it as a prelude to national health insurance. In an effort
to placate the medical profession, legislators inserted language into the law that Medicare would in no way alter the
traditional practice of medicine—meaning it would not be
used as a vehicle for changing the system of usual and customary fees. For the moment, there is limited support for national
health insurance, but physicians have good reason to be worried. With the move toward cost containment there is pressure
on the part of the federal government to force physicians to
accept Medicare payments as full reimbursement for physician
services. There are likely to be additional efforts by the Health
Care Financing Administration (HCFA), which administers
the Medicare program, to reduce the fees that physicians can
charge for the care of patients covered by Medicare.

Attitude of Organized Labor and Industry. By the end of the
1930s, the strength of national labor unions was well established. An important goal of organized labor was to improve
access to health care for union members and those who had
retired, and it became customary in contract negotiations with
industry to bargain for better health benefits, with considerable success. Industry did not at first see this as a threat to
profitability, since the cost could be passed along to the consumer, and if better benefits resulted in a healthier work force
so much the better. Unions were sympathetic to the idea of
prepaid medical care, not because it controlled costs but be-

cause it provided a full range of services under one roof. The United Mine Workers for a time organized their own health care system, but this had to be abandoned when the industry began to experience hard times and the cost of the system became too great. Although many union leaders were unsympathetic to an open-ended fee-for-service system, they accepted it as a necessary evil as long as their members received adequate care. Industry did not care, with the result that physicians were free to set their own fees without worrying that the corporate world would object. Fringe benefits for health care had become the rule even in new industries that were not unionized. Until the 1980s no one in industry worried enough about charges for physicians' services to try to control them.

The Attitude of Individuals. Individuals only feel the true cost of medical care when they pay for it out-of-pocket, and few pay the full cost in that way. Initially, most health insurance was only for hospital care, but as the cost of ambulatory services rose, insurance coverage was extended to cover many of the charges incurred in the physician's office and in the hospital emergency room. As long as health care was to a large extent a tax free fringe benefit with only marginal charges to the patient, few individuals objected to its cost. If someone else paid most of what the physician charged, why object to usual and customary fees? In other words, until comparatively recently, none of the payers objected very much to the fees charged by physicians, and the profession controlled to a large extent what those fees should be.

Payment for Procedures. The scientific advances that have made so many new technological procedures for diagnosis and treatment possible have been remarkable, and at times life saving, so patients have not objected to their introduction. But the professional fee for each procedure that requires the supervision of a physician is often much higher than what a physician is paid for taking a history, doing a physical examination, or making a preliminary diagnosis, all of which are time consuming. The specialist who can pass a flexible scope into one or another end of the gastrointestinal tract or can catheterize the heart will be paid much higher fees than the primary care physician who spends most of his or her time talking to patients. Thus technology oriented medicine has spawned substantial gaps between fees received by specialists and those received by primary care physicians.

The Salaried Physician. Historically, the medical profession objected to the concept of a salaried physician. It recognized that certain governmental positions had to be salaried, but it fought against salaries for physicians in civilian practice. For this reason, staff model HMOs that pay salaries to their physicians, and even group models such as Kaiser-Permanente in which the plan contracts with an independent physician group for its services, were looked upon as a corruption of the fee-for-service practice of medicine. Organized medicine no longer officially takes this position, but many physicians are worried that the acceptance of the concept of prepaid medical plans using salaried physicians represents a defeat for the profession.

Factors That Will Affect the Role of the Physician

I believe we have entered a period of more profound change in the role of physicians and their relationship to patients, hospitals, and payers than at any other time since the beginning of this century. There are many reasons for this, but I will comment on only five: cost containment, public attitudes, the information revolution, government policy leading to an excess of physicians, and the commercialization of medicine.

Cost Containment

Cost containment without question will play a central role in what happens to physicians over the next decade, not necessarily because it will be effective, for it may not be, but because of the changes it has already set in motion.

Diagnosis Related Groups. Prospective payment of hospitals for so-called diagnosis related groups (DRGs) has had a profound effect on hospital occupancy even though the system officially applies only to Medicare. Occupancy has dropped dramatically, and this affects physicians in several different ways. If a physician has staff privileges at several hospitals, each hospital will compete with the others for the physician's patients. On the other hand, each is motivated to refuse to admit patients covered by Medicare who do not fit specific criteria for hospitalization. Once the physician has admitted a patient in the appropriate diagnostic group, he or she will be urged to discharge the patient at the earliest possible time.

Hospitals with falling occupancy are actively seeking additions to their medical staffs and are no longer reluctant to extend privileges to physicians working for HMOs. In fact, some hospitals are actively seeking affiliations with HMOs.

Prospective payment also calls for an elimination of the Medicare "pass through" of the cost of new equipment or capital costs for renovation. Thus hospital management now questions the need for new, expensive technologies, and physicians must justify their needs before new expenditures can be authorized. The hospital is no longer thought of as the doctor's workshop. It is an important institution and is fighting for its appropriate place in our changing health care system.

DRGs do not apply to the professional charges made by physicians, but it is rumored that HCFA would like to extend the concept of DRGs to physician fees. Should this happen, it could have a profound effect on the income of specialists, for it would lump together the professional fees for all of the procedures necessary for the diagnosis and treatment of a particular disease group.

Competition. At present, competition as a means of cost containment is among different systems of care—i.e., staff model HMOs, independent practice associations (IPAs), preferred provider organizations (PPOs), and traditional fee-for-service medical practice. Physicians have reacted to this by hedging their bets. If they are in the private, fee-for-service practice of medicine, they may accept contracts with an IPA or become associated with a PPO or, in fact, take a part-time salaried position. As yet, competition has not become intense among physicians in private practice, but as the number of practicing doctors continues to increase, it almost certainly will, and this will have an impact on referrals to specialists and on the ability of solo practitioners, or even small, single-specialty group practices, to survive.

A large unknown in the area of cost containment is the degree to which big industrial payers will take an active role in shaping the health care system in a more rational and cost-effective direction. They have not done so directly until now, but have sought to influence cost by encouraging competition among different systems by seeking discounts for favorable experience ratings, by offering incentives to employees to accept limited benefits, by auditing charges made for medical care, and by jawboning. Until now, cost containment has been a matter of concern largely at the level of the individual company. Little has been done at the industry level or across industries to control health care costs.

Public Attitudes

There are four ways in which public attitudes will affect the role of physicians. The first and most important is consumer satisfaction with what the insured public perceives as the quality of care it is receiving. To use an extreme example, the American public would accept the constraints of the National Health Service of Great Britain only if this country were on the verge of bankruptcy, and possibly not even then. Members of the public may accept some limitation of choice, but there will have to be some real choice, for I doubt that any kind of monolithic system, public or private, would be acceptable. This means that for the foreseeable future we will have fee-for-service systems and prepaid care competing with one another and that each will have its staunch adherents among consumers.

A second and traditional way in which public opinion will

influence what doctors do is by way of special interest groups, especially the elderly. For over a century, we have had powerful lobbies on behalf of those afflicted with specific diseases: tuberculosis, cancer, and heart disease, to name a few. Now the elderly are concerned about those health problems that afflict them, and they will be a powerful force directing physicians to pay more attention to them. They will lobby for more home care, better ambulatory care, and for medical care provided in continuing care communities. They will push for more and better medical care in nursing homes. Cost containment will be secondary to access and quality.

The public's attitude toward privacy is a third way in which the physician's role could be affected. To what degree will the public favor enhancement of the private relationship between doctor and patient or doctor and family on matters that have to do with dying or birth defects, or even abortion? Or will special interest groups succeed in influencing that relationship via government intervention?

Finally, the attitude of the public toward medical care for the poor will influence whether or not we continue to have a segregated system or a one-tiered system for all. Physicians will practice differently according to which approach we favor as a nation.

The Information Revolution

The present generation of computers can handle enormous amounts of data, and the ability to connect personal computers with mainframe computers means that the availability of information can be decentralized. Most hospitals are now computerized for the purpose of billing and for keeping track of patient stays, but the use of computers in the practice of medicine is still in its infancy. Even after more than a decade of experience with computerized records at the Harvard Community Health Plan—a staff model HMO—its system, called Costar, has not been widely disseminated. Yet the potential is great. If we are to develop effective systems of quality assurance for ambulatory care as well as hospital care, it will be essential to make full use of computerized record keeping.

Various systems have been developed that use computers as an aid to diagnosis, but here again, the models that have been developed have not been widely used. Perhaps the slowness of the medical profession to utilize computer technology reflects the average age of physicians in practice, many of whom are computer illiterates. The younger generation of physicians now finishing their training may be much more comfortable in a computerized world of medicine. Progress may be slow at present, but without question the computer will ultimately profoundly influence the way in which the physician practices.

An Excess of Physicians

The predictions of the Graduate Medical Education National Advisory Committee appear to be coming true, at least in the minds of physicians. Until the GMENAC report in 1980, there were concerns among physicians that certain specialties were overcrowded, but little worry was expressed about an overall excess of physicians. Six years later, everyone was worried. Even though it is absurd to think that in six years the medical profession had suddenly become massively overcrowded, the perception of many physicians, particularly those just entering practice, is that an oversupply exists now. Obviously, this affects their thinking about where and how to practice.

The Commercialization of Medicine

The most apparent sign of the commercialization of medicine is the success of the large for-profit hospital corporations such as Humana, Health Corporation of America (HCA), and American Medical International (AMI), but there is other evidence as well. Even not-for-profit hospitals are marketing aggressively, as are HMOs and other providers. Academic health centers are heavily dependent on income from faculty group practices, and they, too, actively market their services. The inevitable emphasis on profit that accompanies commercialization will result in more attention to those who can pay and in avoiding those who cannot. Hospitals will prefer to be known as centers for high-priced procedures such as open heart surgery rather than low-priced services such as family medicine.

To What Degree Will Corporate Organization Influence the Practice of Medicine?

Toward the end of the nineteenth century, the medical profession feared the corporate practice of medicine and successfully fought efforts of companies to establish themselves as corporate providers of care. For much of this century, however, physicians were powerful enough to control how medicine was practiced by the majority of physicians, although they were unsuccessful in stopping the creation of health maintenance organizations. Today, once again, there is a rising level of fear among physicians that corporations will take over the practice of medicine. How realistic are those fears?

Environmental Factors

None of the environmental factors I have just discussed will in itself lead to the corporatization of medical practice, but each could promote it. Cost containment does not depend on the provision of care by large organizations, and one could argue that the corporate practice of medicine could be more rather than less expensive. At present, public attitudes are probably more sympathetic to small rather than large organizations in the health field. The information revolution could help the solo practitioner as well as the large provider. An excess of physicians would not inevitably lead to care provided by large organizations, but would make it easier for such large providers to recruit. And finally, commercialism does not distinguish between large and small organizations.

If none of these factors will lead to the creation of the corporate provision of care, what will?

Factors Favoring Corporate Organization

Corporate medical service organizations can be either for-profit or not-for-profit. Large corporate organizations already exist as delivery models that can be emulated. Among HMOs, Kaiser is the flagship; of multispecialty group practices, the Mayo Clinic is one of the oldest; among academic medical centers, Duke University and the University of Chicago are notable examples; and, of course, there are several examples in the for-profit hospital field. The latter, however, tend to have a more traditional relationship with their physicians.

Access to Capital. Both for-profit and not-for-profit health care corporations have access to capital, but here the for-profits have an advantage because they can use the equity market. Nevertheless, the not-for-profits have the advantage of access to tax free bond issues as well as the traditional debt market. Because the technology of medicine is expensive, both to buy and to service, large organizations have an advantage that individuals or small groups do not have, namely, the ability to negotiate for credit on favorable terms and to service debt more easily.

The Ability to Rationalize the Use of Expensive Resources. Not only is a large organization likely to be able to purchase expensive equipment and provide expensive services, but it also is in a position to use these resources efficiently without unnecessary duplication. The greater the integration of services within one corporate structure, the more likely this is to be true. For example, an HMO that has multiple centers can calculate the need for subspecialists and the technology they require based on the demography of the population cared for and can provide necessary services more economically than is possible in a less well integrated system of medical care.

The Ability to Bargain with Payers and Providers. A large HMO that is at risk for expenses that exceed premiums, but has stop-loss insurance for losses beyond a stated amount, is an example of an organization that cannot effectively bargain with the federal government but can with state government for the care of Medicaid patients. It can also offer both large industrial groups and smaller professional groups contracts that are competitive yet profitable. By marketing directly, it can be more sensitive to market conditions than would be the case if a third party were doing the negotiating.

Assume for the purpose of this example that the HMO does not own a hospital. If the HMO is large enough and can guarantee a significant number of admissions, it is in a favorable position to negotiate special terms with a hospital or hospitals of its choice. Most important, a large staff model HMO is in an excellent position to compete for a skilled work force, including physicians, in terms both of salaries and the provision of expensive resources.

Modern Communications. Although modern communications systems do not necessarily favor large corporate organizations, they do enable them to operate more efficiently and effectively than in the past. In particular, modern computers make it possible to monitor the use of expensive resources and in the future will facilitate quality assurance.

The Ability to Compete. For years neither hospitals nor physicians had to worry much about competition, but in the 1980s the world changed. Bed occupancy began to fall and an impending oversupply of physicians was recognized. Suddenly physicians, hospitals, and HMOs recognized that they were living in a much more competitive environment and that the success of one provider might be at the expense of another. Under these circumstances, the large corporate health care provider has certain advantages. It can compete by underpricing smaller competitors, either by accepting a smaller margin of profit or by taking a loss for a limited period of time as a means of eliminating a competitor. It also has greater flexibility in tailoring the provision of care to the special needs of the payer. And, finally, it can control the practice environment to reduce the risk of malpractice suits.

Managing the Regulatory Environment. No matter what is said about competition and the virtues of the marketplace, providers of health care services will be subject to regulation that is likely to become more, rather than less, rigorous. Large corporate providers of care can afford the experts needed to deal expeditiously with complex regulations.

The Impact of Change on Physician Relationships and Behavior

Although it is impossible to say to what degree care will be provided by large corporate entities in the future, the behavior of physicians and their relationships to others will change because of the profound changes occurring in the world of medical practice.

Who Will Be in Control?

Physicians no longer control the medical care system to the degree they did in the relatively recent past, and they are likely to have even less control in the future. Any large provider, whether a hospital, an HMO, or even a large multispecialty group practice, requires a level of management skill equivalent to that found in other major industries. People who qualify for top management positions in industry are unlikely to work *for* a group of doctors, although they will be quite willing to work *with* them.

This does not mean that physicians will lose all control and will work as hired hands, but it does mean that they will have to share control with others to a degree unprecedented in this century.

How Will Physicians Be Paid? The fee-for-service system continues to be sufficiently robust to survive for some time to come. But it should be remembered that fee-for-service can be used both by individual physicians as well as by large providers that pay their physicians' salaries. The number of salaried physicians will probably continue to increase in the decades ahead, and more and more will be on full-time salaries. This is the present situation in staff model HMOs, but not in IPAs. What will determine the balance between salaried and un-salaried physicians will be the success of large corporate providers versus individual physicians or small groups.

How Will Physicians React to an Increase in Salaried Positions? Their reactions will be mixed. Many will seek salaried positions in a world of practice that is becoming more competitive. They will welcome the security, the more regular hours, and the fringe benefits. Women, in particular, will find salaried positions attractive if they have families to raise.

As a result, the medical school applicant of the future may present a different profile. Many young men and women chose medicine because they felt it was one of the few prestigious jobs in our society that permitted the individual to be his or her own boss. These were the strong individualists who valued their independence and sought to control the environment in which they worked. It is becoming increasingly difficult for the individual to exercise that kind of control, and, as a consequence, a career as a physician becomes less attractive to such individuals. In contrast, medicine becomes a more attractive career for people who like to work in organizations.

The Doctor-Patient Relationship

In one sense the doctor-patient relationship will not change, for no matter how practice is organized and paid for, there will always be a one-to-one relationship between doctor and patient. The relationship, however, may be more clearly defined, and that should be all to the good.

Choice of Physician. Physicians in the fee-for-service practice of medicine are quick to point out that the patient enrolled in an HMO is assigned a physician and has no choice, and is lucky

to see the same physician twice. This assumes that the opposite is true in fee-for-service medicine. The fact is that there
are problems in both systems. The major problem is identifying a primary care physician who will guide the patient
through the complexities of modern specialty oriented medicine. Initial choice is a hit-or-miss matter in both systems.
What is important is that a good match should be made even
if it means changing physicians, for the needs of patients vary
as much as the personalities of physicians.

Understanding the Patients' Needs. There is increasing awareness that the needs of patients go well beyond the immediate
physical or emotional impairment that precipitates a visit to
the physician. I believe that in a more competitive world the
edge will go to those providers who recognize the importance
of knowing the patient as well as his or her disease. One might
have hoped that compassion rather than commercial interest
would have been the force for this change. But whatever the
motivation, it is significant that an approach to patient care
that places a high value on understanding the patient as well
as the disease is emerging.

The Physician and the Hospital

The relationship of the physician to the hospital is already
changing. Physicians are having to accept the new reality that
the community hospital or the voluntary hospital is no longer
considered their workshop and nothing more. The hospital
itself is in the process of change; more and more hospitals will
seek associations with other providers so as to become parts
of integrated systems of care.

Physicians and Payers

Despite all the changes that are occurring, solo practitioners
and small group practices will continue to play important
roles. Physicians in these practices will maintain their present
relationship to insurers and payers. If there is a trend toward

larger corporate providers, however, most physicians will have little or no direct relationship with payers.

How Well Prepared Are Physicians to Manage Change?

Physicians as individuals are poorly prepared for change. The acculturation process described earlier is predicated on stability and not change. Neither by temperament nor by education do physicians think much about change. They have little control over the changes that are occurring or have occurred, and they are not helped much by those who educate them and represent them.

Medical Education

The academic health centers that control medical education have revolutionized the practice of medicine through the scientific and technological advances they have pioneered and the specialty practice of medicine they have fostered. AHCs trained the specialists who were recruited to community hospitals and who in turn modeled the community hospital practice of medicine on the academic medical center.

But the AHCs stopped there. They not only failed to go the next step, which would have been to develop integrated systems of care, but they actually opposed the development of HMOs. The result is that the AHCs are no longer in the vanguard, but are fighting a rear-guard action to keep things as they are. They are not in a position to provide the leadership for change, and they are not even in a good position to train physicians for the future. They have done a superb job of training hospital-based specialists but a poor job of training generalists.

Professional Organizations

Unfortunately, the organizations that represent the medical profession in the United States have been reactive rather than

proactive for much of this century, and they are not viewed by
the general public as particularly progressive forces in our
society. Nevertheless, the AMA, which has the largest physician constituency in the country, has recognized the changing
world and has tried to change with it. It is attempting to provide for its membership the best advice it can muster on practice arrangements in all systems of care. The staff of the AMA
is well informed, conscientious, and no more biased than any
other staff concerned with public policy.

But one wonders whether traditional professional organizations will be up to the challenges of the changing world of
medicine. Will physician unions develop as more and more
doctors are salaried? Will U.S. physicians use the threat of a
strike as do their Canadian counterparts? Only time will tell.

Conclusion

Physicians live and practice in a changing world over which
they will have less and less control. This will cause the profession to appear less attractive to some physicians. Young men
and women who seek a career in medicine because it is both
humanitarian and intellectually stimulating, however, will find
that control will be less important than the potential to do so
much more to help patients than was possible a generation
ago. To them I say: let someone else worry about management
of the system as long as you can provide the best and most
humane care for your patients.

6

The Interaction of
Population Aging and Health
Transitions at Later Ages:
New Evidence and Insights

KENNETH G. MANTON

Introduction

A number of demographic factors have contributed to the rapid growth of the elderly (aged sixty-five and over) and extreme elderly (aged eighty-five and over) population in the United States. For example, reductions in fertility mean that future elderly cohorts will be more nearly equal in size to new birth cohorts, with the net effect of increasing the proportion of the population at advanced ages. In addition, we have

KENNETH G. MANTON has an extensive history of affiliation with Duke University. He is currently a senior fellow in the Center for the Study of Aging and Human Development as well as a medical research professor in the Department of Community and Family Medicine at the Duke University Medical Center. He also serves as assistant director of the Center for Demographic Studies and research professor of demographic studies at Duke. Dr. Manton has lectured and published widely on topics concerning aging, mortality, and chronic disease and the relationship of these issues to health care costs.

The research in this chapter was supported by NIA grant no. AG 01159 and HCFA grant no. 18-C-98641.

recently observed large increases in life expectancy at advanced ages (e.g., males at age sixty-five lived 1.6 years more in 1982 than in 1960 [12 percent increase] and females 2.9 years more [an 18 percent increase]; at age eighty-five the corresponding increases are 0.7 and 1.7 years, or a 15 percent increase for males and 33 percent increase for females)—increases that were not anticipated. Thus those persons who survive to more advanced ages will live even more years at those ages where there is currently a high prevalence of chronic disease and disability.

Population aging raises concerns that a greater burden will be placed on private pension systems and Social Security benefits and that there will be large increases in acute, postacute, and long-term health care costs. In 1984 B. B. Torrey projected that by the year 2000, the population over age eighty will consume $85.5 billion (in 1984 dollars) in federal benefits, thereby becoming the largest single federal entitlement group.

Population aging with its implications for income security and health care costs and their impact on general economic productivity and growth is not a phenomenon restricted to the United States. Many major economic powers will be subjected to similar pressures. For example, the rate and level of population aging in Canada will be nearly the same as in the United States. Japan will experience even more rapid population aging, with nearly a quarter of its population projected to be over age sixty-five in 2025, according to the Nihon University Population Research Institute. It is expected that the economic and social consequences of population aging and life expectancy increases will affect most highly developed countries of the world.

Ironically, these consequences will be a result of conscious efforts to achieve highly desirable goals, i.e., control fertility and population growth, reduce mortality, and increase life expectancy. This apparent conflict between the consequences of population aging and a high degree of success in population control and mortality reduction has raised questions about the best way to balance the effects of controlling population growth and the effect of population aging. At times these concerns have even led to questions about the desirability of strict population control and continuing mortality reductions.

In this chapter I suggest that appropriate policy responses can help mitigate many of the negative impacts of population aging. These policy responses will require consideration of new concepts and models of chronic disease, disability, and health changes at advanced ages and of new scientific evidence about the potential for improving health and functional status at advanced ages. It will also be necessary to develop appropriate and coordinated policy responses with respect to health, retirement, and pension issues.

A Model of Health Changes at Advanced Ages

Health changes at advanced ages are difficult to describe because they are intrinsically more complex than those at younger ages. Typically, we view most younger persons as being healthy until they acquire a well-defined disease or pathological condition which either can be cured or may cause death. We should probably view chronic diseases at later ages as processes (rather than events) that may be controlled or delayed rather than cured. We can expect that there will be multiple interacting diseases operating in someone whose vital physiological status has been generally reduced by basic aging processes. The difficulty in describing such complex health changes has led to debates among a number of authors about the implications of recent life expectancy gains at advanced ages for the elderly population.

To resolve these difficulties and to create a relatively simple conceptual model for health planners, in 1984 a World Health Organization scientific advisory group on the epidemiology of aging developed a conceptual model of illness, disability, and death based on simple life table concepts. The scheme they developed is presented in Figure 1.

In this figure, age is represented along the horizontal axis and the probability of surviving to a given age along the verti-

FIGURE 1. The Observed Mortality and Hypothetical Morbidity and Disability Survival Curves for Females in the United States of America in 1980

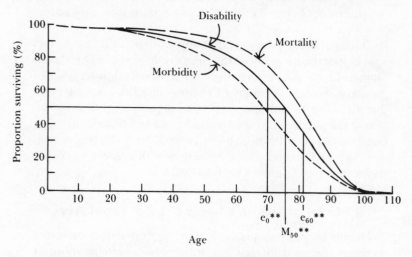

e_0^{**} and e_{60}^{**} are the number of years of autonomous life expected at birth and at age 60, respectively. M_{50}^{**} is the age to which 50% of females could expect to survive without loss of autonomy.

SOURCE: The Uses of Epidemiology in the Study of the Elderly, Technical Report Series 706, WHO, Geneva, 1984.

cal axis. Thus a birth cohort starts with 100 percent survival at age zero and, as mortality operates, the proportion surviving to any given age monotonically declines. This decline in survival with age is represented by the outermost curve, labeled "mortality." The innermost curve, labeled "morbidity," represents the probability of surviving to a given age free of disease. The area under the curve represents the number of years that a member of the birth cohort can expect to live disease free, i.e., his or her "healthy" life expectancy. The middle curve, labeled "disability," represents the probability of surviving to a given age free of disability. The model assumes that disability must be generated by an underlying disease process. The area under the disability curve represents what has been referred to as "active" life expectancy, whereas the area between the disability and mortality curves represents the number of years a member of a cohort can expect to live in a disabled, dependent state. Someone in this state will likely require both acute and long-term health care services, whereas someone in the morbid state is likely to be at risk primarily for acute health care services.

With the recent increases in life expectancy (i.e., the mortality curve moving farther to the right), how have the morbidity and disability curves changed? If improvements in mortality proceed faster than improvements in health, the mortality curve may shift to the right faster than the morbidity and disability curves. This will increase the area between those curves and the mortality curve and thereby increase the number of years a member of this cohort can expect to live in a health-impaired state at higher risk of need for significant acute and long-term health care services.

The figure can be used to focus both policy and scientific questions about the impact of population aging. The policy issues are likely to focus on such matters as changes in health that have resulted in increasing numbers and proportions of people surviving to even more advanced ages and the implications of increases in entitlement age for Social Security. They will also need to address whether health will improve enough at ages sixty-five to sixty-seven (or older) to determine whether it is feasible for private health insurance to take over coverage as the entitlement age for Social Security is increased and these age groups continue in labor force activities, and if the entitlement age for Medicare can be increased to parallel Social Security and pension programs. These questions will also be important in deciding whether reimbursement incentives can be built into private health insurance (or into Medicare and Medicaid) such that physicians will have incentives to prevent disease and promote health and functional independence at ever greater ages.

Associated with such policy questions are scientific questions that revolve around the question of the degree to which the health of elderly persons can be altered. That is, at what ages are health changes more a function of basic aging pro-

cesses than of age related disease processes that are to some
degree controllable? At one extreme, most aging changes
might be viewed simply as the accumulation over time of adverse environmental exposures and multiple chronic diseases.
One might then try simply to control the rate of such exposure
to minimize the adverse effects. Alternatively, chronic disease
and aging degeneration might be viewed as biologically pro-
gramed at the cellular level as a fixed function of time—as a
process totally beyond the control of the individual. Probably
both types of changes—environmental and physiological—
occur and interact, but current scientific knowledge cannot tell
us to what degree. Most recent scientific findings have tended
to shift the balance more toward a large environmental component of aging changes that is potentially controllable.

In the following I examine the scientific evidence on the
feasibility of modifying health at very advanced ages in order
to minimize the acute and long-term care demands of population aging. I first use the conceptual model presented in Figure 1 to review several different researchers' views on the
dimensions of health that can be changed, the degree to which
they can be changed, and the types of interventions that can
be used. Next I review the health survey and epidemiological
data on the health changes that have probably occurred with
the current increases in life expectancy at advanced ages—and
discuss what future changes are feasible. Then I examine evidence on how these factors translate into health service demands of several types and evaluate some possible strategies
for modifying the level of demand.

Models of Health Changes at Advanced Ages

Figure 1 implies that changes in mortality do not simply
translate into qualitative improvements in health, and the relation of morbidity, disability, and mortality is variable with age.
There are several different perspectives on how the relation of
morbidity, disability, and mortality has changed as life expectancy has increased at advanced ages.

One model (the one apparently assumed in the decision to

increase the Social Security entitlement age) suggests that as
life expectancy increases and mortality declines, the morbidity
and disability curves move as rapidly to the right as the mortality curve. If the curves in Figure 1 represent the cumulative
impact of *multiple* diseases and conditions, each with differing
relations to mortality and disability, the relations between the
morbidity and disability curves and mortality are probably so
complex that it is hazardous to make any assumption without
a detailed evaluation. This point was made by J.J. Feldman in
1982 in a minority report to the National Commission on
Social Security Reform. He argues that it is equally plausible
to assume that life expectancy has increased because death is
averted for people who are already sick and disabled—especially since American medicine is typically oriented to the
treatment and management of chronic disease rather than to
its prevention.

Similarly pessimistic views were espoused by E.M. Gruenberg in 1977 in the *Milbank Memorial Fund Quarterly* and by M.
Kramer in 1981 at the National Conference on the Elderly
Deinstitutionalized Patient in the Community. Kramer and
Gruenberg also cite the strong focus of biomedical research on
the treatment of disease and the prevention of death—rather
than the prevention of disease or the promotion of health.
They identify numerous disease-specific examples (e.g., successful cardiac surgery to correct congenital defects in children with Down's syndrome) where the life expectancy of
severely impaired persons has been greatly increased without,
they suggest, an appropriate and simultaneous emphasis on
health promotion. Like Feldman, they believe that the mortality curve has been shifted to the right without significant and
compensating movement in the morbidity and disability
curves. Thus aging people spend more years in a morbid or
disabled state, resulting in both higher acute and long-term
care costs.

A dramatically different view was offered in 1975 by B.L.
Strehler at the Fifty-eighth Annual Meeting of the Federation
of American Societies for Experimental Biology. He suggests
that by 2010 biological science will provide techniques to con-

trol basic aging processes so that the human life span could increase by 25 percent to 125 or more years. Strehler argues that because this would be accomplished by changing the intrinsic rate of aging, there would not be any increase in the number of years spent in morbid or disabled health states; that is, the three curves would all move to the right by twenty-five years. This suggests that the amount of acute and long-term care services required by any individual would not increase but that his or her potential for remaining economically active would be preserved for many years. The problem for society would then be how to harness these additional health years in productive economic and voluntary roles.

A very different concept has been offered by J.F. Fries. He suggests that in the United States and other developed countries further increases in life expectancy will be difficult due to intrinsic biological limits; that when the biological limits of life expectancy in a population are approached, death will be increasingly "natural" (i.e., due to biological senescence); that the causes of natural death are independent of those of premature death (i.e., death resulting from major acute disease processes); and that death from biological senescence can occur without prolonged morbidity and disability. The Fries model suggests that we are currently near the biological limits to life expectancy, so that the mortality curve in Figure 1 has become nearly square (i.e., "rectangularized"), that is, most people will survive to very advanced ages and then die in relatively short intervals. He also suggests that the morbidity and disability (but not the mortality) curves are changeable with current technologies. Thus we could cause the morbidity and disability curves to move to the right, reducing the number of years spent in morbid and disabled states as they moved to compress the area between them and the morbidity curve.

The Fries model has appealed to many people because of its simplicity and because it offers an attractive vision to some, i.e., that people will live to a ripe old age and then die a natural death free of disease or disability. This is also attractive because it frees us from the responsibility of providing ever-increasing resources for acute and long-term care health services at advanced ages. Unfortunately, there are a number of problems with the Fries model.

First, we cannot scientifically validate the concept of natural death. Autopsy studies of very elderly persons show multiple pathologies, so it is difficult to select the cause of death—but the pathologies are clearly present. Fries has admitted that the distinction between natural and premature death is an arbitrary one that can change depending on one's definition. We do not know if controlling a premature cause of death will increase the upper bound to life expectancy, that is, that curing or preventing a disease will always produce corresponding reductions in mortality as well as morbidity and disability. This makes the concept difficult to verify empirically.

Second, it is difficult to imagine how the gap between the morbidity and disability curves and the mortality curve can be closed rapidly enough to cope with the projected numerical increase in the elderly and extreme elderly populations. Related to this is the fact that prevention is neither cost free nor completely effective.

Health promotion activities tend to be adopted by higher socioeconomic groups. Indeed, we see a nearly spontaneous adoption of health promotion behavior among young professionals, whereas other socioeconomic groups are relatively resistant to such intervention efforts. It is not inconsequential that the groups least susceptible to such efforts tend to be least able to pay for health services and to have inadequate or no health insurance coverage, have the highest health resource demands, and are subject to multiple health risks (e.g., the U.S. Department of Health and Human Services reported in 1985 that some black urban subpopulations have increased alcohol and drug consumption, have poor nutrition, have inadequate health care services, and smoke).

Thus the Fries model is most applicable to specific higher socioeconomic population groups. We may also not be that close to the biological limits on life expectancy. Evidence presented in the next section suggests that life expectancy may continue to increase even at very advanced ages.

Another model suggests that the physiology of older persons can be improved more than most past evidence of age related functional loss would suggest. Because in this model the relation of the three survival curves is not fixed as life expectancy increases, we must carefully evaluate interventions on specific diseases to determine how they would affect the relation of the curves. For example, certain types of cancers are rapidly lethal once they reach the stage where they produce significant disability. If these cancers could be prevented, the number of persons surviving to advanced ages is likely to increase, but other diseases will then be prevalent. In contrast, conditions like arthritis and Alzheimer's disease (or urinary incontinence) are much less lethal but produce significant disability for a considerable period of time. Successful prevention of these diseases might have only a small impact on survival but would make a large impact on disability.

Evidence on Individual and Population Health Transitions

Table 1 summarizes anticipated changes in the size of the old and oldest-old population for the years 1985, 1990, 2000, 2020, and 2040. The growth of the elderly (aged sixty-five plus) and oldest-old (aged eighty-five plus) population is quite irregular. For example, the fastest growth of the population

TABLE 1: Projections of the U.S. Population Aged 65+ and Aged 85+ 1985–2040, by Sex (in Thousands)

	Males Age 65+	Age 85+	All Ages	Females Age 65+	Age 85+	All Ages
1985	11,608	802	121,198	17,639	2,052	126,611
1990	12,946	973	126,550	19,625	2,590	132,262
2000	14,357	1,388	135,669	21,827	3,773	141,782
2020	22,404	2,003	150,782	30,869	5,139	157,703
2040	28,565	3,984	157,838	40,283	9,101	167,802

SOURCE: SSA Office of Actuary: Social Security Area Population Projections, 1984. Actuarial Study No. 92. SSA Pub. No. 11-11539, 1984 (Alternative II Projections).

age sixty-five plus occurs between 2000 and 2020 when the post–World War II baby boom cohorts reach age sixty-five. The fastest growth of the population age eighty-five plus, the group with the highest long-term care needs, occurs roughly twenty years later when those cohorts begin to pass age eighty-five. Not only are these populations large in absolute terms, but they also comprise very large proportions of the total U.S. population. For example, in the United States in 2040, 18.1 percent of males and 24 percent of females will be over age sixty-five. The population age eighty-five plus is projected to grow by a factor of 4.6 from 1985 to 2040. By 2040 4 percent of the total U.S. population will be over age eighty-five, suggesting major increases in the demand for long-term health care services unless there are mitigating qualitative social and health changes. Because the population age eighty-five plus is primarily female, the social and economic characteristics of this population will be predominantly those of surviving females.

Table 2 shows that many developed countries have female and male life expectancies significantly greater than those of the United States. Japan, in particular, has a life expectancy of

TABLE 2: Life Expectancy at Birth for 11 Developed Countries, Males and Females

Country	Year	Males	Females
Canada	1982	72.0	79.0
United States	1980	70.1	77.8
Japan	1982	74.5	80.2
Denmark	1982	71.8	77.9
Finland	1980	69.2	78.0
France	1981	70.9	79.1
Greece	1982	73.6	78.3
Netherlands	1982	72.8	79.7
Norway	1982	72.7	79.8
Sweden	1982	73.5	79.6
Australia	1981	71.4	78.7

SOURCE: World Health Statistics Annual: 1984. WHO, Geneva, 1984.

TABLE 3: Education and Income Statistics for the U.S. Elderly.

Education Attainment, by Age and Sex, 1979[1]

Age	ELEMENTARY		HIGH SCHOOL		COLLEGE			Median Years
	1-7 Years	8 Years	Some	4 Years	Some	4 Years	5 Years & Over	
Males								
30-34	3.5	2.6	8.5	33.4	22.0	16.1	13.8	13.3
35-39	4.2	4.2	11.0	37.6	16.8	11.4	14.8	12.8
40-44	6.7	5.0	13.3	36.8	15.8	11.3	11.0	12.7
45-49	8.9	7.4	14.7	35.3	12.1	10.0	11.5	12.5
50-54	9.5	9.7	17.1	33.4	12.3	9.4	8.6	12.4
55-59	11.7	10.6	14.8	33.8	13.1	8.7	7.3	12.4
60-64	14.8	14.4	16.1	31.6	11.0	6.8	5.3	12.1
65-69	21.0	17.3	17.6	25.1	8.6	5.9	4.2	10.7
70-74	23.8	21.7	16.8	21.4	7.0	5.1	4.0	9.8
75+	33.3	23.9	11.3	14.6	7.5	5.5	3.7	8.7
Females								
30-34	3.3	2.4	12.1	44.5	18.4	12.1	7.3	12.7
35-39	4.1	3.1	14.7	45.9	15.8	9.0	7.2	12.6
40-44	5.5	4.5	15.7	47.3	13.3	8.5	5.0	12.5
45-49	7.2	6.0	16.7	45.5	13.3	6.5	4.8	12.4
50-54	11.7	7.4	17.2	45.4	11.9	6.3	3.6	12.4
55-59	10.0	9.4	16.2	43.4	13.0	4.9	3.2	12.3
60-64	12.5	13.4	17.8	38.8	9.1	4.9	3.4	12.2
65-69	16.3	17.4	18.5	29.9	9.0	5.6	3.2	11.5
70-74	19.3	19.7	16.8	27.2	8.6	4.8	3.3	10.7
75+	27.5	25.1	13.4	19.3	8.2	4.5	1.9	8.9

Total Income of Persons 65 Years of Age and Over, as Percent of GNP (Billions of 1972 Dollars)[2]

	1980	2000	2020	2050	RATE OF GROWTH (Average Annual) 1980 -2020	1980 -2020 ...		

	1980	2000	2020	2050	1980 -2020	2020 -2050	1980 -2050
Total Income	$ 100.6	$ 182.0	$ 350.2	$ 590.2	3.12%	1.74%	2.53%
Income as GNP	1423.4	1988.4	2526.9	3195.2	1.43	0.78	1.16
Percent of GNP	7.1%	9.1%	13.9%	18.5%	1.68	0.95	1.37

SOURCES: [1]U.S. Bureau of Census, 1980. "Educational Attainment in the United States: March 1979 and 1978." *Current Population Reports*, Series P-20, No. 356, Table 2. [2]The National Institute on Aging, 1984. *Macroeconomic-Demographic Model*, Table 10-34.

74.5 years for males and 80.2 years for females. In the Japanese prefecture of Okinawa, females had a life expectancy of 81.7 years in 1980. Thus life expectancies significantly higher than those in the United States have already been observed in many countries. Evidence suggests that we have not begun to observe the effect of rectangularization on life expectancy increases at advanced ages. If we were near an upper bound to life expectancy, the variance of the age at death would decrease (because the ages at death distribution would be truncated on the high side). Such truncation was not observed from 1962 to 1979, suggesting that the number of years remaining to be lived was increasing even at the most advanced ages. We can expect the number of years expected to be lived by persons between the ages of sixty-five and eighty-five to continue to increase.

One factor that will help reduce the unfavorable consequences of population aging is that the cohorts reaching ages sixty-five and eighty-five in the future will be better educated and have higher lifetime earnings than those currently reaching those ages. This is illustrated in Table 3, which presents educational and income statistics for elderly cohorts. In thirty years, for example, the median education of persons sixty-five to sixty-nine will increase 2.1 years for males (from 10.7 to 12.8 years), and they will have higher earnings than current elderly cohorts. (Income of the elderly as a percentage of gross national product will increase an average of 1.37 percent per annum compared with a projected 1.16 percent for total GNP.) This advantage will be partly offset by smaller family size, which means, at least for the oldest-old, fewer informal care resources. Furthermore, although future cohorts of elderly, on average, will be better off in terms of personal and economic resources, there will be significant numbers of elderly in certain subgroups who, because of low socioeconomic status (due possibly to chronic unemployment resulting from technological changes in occupation), are likely to suffer poorer health status and have inadequate access to medical services.

What is the quality of life likely to be for older populations

in the coming decades? Table 4 shows changes between 1951
and 1978 in Canada, in life expectancy as well as life expectancy free of major activity limitations. Although life expectancy increased 6.0 years over this period, more than 83 percent of that increase (4.7 years) was in an activity-limited state.
It could be said that in Canada, while there was significant
movement of the mortality curve, there was much less change
in the disability curve. More recent studies of Canada that used
health insurance data suggest that, while much of the life expectancy increase occurred in an impaired state, the level of

TABLE 4: Health Expectancy at Birth by Sex, Canada, 1951 and 1978
(Years)

Health Expectancy	Males	Females	Total
Life expectancy[a]			
1951	66.3	70.8	68.6
1978	70.8	78.3	74.6
Change: 1951–1978	+4.5	+7.5	+6.0
Disability expectancy[b]			
1951	6.6	6.1	6.3
1978	9.7	12.2	11.0
Change: 1951–1978	+3.2	+6.1	+4.7
Disability free life expectancy[c]			
1951	59.8	64.7	62.2
1978	61.1	66.1	63.6
Change: 1951–1978	+1.3	+1.4	+1.3
Quality-adjusted life expectancy[d]			
1951	63.1	67.8	65.4
1978	66.0	72.2	69.1
Change: 1951–1978	+2.9	+4.4	+3.7

Notes: a. All states of health combined.
   b. Long-term disability or activity limitation, excluding institutionalization and purely short-term
      disability.
   c. Life expectancy less disability expectancy.
   d. Disability expectancy counted as 50 percent of disability free life expectancy.

SOURCE: Wilkins, R. and Adams, O.B. *Healthfulness of Life.* Institute for Research on Public Policy,
   Montreal, 1983.

activity limitation was generally small. Thus, for a well-educated population involved in professional and technical occupations there should be relatively little impairment of work ability—whether in the regular labor market or in voluntary roles.

There are no comparable models and longitudinal studies at the national level for the United States. The Canadians produce this type of national health assessment regularly as a part of their labor economic surveys to evaluate the state of human capital. The Japanese also conduct such studies as part of the evaluation of their social security and health insurance systems as well as to serve a population projected to be 24 percent over age sixty-five by 2025.

The lack of similar comprehensive national studies in the United States is, in large part, a function of the available data. For example, although the National Health Interview Survey has collected limited data on disability from 1957 to the present, the measures used are probably not completely comparable across time. As a consequence, cross-temporal U.S. data have to be gleaned from a variety of sources and studies and then integrated to assess the U.S. situation.

One type of data with an adequate, nationally representative time series is cause-specific mortality data. These data can be used with population data to calculate cause-specific life table parameters that describe how a given disease affects survival with the effects of population composition removed. Two types of statistics from such life tables are presented in Table 5: the mean time to death from a given disease in the life table population and the probability of dying of the disease in a population cohort. These statistics are presented for the life table population at birth and at ages sixty-five and eighty-five.

The mean time to death at all ages and for all diseases is increasing. It appears that most chronic diseases are being delayed two to three years at birth and between four-tenths and seven-tenths of a year at age eighty-five. This upward shift in the age at death can be contrasted with data on Medicare expenditures, which show no apparent trend in the amount of health expenditures in the final year of life—even for more intensive medical treatment. Indeed, Medicare expenditures in the final year of life tend to decrease with age. Thus these data suggest that the increase in the mean time to death, shown in Table 5, was not associated with large increases in acute care costs. Perhaps old people are not living longer in severely morbid states as their life expectancy increases. This appears to be true in Canada, according to N.P. Roos, E. Shapiro, and B. Havens in the Economic Council of Canada's 1986 Colloquium on Aging with Limited Health Resources.

In Table 5 we can also identify conditions that are more frequent causes of death at advanced ages. For example, diabetes tends to decrease after age sixty-five while stroke and hip fractures increase in importance. To evaluate these disease processes in greater detail, I examined data from the 1982 National Long Term Care Survey (NLTCS), a nationally representative survey of chronically disabled elderly in the United States. Chronic disability was defined as having at least one "activity of daily living" (ADL) or "instrumental activity of daily living" (IADL) impairment for at least ninety days. A telephone screen of 36,000 persons drawn at random from the Health Insurance Master File listing all Medicare beneficiaries was conducted; it identified 6,393 persons who fulfilled the disability criterion. These persons were then given an in-depth personal interview. The two-stage procedure yielded more detailed information from a representative population of disabled persons than can be obtained from an effectively much larger sample.

Table 6 shows the diseases that were reported by respondents in the NLTCS as causing disability for persons at various levels of disability. Diseases thought of as being the major lethal conditions were reported relatively infrequently as causes of disability. For example, cancer and ischemic heart disease were associated with only 4.8 percent and 5.08 percent of chronic disability above age sixty-five—but caused 22.5 percent and 63.3 percent of the mortality (see Table 5). The most frequently reported conditions were arthritis (36.95 percent), arteriosclerosis (35.34 percent), stroke (30.25 percent), and

TABLE 5: Mean Time to Death and Probability of Dying From Diseases for U.S. White Male and Female Life Table Population at Birth, Age 65 and Age 85, 1968–1980

White Males

Disease	Mean Time To Death 1968	1974	1980	Probability (%) 1968	1974	1980
AT BIRTH						
Hip Fracture	81.47	83.23	84.07	0.8	0.9	0.7
Stroke	75.46	76.67	78.10	15.0	15.1	12.5
Influenza/Pneumonia	71.91	74.44	77.34	12.1	11.0	9.3
Diabetes	71.35	72.64	73.44	5.5	6.1	5.8
Cancer	69.43	70.43	71.59	17.0	19.3	22.2
Chronic Obstructive Lung Disease	71.85	73.31	75.00	6.6	8.1	9.8
Heart Disease	71.76	72.96	74.19	52.7	54.5	58.3
AT AGE 65						
Hip Fracture	18.30	19.41	20.12	1.2	1.2	0.9
Stroke	14.39	15.19	15.98	19.1	18.9	15.4
Influenza/Pneumonia	14.46	15.44	16.58	13.9	12.9	11.0
Diabetes	11.60	12.36	12.98	6.1	6.8	6.3
Cancer	11.16	11.73	12.31	17.3	19.6	22.5
Chronic Obstructive Lung Disease	11.01	11.85	12.88	7.7	9.6	11.5
Heart Disease	12.91	13.74	14.46	57.8	59.6	63.3
AT AGE 85						
Hip Fracture	5.26	5.72	5.95	2.6	2.7	1.9
Stroke	4.51	4.78	4.94	23.8	18.9	19.4
Influenza/Pneumonia	4.91	5.31	5.34	18.5	17.0	15.7
Diabetes	3.88	4.11	4.31	4.2	5.1	4.8
Cancer	3.96	4.16	4.34	11.1	13.0	15.4
Chronic Obstructive Lung Disease	3.96	4.05	4.22	4.4	5.9	8.2
Heart Disease	4.63	5.00	5.06	58.3	62.3	60.9

White Females

Disease	Mean Time To Death 1968	1974	1980	Probability (%) 1968	1974	1980
AT BIRTH						
Hip Fracture	85.15	86.17	86.65	2.2	2.2	1.5
Stroke	80.29	81.68	83.01	22.7	23.2	19.7
Influenza/Pneumonia	78.42	80.27	82.92	12.3	10.9	9.7
Diabetes	75.45	76.87	77.62	8.3	8.7	7.8
Cancer	70.34	71.32	72.32	15.7	17.1	19.0
Chronic Obstructive Lung Disease	74.13	74.66	75.98	2.0	2.7	4.2
Heart Disease	79.31	80.45	81.22	52.9	55.2	60.5
AT AGE 65						
Hip Fracture	20.69	21.61	22.28	2.7	2.6	1.7
Stroke	17.67	18.78	19.78	25.6	26.1	22.0
Influenza/Pneumonia	18.81	19.70	20.85	13.2	11.6	10.5
Diabetes	13.59	14.81	15.66	9.2	9.2	8.1
Cancer	13.33	13.91	14.26	13.1	14.3	16.1
Chronic Obstructive Lung Disease	14.78	14.39	14.66	1.9	2.6	4.2
Heart Disease	17.14	18.19	18.97	58.1	60.3	65.0
AT AGE 85						
Hip Fracture	5.70	6.21	6.29	4.1	3.8	2.5
Stroke	5.35	5.69	6.04	27.6	28.7	25.1
Influenza/Pneumonia	6.08	6.34	6.71	16.4	14.2	13.3
Diabetes	4.34	4.54	4.99	4.8	5.9	5.5
Cancer	4.72	5.02	5.23	7.6	8.4	9.6
Chronic Obstructive Lung Disease	5.02	5.27	5.30	1.4	1.6	2.6
Heart Disease	5.67	5.97	6.28	59.5	62.9	68.6

TABLE 6: Age-Specific Conditional Probabilities of Having a Specific Medical Condition for Persons Aged 65+ with a Given Disability Level

Condition	IADL	1–2 ADL	3–4 ADL	5–6 ADL	Total
		Number of Persons With Condition			
Cancer	66,327 (4.51)	69,032 (4.23)	24,240 (3.49)	63,630 (7.48)	223,229 (4.80)
Diabetes	91,049 (6.19)	125,931 (7.72)	52,079 (7.50)	95,567 (11.23)	364,626 (7.84)
Senility	190,854 (12.97)	208,260 (12.77)	70,036 (10.09)	145,733 (17.12)	614,883 (13.23)
Emphysema & Bronchitis	94,310 (6.41)	80,903 (4.96)	36,884 (5.31)	56,358 (6.62)	268,455 (5.78)
Ischemic Heart Disease	83,844 (5.70)	70,217 (4.31)	27,850 (4.01)	53,977 (6.34)	235,888 (5.08)
Hypertension	184,169 (12.51)	174,027 (10.67)	79,752 (11.49)	82,762 (9.73)	520,710 (11.20)
Arteriosclerosis	428,105 (29.08)	481,659 (29.53)	260,626 (37.55)	472,290 (55.50)	1,642,680 (35.34)
Arthritis	445,808 (30.29)	698,026 (42.80)	311,532 (44.89)	262,217 (30.81)	1,717,583 (36.95)
Cerebrovascular Disease	372,984 (25.34)	423,743 (25.98)	223,149 (32.15)	386,313 (45.40)	1,406,189 (30.25)
Hip & Other Fractures	287,563 (19.54)	446,400 (27.37)	209,431 (30.18)	189,200 (10.48)	1,132,594 (24.37)
Total Number of Persons	1,472,000	1,631,000	694,000	851,000	4,646,000

NOTE: Figures in parentheses are percent of total population at given disability level with condition.

hip and other fractures (24.37 percent). Above age eighty-five, senility was reported most often.

Of course, these relations are variable with age. It may be that those conditions that cause the greatest disability around age sixty-six or sixty-seven (i.e., the age where we should currently target our initial efforts at health promotion) are different from those that cause problems at seventy-six or seventy-seven. Also, simple analysis of the level of disability may hide important qualitative changes in the relation of morbidity and disability, in that certain conditions causing disability may be temporary or may not significantly inhibit the performance of certain types of jobs. For example, even at younger ages a person may have long-term serious disability from, say, a broken leg that will eventually mend. Among the elderly, too, hip fracture is a potentially rehabilitatable condition—and one that may be preventable by treating the underlying condition of osteoporosis. Furthermore, muscoskeletal problems might not interfere with the performance of certain types of sales, marketing, and technical jobs that could be done at home using new telecommunication technology.

To examine the health disability relation more precisely, I used the disability data from the NLTCS in a series of multivariate analyses. I subjected the full set of ADL, IADL, and IADL2 measures to a multivariate pattern recognition procedure called the grade of membership (GOM) analysis. This procedure examines the relations among those functional status measures to identify a small number of basic disability profiles that "explain" individual variation on the observed measures by assigning a weight for each person to each of the profile types. The weights for any given individual sum to 1.0 and range between 0.0 and 1.0.

GOM analysis is akin to another well known multivariate procedure called "factor analysis," where two types of coefficients are estimated. One type of coefficient in factor analysis is called the factor loading. It describes the correlation of observed variables and analytically determined factors. In the GOM model similar coefficients are calculated, except that they describe the probability that a person of a given type has a particular attribute. The second coefficient calculated in factor analysis is the factor score. It describes how well a person is described by a particular factor determined by the observed variables. These coefficients are similar to the individual weights calculated in GOM analysis, except that the weights in GOM are constrained to sum to 1.0 and to be positive, whereas the factor scores do not have such properties. Furthermore, in the GOM model, because the individual weights are calculated simultaneously with the profile coefficients, no distributional assumptions are required.

In the GOM analysis of the disability data from the NLTCS, I generated five different disability profiles. The Type 1 profile represented a baseline "unimpaired" category with few disabilities. The Type 2 profile represented persons with mobility problems associated with fracture and degenerative joint conditions. The Type 3 profile was characterized by greater impairment, apparently due to cardiopulmonary diseases. The Type 4 profile was characterized primarily by cognitive impairments. The Type 5 profile represented cognitive impairment plus a wide range of acute medical problems; these were the "frail" elderly.

Each person in the sample had a score on each of the five disability profiles that indicated the degree to which he or she was subject to the disabilities of that type. Because each disability profile is associated with a different likelihood of being able to perform different tasks, it defines both the potential work ability of the person and his or her requirements for long-term care. Thus the higher a disabled elderly person's score in Profile 1, the lower his or her requirement for long-term care.

I regressed the individual score for each of the five disability profiles on a set of twelve dummy variables describing whether a person had a specific disease. In the regression each coefficient was an interaction term involving age:

$$g_{ik} = [B_{iD} \text{ age}] \, X_{iD} + e_{iK},$$

where $[B_{iD} \text{ age}]$ is the age-specific change in the Kth disability score owing to the presence of the Dth condition (i.e., $X_{iD} =$

1.0). By including age in this way I can calculate the effect of changing disease prevalence at specific policy relevant ages, for example, sixty-six or sixty-seven.

The coefficients in Table 7 show the impact of changing disease prevalence at age sixty-seven. Elimination of any disease will increase the prevalence of Type 1. Even if all twelve diseases were eliminated, however, only 47.6 percent of those age sixty-seven would be in Profile 1. Clearly there are additional disease and aging factors that generate disability that are not captured by the model. Also, there is a relatively large impact of senility on Types 4 and 5—the least active types. The coefficients in Table 7 show us what diseases should be emphasized in a disability reduction program, i.e., have the greatest impact on the prevalence of Type 1 (senility, stroke, rheumatism, hip fracture).

The potential impact of even a modest improvement in health status is suggested in Table 8 where the disability rates from the NLTCS are multiplied by the 1980 Social Security population projections under the assumptions that the age- and sex-specific disability rates do not change, and the disability rates decline as rapidly as the mortality rates. As can be seen in Table 8, both the number of disabled and the number of hours of informal care are dramatically reduced (by about 30 percent by the year 2040) using this procedure. The morbidity reduction assumption simply reflects the disability survival curve in Figure 1 moving as rapidly to the right as the overall survival curve is projected to move under the 1980 Social Security mortality assumptions.

Given the desirability and importance of reducing disability in conjunction with mortality rate reductions, we are faced with the problem of how these changes can be instituted—a problem that has to be addressed on both the scientific and the public policy levels. On the scientific level, recent research findings indicate much greater potential for health improvement at advanced ages than was previously thought. For example, at the National Institute on Aging Gerontological Research Center in Baltimore, numerous studies show that the cardiovascular function of persons in their seventh and eighth

TABLE 7: Regression Coefficient Multiplied by Age 67, Crude Prevalence by Type (in parentheses), and Intercept

Disease	Proportion in Total Sample With Trait	REGRESSION COEFFICIENTS				
		Type 1 "Healthy" (31.4%)	Type 2 Mobility Limited (20.7%)	Type 3 Circulatory and Respiratory Impaired (19.3%)	Type 4 Cognitive Impaired (11.4%)	Type 5 Acute Medical Problems (17.2%)
Rheumatism	73.2	−8.04	1.97	6.69	−2.61	2.01
Diabetes	16.6	−7.01	−1.47	1.88	0.61	6.03
Cancer	6.4	−3.62	−0.21	−1.74	−0.61	6.23
Arteriosclerosis	31.4	−6.63	−2.41	1.21	2.68	5.16
Senility	9.2	−15.41	−10.72	−7.84	10.18	23.85
Heart Attack	6.2	−7.37	0.72	4.29	0.29	2.08
Hypertension	47.1	−1.34	0.64	3.35	−1.41	−1.22
Stroke	6.6	−10.39	−0.87	−2.55	−0.35	14.07
Bronchitis	12.9	−5.23	−3.28	7.34	−1.34	2.35
Emphysema	9.9	−1.81	−1.76	1.27	0.01	2.28
Hip Fracture	2.3	−13.67	14.74	−5.16	−4.76	8.84
Other Fractures	5.5	−6.50	0.88	3.75	−2.88	4.71
Intercept (%)		47.6	21.2	10.7	12.6	7.8

TABLE 8: Number of and Hours of Care Per Week Per Helper Devoted to the U.S. Noninstitutionalized Elderly under Two Assumptions, 1980–2040

	Assuming Unchanged Disability Rates	Assuming Declining Disability Rates
	Number of Persons (in Thousands)	
1980	4,427	4,427
1985	4,992	4,612
1990	5,638	4,887
2000	6,717	5,427
2020	9,363	6,974
2040	13,147	9,179
	Hours of Care Per Week Per Helper (in Thousands)	
1980	112,167	112,167
1985	126,934	117,342
1990	143,919	124,799
2000	173,518	140,161
2020	242,225	180,430
2040	344,512	240,400

SOURCE: Tabulations of 1982 NLTCS

decades can be the same as that of thirty-year olds. Furthermore, although cross-sectional studies suggest a systematic decline in intellectual functioning at advanced ages, new and more valid longitudinal studies show that, at the individual level, most persons experience intellectual decline in the period just prior to death. Thus the cross-sectional studies may contain population artifacts; that is, because mortality rates increase with age, at more advanced ages there are larger proportions of the surviving population in the terminal decline period. Indeed, as R.W. Besdine pointed out in 1984 at the Fifth Annual Invitational Symposium on the Elderly and their Health, much of our prior scientific understanding of functional decline with age has had to be revised because the early studies were conducted on populations that had high prevalences of multiple chronic degenerative diseases. This is

precisely the wrong population to study if one wishes to determine functional decline caused solely by intrinsic biological
aging processes. In summary, recent scientific evidence suggests that health is more malleable at advanced ages than
previously believed and that there is much greater potential
for retrieving functional capacity at later ages than previously
thought.

Given the scientific evidence on the mutability of health at
advanced ages, how will future health improvements be produced? There is major interest in controlling the traditional
risk factors for chronic diseases, for example, smoking, hypertension, obesity, cholesterol. It had been thought that traditional risk factors lost their potency past age sixty-five. These
findings appear also to be in error, in part because the survival
analyses used to assess the effects of certain risk factors measured those effects relative to an underlying hazard rate. Because mortality rates at advanced ages double every eight to
nine years, if the absolute effect of a risk factor on mortality
increased, its proportional contribution to mortality would
decline unless it were doubled every eight to nine years. Evidence in 1986 from the Brookings Institution suggests that the
size of the absolute effect of risk factors increases for cardiovascular mortality and is constant for stroke. In my own reanal-
ysis of data from a series of well known longitudinal studies
(e.g., Framingham, the Finnish East-West study, a WHO-
sponsored study in Kaunas, Lithuania), I found no significant
difference in the effect of a range of risk factors on total mortality above and below age sixty-five.

Risk factors may also appear to lose their potency at advanced ages because of mortality selection. Mortality selection
simply means that people who have elevated risk factor levels
(and possibly jointly elevated risk factor levels) may not survive to more advanced ages. Thus most heavy smokers and
diabetics may die before age seventy-five, leaving a population
with much lower risk factor levels.

Table 9 presents the results of a series of simulations of the
effects of mortality selection on risk factor distributions. The
age-specific impact of eliminating three broad disease classes

TABLE 9: Age-specific contributions (in years) to life expectancy gains from the elimination of cancer, circulatory disease, or residual disease operating independently (A), after eliminating smoking (B), or where dependent on common risk factors (C), for Framingham males

	CANCER			CIRCULATORY DISEASE			RESIDUAL DISEASE		
Age Interval	A Baseline	B Smoking Eliminated	C Risk Factor Dependent	A Baseline	B Smoking Eliminated	C Risk Factor Dependent	A Baseline	B Smoking Eliminated	C Risk Factor Dependent
30–39	0.158	0.117 (−26.0)	0.158 (0)	0.357	0.270 (−24.0)	0.357 (0)	0.119	0.113 (−5.0)	0.119 (0)
40–49	0.250	0.118 (−53.0)	0.250 (0)	0.704	0.540 (−23.0)	0.704 (0)	0.187	0.188 (1.0)	0.187 (0)
50–59	0.380	0.304 (−20.0)	0.378 (−1.0)	1.183	0.960 (−19.0)	1.182 (0)	0.300	0.291 (−3.0)	0.299 (0)
60–69	0.521	0.458 (−12.0)	0.514 (−1.0)	1.808	1.603 (−11.0)	1.799 (0)	0.431	0.411 (−5.0)	0.425 (−1.0)
70–79	0.572	0.563 (−2.0)	0.547 (−4.0)	2.450	2.385 (−3.0)	2.402 (−2.0)	0.474	0.470 (−1.0)	0.452 (−5.0)
80–89	0.365	0.396 (8.0)	0.332 (−9.0)	2.513	2.614 (4.0)	2.395 (−5.0)	0.278	0.304 (9.0)	0.247 (−11.0)
90–99	0.076	0.084 (11.0)	0.062 (−18.0)	1.487	1.564 (5.0)	1.197 (−20.0)	0.050	0.055 (10.0)	0.038 (−24.0)
100+	0.002	0.002 (*)	0.001 (*)	0.384	0.410 (7.0)	0.199 (−48.0)	0.001	0.001 (10.0)	0.001 (*)
Total	2.324	2.112 (−9.0)	2.242 (−4.0)	10.885	10.345 (−5.0)	10.186 (−6.0)	1.840	1.834 (0)	1.768 (−4.0)

*Estimate too imprecise at this advanced age
Figures in parentheses are percentage differences between columns A and B or C.

is shown in three different ways. Column A shows what the gain in life expectancy would be if the disease were eliminated in a way that did not affect other diseases or the distribution of risk factors. Column B shows the effects of eliminating the disease if no one smoked in the population. Without smokers, the effect of cancer and circulatory disease at early ages is reduced (e.g., the effect of cancer at ages forty to forty-nine is reduced 53 percent). The increase in the effects of these diseases among nonsmokers at later ages is due to the delay of death. Column C shows the effects of eliminating the disease and modeling the increased survival of smokers who would have died of the eliminated disease. Clearly, for example, eliminating cancer allows more smokers to survive to advanced ages. Because other diseases are affected by smoking, surviving smokers will have elevated risks from those other causes—but at more advanced ages. It will be more difficult to detect the health effect of any single risk factor with this accumulation of higher risks at later ages.

The increase in life expectancy owing to the control of individual major risk factors is somewhat less in this model than in other evaluations because of the numerous major individual physiological and population effects (e.g., dependence of mortality risks through common risk factors, modeling of random effects on risk factor levels, etc.) in the model. The current level of effect seems to be more consistent with the impact of risk factors observed after interventions in community populations.

Table 10 summarizes a number of risk factor control scenarios involving both a reduction of the variance of individual differences in risk factor levels and control of the age related increase in risk factor levels with age. Controlling the variance of risk factor levels has a greater impact at early ages, whereas control of the age increase of risk factors has a greater impact at later ages. Perhaps the most interesting value in the table is that for the simultaneous control of a large number of risk factors (i.e., diastolic blood pressure, cholesterol, smoking, vital capacity, relative weight, hemoglobin, blood sugar, pulse pressure). Males who control these factors have a life expect-

TABLE 10: Changes in Age-Specific Life Expectancy after Different Interventions on Risk Factors Using the 20-Year Experience of Framingham Males

Age	Framingham Baseline	U.S. White Males 1982	No Age Increase of Diastolic Blood Pressure or Pulse Pressure	No Variance of Diastolic Blood Pressure or Pulse Pressure	Both Controls on Diastolic Blood Pressure or Pulse Pressure	Age Controls on All Variables	Both Controls on All Variables
30	44.5	43.8	45.6	46.6	47.5	48.9	57.3
			(1.1)	(2.1)	(3.0)	(4.4)	(12.3)
60	18.3	17.9	19.5	19.8	20.9	22.3	29.2
			(1.2)	(1.5)	(2.6)	(4.0)	(10.9)
70	11.5	11.6	12.8	12.6	13.9	15.4	21.0
			(1.3)	(1.1)	(2.8)	(3.9)	(9.5)
80	6.4	7.0	7.7	7.0	8.3	10.0	14.1
			(1.3)	(0.6)	(1.9)	(3.6)	(7.7)
90	3.1	—	4.1	3.3	4.3	6.3	8.9
			(1.0)	(0.2)	(1.2)	(3.2)	(5.8)
100	1.70	—	2.5	1.8	2.6	4.8	6.7
			(0.8)	(0.1)	(0.9)	(3.1)	(5.0)

ancy at age 30 of 87.3 years—12.3 years greater than without interventions. Although we are unlikely to achieve this degree of risk factor control in a large population, it does indicate the tremendous potential for increasing life expectancy at later ages by controlling traditional risk factors.

There are a number of chronic conditions that produce large amounts of disability that, as far as is known, are not strongly influenced by traditional risk factors. Two such conditions are senile dementia and hip fracture. Nonetheless, new research is providing insights and leads about risk factors for these diseases that might be subject to control. For example, the role of nutritional supplementation with calcium is being investigated to control osteoporosis and resulting hip and other fractures. For senile dementia it is speculated that as much as a third may be due to micro cerebral infarcts. Such micro infarcts might be eliminated by hypertension control.

One example of the implications of control of these conditions can be seen in Figure 2, which presents the increase in the incidence of hip fracture with age. The incidence of hip fracture increases roughly exponentially with age, with a doubling time of about five years. The incidence of hip fracture could be halved by delaying the rate of incidence by five years. In 2050, without an increase in life expectancy, this would mean about 300,000 fewer hip fractures with their attendant acute and long-term care costs. Conversely, if the incidence rate is not delayed, and if life expectancy increased five years, the incidence of hip fracture could double, that is, increase to 1.3 million.

Recall that in 1980 older people suffering from most major chronic diseases, including cancer, could expect to live two or more years longer than their counterparts in 1968 (see Table 5). This correlation in the age assault pattern of chronic disease has tended to keep the prevalence of disability at later ages in control. Unfortunately, we do not know what factors contributed to this pervasive shift. Some have speculated that it may be due to yet unidentified cohort factors such as better nutrition. Whatever may account for this shift, it will be important to monitor future trends of different diseases to ascertain

FIGURE 2. Projected Number of Hip Fractures Annually in the U.S. by Age: 1980–2050

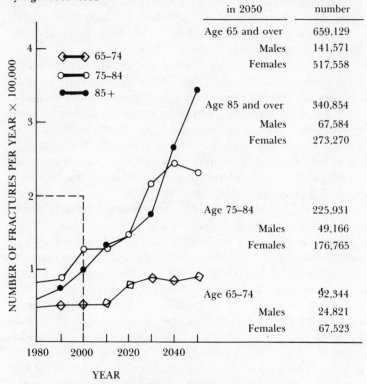

in 2050	number
Age 65 and over	659,129
Males	141,571
Females	517,558
Age 85 and over	340,854
Males	67,584
Females	273,270
Age 75–84	225,931
Males	49,166
Females	176,765
Age 65–74	92,344
Males	24,821
Females	67,523

SOURCE: NCHS and U.S. Bureau of Census projections. Reported in Brody, J. A., Decreasing Mortality and Increasing Morbidity in the 20th and 21st Centuries. Forthcoming in *Philosophy and Medicine Series*, D. Reidel Pub. Co., 1986, Figure 3.

whether such an equilibrium is likely to continue.

How can incentives be built into both private and public health insurance programs and health service delivery systems to improve and promote health at later ages? Perhaps some incentives can be built directly into the health service delivery system for the elderly. For example, proper design of housing and the physical environment can reduce the risk of falls and hip fractures. Hypertension control—part of standard medical practice—could be monitored even more carefully in the elderly. Geriatric evaluation units could help assess the total physical status of the elderly person and define current physiological and functional deficiencies and either ameliorate those conditions by a broad range of actions or attempt a broad range of preventive actions or both. Thus an important policy question is how such geriatric evaluation and assessment functions can be reimbursed and how prospective reimbursement can be specially structured for persons with multiple, interacting chronic diseases and attendant functional impairments. Such geriatric problems do not fit well into current standard diagnosis-specific models of medical management and reimbursement systems.

It is even more difficult to build in incentives for primary prevention and health promotion at younger ages whose major impact will be at later ages. One suggestion has been to reduce payments for preventable diagnosis related groups and shift those funds into more prevention oriented activities. The problems of implementing such incentives in a medical delivery system oriented toward illness in older populations would be considerable.

Health maintenance organizations (HMOs) have potential for promoting health, although more recently HMOs have been oriented more toward cost control than health promotion. The HMO is one of a general class of reimbursement strategies that may be collectively called capitation systems. Using a Blue Cross and Blue Shield Plan as the Medicare insurer for an entire state has been examined as a type of "area capitation" system in Maryland. Another type of capitation model reimburses physicians who triage patients to different specialists. Such "gatekeeper" models involve risk incentives at two levels—for the physician gatekeeper and the specialist provider of care.

Some special problems arise in establishing capitation systems for elderly populations, for example, in adjusting reimbursements for elderly populations that have a much higher level of service needs. The Medicare program uses the actuarial index called the average adjusted per capita cost (AAPCC) in setting payments for "at risk" HMOs who have contracted to provide care to the elderly. This index scales the capitation rates for age, sex, and institutional and welfare status. Health status, however, is not directly included as an underwriting factor. It is possible to include specific risk sets or groups in the capitation rates to adjust payments to reflect health status differentials. They could also be used, as in the DRG system, to provide incentives to reduce the risk of certain preventable events and conditions.

Designing such case mix measures for long-term care services that target the *functional* status of elderly persons raises special problems. Currently, Medicare—and other payers— does not reimburse for medical and other care that improves or maintains general functional capacity—even though this is the primary goal of geriatric medicine. Additionally, the development of a long-term care case mix measure requires that the chronicity of a service episode be taken into account. Such measures are intrinsically more complex, in terms of measuring functional status (measuring current level of service need) and diagnosis (indicating chronicity or trajectory of change of service need).

It will be interesting to see how HMOs will respond to the challenges presented as their populations eventually age into higher service and age categories. They should have special incentives to control disability and dependence-generating conditions. There already are certain incentives in capitation systems that treat very old and high-service-use populations. One such incentive exists where capitation rates are set to reflect the predictably higher average cost of a high-service-use population; this reduces the financial risks of caring for older, high-service-use populations.

The effects of aging on the flow of expenditures over time in an HMO are illustrated in Table 11, which shows the expected costs for two HMO cohorts with different life expectancies. Initially the high–life expectancy cohort (Davis County) has lower expenditures but the cost differential shifts at more advanced ages, because eventually that cohort will have more

TABLE 11: Annual Per Capita Costs Due to the Mortality Process

Age	Benton County	Davis County	Ratio Benton/Davis
70	$342	$323	1.06
71	397	348	1.14
72	463	368	1.26
73	528	384	1.38
74	578	400	1.45
75	606	418	1.45
76	595	447	1.33
77	554	493	1.12
78	508	534	0.95
79	477	587	0.81

SOURCE: Tolley, H.D., Manton, K.G. "Assessing health care costs in the elderly."
TRANSACTIONS of the Society of Actuaries 36:579–603, 1984, Table 10.

deaths with their higher attendant terminal care costs. Such shifts result from the fact that medical costs tend to be concentrated in the last year or two of life.

HMOs and other capitation systems may be stimulated to provide primary prevention services by grouping members according to risk and adjusting the reimbursement of groups for preventable diseases. This still leaves the more basic problem of "primordial prevention"—that is, the prevention of adverse risk factors. Some medical services cannot now be specifically reimbursed for "treating" many chronic disease risk factors—especially risk factors that have a long-term impact on multiple disease outcomes. A number of community-based capitation programs are experimenting with providing services for long-term disease prevention. The cost effectiveness of these efforts has been challenged; also, they often do not take into account that primary prevention at advanced ages may require entirely different methods and goals than at earlier ages. Specifically, the current evidence suggests that the optimal value for many risk factors may be age variable. Thus it may be desirable, for example, to have higher relative body weight and blood pressure at advanced ages to compensate for basic aging changes (a subject of controversy in the prevention field). Also, geriatric medicine probably should treat and manage disorders like hypertension and diabetes differently from treatment for the rest of the population because of physiological differences; an otherwise deviant physiological value may be quite adaptive for old people.

There will also need to be changes in employment, pension, and health insurance to respond to an aging population. It may be that, despite higher health care costs, an elderly person may be capable of remaining economically active (i.e., the morbidity curve in Figure 1 may be unchanged but interventions may move the disability curve to the right). It may also be possible that elderly persons would continue to work part-time if appropriate adjustments in pension and Social Security policy provided necessary incentives. The skill requirements of certain jobs might be modified to permit a partially disabled elderly person to continue to fill an economic role. Finally, perhaps incentives could be created to encourage older persons to participate in voluntary activities. They could make a major impact providing informal care services to less healthy older people. A small increase in the provision of informal care could have a large impact on long-term care expenditures—the component of health care expenditures which is most affected by population aging.

Summary

This chapter has reviewed the demographic factors that contribute to population aging in the United States and other developing countries. The most significant of these are fertility control, which eventually causes elderly cohorts to be the same size as younger cohorts, and life expectancy increases. The net impact is a projected increase in the elderly and oldest-old population that will have serious consequences for the acute and long-term care service systems.

The qualitative changes in the health and functional status

of the elderly associated with the life expectancy increase have not yet been well studied. If there were a significant improvement in health and functioning at later ages, there would be both direct benefits (i.e., reducing an individual's service needs) and indirect benefits (i.e., making more elderly available for providing informal long-term care services). Changes in health associated with recent life expectancy gains is debated by different authors. More extensive longitudinal data from other countries and specially studied populations in the United States suggest that most increases in functional dependency at later ages are caused by moderate types of impairment. This, coupled with the improving socioeconomic status of the elderly (on average), should attenuate the health service demands of an aging population—especially if incentives can be built into the current reimbursement system to promote health at later ages.

Bibliography

Blanchet, M., "Advances in Preventive Medicine." Paper presented at Colloquium on Aging with Limited Health Resources, Economic Council of Canada, Winnipeg, Manitoba, May 5–6, 1986.

Fries, J.F., "Aging, Natural Death, and the Compression of Morbidity," *New England Journal of Medicine*, 303 (1980), 130–135.

————, "The Compression of Morbidity," *Milbank Memorial Fund Quarterly*, 61 (1983), 397–419.

Kannel, W.B., and T. Gordon, "Cardiovascular Risk Factors in the Aged: The Framingham Study," in *The Second Conference on the Epidemiology of Aging*, eds. S.G. Haynes and M. Feinleib. NIH Pub. No. 80–969, Washington, D.C.: U.S. Government Printing Office, 1980.

Katz, S., L.G. Branch, M.H. Branson, J.A. Papsidero, J.A. Beck, and D.S. Greer, "Active Life Expectancy," *New England Journal of Medicine*, 309 (1983), 1218–1223.

Katzman, R., "Aging and Age-dependent Disease: Cognition and Dementia," in *Health in an Older Society*, U.S. Committee on an Aging Society. Washington, D.C.: National Academy Press, 1986.

Kuroda, T., Comment on IUSSP–NIRA Seminar on Biological and Social Correlates of Mortality. Nihon University Population Research Institute, Japan, 1984.

Lakatta, E.G., "Health, Disease and Cardiovascular Aging," in *Health in an Older Society*, U.S. Committee on an Aging Society. Washington, D.C.: National Academy Press, 1986.

Lubitz, J., and R. Prihoda, "Uses and Costs of Medicare Services in the Last Year of Life," *Health, United States, 1983*, Department of Health and Human Services Pub. No. (PHS) 84–1232, Washington, D.C.: U.S. Government Printing Office, 1983.

Manton, K.G., and T. Hausner, "Prospective Reimbursement System for LTC: An Illustration of a Case Mix Methodology for Home Health Services," in review at *Health Care Financing Review*, 1986.

McClure, W., "On the Research Status of Risk Adjusted Capitation Rates," *Inquiry*, 21 (1984), 205–213.

Minaker, K.L., and J.W. Rowe, "Health and Disease among the Oldest Old: A Clinical Perspective," *Milbank Memorial Fund Quarterly*, 63 (1985), 324–349.

Myers, G.C., and K.G. Manton, "Compression of Mortality: Myth or Reality?" *Gerontologist*, 24 (1984), 345–353.

———, "Recent Changes in the U.S. Age at Death Distribution: Further Observations," *Gerontologist*, 24 (1984), 572–575.

Myers, G.C., K.G. Manton, and H. Bacellar, "Sociodemographic Aspects of Future Impaired Productive Roles," in *America's Aging: Productive Roles in an Older Society*, Washington, D.C.: National Academy Press, 1986.

Riley, G., J. Lubitz, R. Prihoda, and M.A. Stevenson, "Changes in the Distribution of Medicare Expenditures among Aged Enrollees, 1969–1982," Department of Health and Human Services HCFA ORD Working Paper Series No. 85–12, April 1, 1985.

Riley, M.W., and K. Bond, "Beyond Ageism: Postponing the Onset of Disability," in *Aging in Society: Selected Reviews of Recent Research*, eds. M.W. Riley, B.B. Hess, and K. Bond. Hillsdale, N.J.: Lawrence Erlbaum Associates, 1983.

Russell, L., *Is Prevention Better than the Cure?* Washington, D.C.: Brookings Institution, 1986.

Shock, N.W., R.C. Greulich, R. Andres, D. Arenberg, P.T. Costa, E.G. Sakatta, and J.D. Tobin, *Normal Human Aging: The Baltimore Longitudinal Study of Aging*. NIH Pub. No. 84–2450, Washington, D.C.: U.S. Government Printing Office, 1984.

Siegel, J.S., "Recent and Prospective Demographic Trends for the Elderly Population and Some Implications for Health Care," in *Epidemiology of Aging*, eds. S.G. Haynes and M. Feinleib. NIH Pub. No. 80–969, Washington, D.C.: U.S. Government Printing Office, 1980.

Tolley, H.D., K.G. Manton, and J.C. Vertrees, "Structural Strategies in Controlling Fiscal Risks in HMOs: Enrollment Size and Composition," in review at *Inquiry*, 1986.

U.S. Committee on an Aging Society, *Health in an Older Society*. Washington, D.C.: National Academy Press, 1986.

Woodbury, M.A., and K.G. Manton, "A New Procedure for the Analysis of Medical Classification," *Methods of Information in Medicine,* 21 (1982), 210–220.

World Health Organization, *WHO Consultation on an Integrated Programme for Community Health in Noncommunicable Diseases.* December 16–18, 1985, Geneva.

7

Meeting the Long-Term Care Needs of an Aging Population

DIANE ROWLAND

Introduction

Long-term care for the elderly has emerged as one of the most important and challenging social policy issues facing the United States today. Currently more than 3 million older people need the help of at least one person to live independently in the community. With the aging of the population, the number of older Americans requiring assistance to continue living among friends and family in later life is expected to reach 5 million by the year 2000. Substantial modifications in

DIANE ROWLAND is a research associate at the School of Hygiene and Public Health, the Johns Hopkins University, and associate director of the Commonwealth Fund Commission on Elderly People Living Alone. Previously, she served on the staff of the Subcommittee on Health and the Environment of the U.S. House of Representatives Committee on Energy and Commerce and was a consultant at the Center for Policy Studies at the Georgetown University Medical Center. She has also served as deputy assistant secretary for Planning and Evaluation/Health in the Department of Health and Human Services and as special assistant to the administrator of the Health Care Financing Administration.

existing programs coupled with new and innovative ways to reform the long-term care system are required to meet the demands of this rapidly aging population.

Yet developing and improving long-term care coverage in America is a saga of recurring gloom and doom about the future. This pessimism is coupled with inability to take positive action in the present to avert the dire predictions for the future. Why is long-term care reform so difficult? Why has long-term care stayed on the back burner while substantial progress has been made in other areas where the affected constituency is smaller and has notably less political clout?

In part, the dilemma in dealing with long-term care is that the relatively simple concept of providing services to assist individuals with chronic impairments and illnesses gets very complex as soon as one tries to translate that goal into program specifics. It is difficult to specify who needs care because the kind of care required depends not only on health impairment, but also on the availability of family and friends to offer assistance. It is difficult to specify and define a service package because service needs range from very technical medical care, such as parenteral nutrition, to basic help, such as home companions and chore services. Finally, in an era of constrained resources, it is difficult to determine how to pay for these services and whether financing should come from public or private resources.

Implementing a strategy for long-term care reform will not be easy. There are no simple answers or noncontroversial approaches. The price of genuine reform that eases the financial burden for the cost of long-term care suffered by the elderly and their families will be high. In 1985 spending for nursing home care was $35 billion, of which half was publicly financed and the remainder financed from the personal resources of the elderly and their families. Nursing home care outlays are just the tip of the iceberg in terms of real costs for long-term care because they fail to account for either the informal and unpaid help provided by family and friends or the needed services that are not obtained. Finding funds both to fill current gaps in coverage and to meet the growth in demand as our population ages is the major stumbling block to long-term care reform.

This chapter attempts to provide a framework for examining long-term care. It begins by describing the major programs that offer long-term care assistance and the flaws in the current system. The major policy options that could be employed to redirect our long-term care system for the future are then discussed and their potential contribution to long-term care reform evaluated.

The Current Patchwork of Long-Term Care Programs

As the population ages, a growing number of elderly people will require assistance to continue living in their homes and the community. Without restructuring, today's programs are inadequate to meet tomorrow's needs. Despite the billions of dollars currently spent on nursing home and other long-term care services, there is no single or systematic approach for financing and delivering long-term care services. A variety of public programs with varying eligibility criteria, benefits, and reimbursement policies are available to assist some of the frail elderly, but most long-term care is still provided informally by family and friends.

The current programs leave critical gaps in the long-term care safety net for the elderly. Medicare, the primary acute care financing program for the elderly and the disabled, is not designed to provide chronic care assistance although its home health and skilled nursing facility (SNF) benefits are important adjuncts to the elderly's acute care coverage. Although Medicaid pays for over 40 percent of all nursing home care, it is available only to those who deplete their income and assets to impoverishment and offers little assistance to those struggling to remain in the community. Other long-term care programs provide assistance with social and nutritional services, but are highly targeted and have limited funding. The scope and role of the major long-term care programs are reviewed below.

The Medicaid Program

Medicaid is jointly financed by the federal and state governments and provides health financing for 27.5 million low-income Americans, including nearly 4 million elderly poor. For the elderly, Medicaid has two roles. For the 3 million elderly poor living in the community, Medicaid supplements Medicare acute care benefits and pays Medicare cost sharing. For the 1 million elderly in nursing homes, Medicaid pays for care once personal assets and income have been depleted.

Medicaid is a means-tested program. To be eligible for Medicaid services, an individual's available income and assets must be below state-determined eligibility levels which are roughly 75 percent of the federal poverty level. Most nursing home residents typically enter a nursing home as a private paying patient, but over time their available resources are consumed by the cost of institutional care. When personal financing is exhausted, Medicaid coverage takes over and pays for the nursing home care. This process of becoming eligible for Medicaid is called "spending down."

Publicly financed long-term care is dominated by the Medicaid program. Medicaid financed $15 billion of the $35 billion spent nationally on nursing home care in 1985. The Medicaid nursing home benefit includes skilled nursing facility care as a required service and intermediate care facility (ICF) care as an optional service. In practice, the less intensive level of nursing home care available in ICFs is covered by every state.

Medicaid acts as a true safety net for those in nursing homes, but its role in providing long-term care to the poor elderly in the community is far less extensive. Although home health care is a required service in the Medicaid benefit package, many states provide only limited coverage. As a result, home health services are provided to less than 500,000 people and account for less than 2 percent of total Medicaid spending. Eighteen states also elect to offer personal care and home-maker and chore services in beneficiaries' homes.

Amendments to the Medicaid statute in 1981 expanded

Medicaid financing for long-term care services in the community. States are now permitted to offer a broad range of community-based in-home services as an alternative to institutionalization as long as spending for those services does not exceed what would otherwise have been spent on nursing home care. These services can be offered on a trial basis in selected areas and require federal approval prior to implementation. Experience with this provision is limited to date, but it offers states a promising way to expand the scope of community services under Medicaid.

The Medicare Program

Medicare is the primary health financing program for acute care services for the elderly and disabled. In 1986 28 million elderly and 3 million disabled beneficiaries depended on Medicare for assistance with hospital and physician bills at an estimated cost of $74.1 billion. Medicare provides reasonable, but not total, protection from the cost of major illness and hospitalization. However, the major gap in Medicare coverage is its lack of coverage for long-term care services.

Yet despite this limitation, most of the home health services provided to the elderly are financed by Medicare. Because of Medicare's focus on acute care, home health care is provided as a follow-up to an acute illness episode rather than as a chronic care benefit. Medicare home health services include part-time or intermittent nursing care under the supervision of a registered nurse; physical, occupational, or speech therapy; medical social services; or services of a home health aide. Services must be ordered by a physician and must be delivered by a certified home health agency.

Medicare provides for an unlimited number of home health visits without copayment, but rigorous criteria are applied in determining who is eligible for home health coverage. Medicare home health services are restricted to recovery from acute illness and can only be furnished to a beneficiary who is homebound and needs either skilled nursing or speech or physical therapy services. Despite these restrictions, in recent years home health services utilization and spending under Medicare have grown significantly from $61 million for 8.5 million visits in 1970 to $801 million for 24.4 million visits in 1981, according to statistics from the Health Care Financing Administration.

Medicare also provides very limited coverage of nursing home care in a skilled nursing facility. This is available only after a hospitalization, limited to 100 days, restricted to those requiring around the clock skilled care, and subject to substantial cost sharing. Payment for custodial care, including help in walking or getting out of bed, is prohibited. The number of days of SNF care provided to the elderly has been declining over time due to increasingly tight administrative requirements on the use of the SNF benefit.

Other Programs for Long-Term Care Assistance

Other federal programs for long-term care pale in comparison to Medicare and Medicaid in volume of funding and number of people served. However, many of these programs provide essential services to specific groups of frail elderly. These programs include the Veterans Administration, the social services block grant, Supplemental Security Income cash assistance, and the Older Americans Act services.

The Veterans Administration (VA) is an important source of long-term care services for aged veterans and provides nursing home care, domiciliary care in VA facilities, personal care and supervision in residential care homes, and hospital-based home care. To receive care in this program, a veteran must be entitled to service related benefits. The families of veterans are ineligible. The VA pays for nursing home care for 40,000 veterans annually in addition to medical, nursing, social, dietetic, and rehabilitation services to homebound and nonambulatory patients.

Some public assistance with nonmedical institutional care is provided through the Supplemental Security Income (SSI) cash assistance program which supports some low-income individuals in residential care facilities. These institutional settings do not provide the medical and nursing services of a nursing home, but they do offer custodial care for the disabled and frail elderly. These benefits are only available to the elderly poor.

Title XX of the Social Security Act, the social services block grant, provides federal financial assistance to states to support the provision of nonmedical social services. States have considerable discretion in the design and delivery of services under this block grant, and many use it to provide homemaker and chore services for the frail elderly. The extent to which the services offered emphasize long-term care depends on the preference of the state. There are large variations in the eligibility criteria for receipt of services and in the range of services covered in each state.

The Older Americans Act is another source of funding for a wide range of community-based long-term care activities for the elderly. Financing is provided for a nationwide network of Area Agencies on Aging that serve as advocates for the elderly and as coordination units for services. The services provided cover a wide spectrum, ranging from home-delivered and congregate meals to information and referral services. In some areas, multipurpose senior centers have been set up to serve as a coordinating point for the delivery of social and nutrition services and to provide a social and recreational center for senior citizens.

The Need for Reform

Most elderly Americans, especially those between age sixty-five and seventy-four, are in relatively good health and need few, if any, long-term care services. However, among elderly people over seventy-four, the likelihood of chronic illness and physical impairment requiring long-term care services increases substantially. Roughly 1.5 million individuals are cared for in the institutional setting of a nursing home. Another 3 to 6 million live in the community and need community-based support services to prevent, delay, or substitute for institutionalization.

The existing system is frequently criticized for failure to provide adequately for elderly Americans needing long-term care assistance. It is characterized by service and eligibility gaps in public programs, an inappropriate service mix, poor quality in nursing homes, and fragmented and uncoordinated programs for the delivery of long-term care. As the population ages and more people need services, the flaws of the current system and the need for revamping will become increasingly apparent.

Eligibility gaps in existing programs create perverse incentives and can lead to impoverishment to obtain needed services. Many people are neither sick enough nor poor enough to qualify for assistance from public programs. Although Medicaid is the largest financier of long-term care services, most older people become eligible for these services only after entering a nursing home and exhausting their personal resources. The focus of programs such as Medicare on acute conditions results in the aged being unable to obtain needed services in the community to avoid institutional care.

Inflexible and often inappropriate services contribute to an institutional bias in the long-term care delivery system. One of the most obvious problems is the predominance of the nursing home as the most easily reimbursable Medicaid service. The lack of reimbursement for and availability of community-based care—such as home health, homemaker, nutrition, and chore services—often creates an incentive to use a nursing home, which can provide for all a person's basic needs. Most of the aged would not choose a nursing home over community-based care, but at the crisis stage of an illness, it is often easier to obtain care in a nursing home than to develop alternatives in the home.

Nursing home supply is another serious problem faced by many of the elderly who need long-term care. Even when a person is eligible for Medicaid reimbursed care, a place in a nursing home may not be available. A 1982 study by Weissert and Scanlon found that in states with the highest nursing home bed to elderly ratio, more than 90 percent of those most in need of care (those who are unmarried, seventy-five years or older, and in need of assistance with all activities of daily living) were in nursing homes. In contrast, only half of this population was receiving nursing home care in the states with the lowest bed to elderly ratio. Moreover, as nursing home supply becomes more limited, patients will be sicker and, therefore, more costly.

Fragmentation among long-term care programs is an under-lying cause of the inability to coordinate service packages and reimbursement in the community. The current system is a patchwork of separate public programs skewed toward the provision of either social services or health services. Rarely are the two types of service integrated, despite the fact that most frail individuals require both types of aid. As a result, it is often impossible for a single provider or reimbursement source to support the total care of a frail elderly person. Lack of effective entry evaluation and of case management leaves many of the disabled and chronically ill elderly without knowledge of available services or access to providers of care. Even when someone qualifies for reimbursement, obtaining and coordinating services may be extremely difficult.

Reform of the current system for financing health and long-term care services for the elderly is long overdue. Surprisingly, Medicare and Medicaid have fundamentally changed little since they began in 1966. Changes have been incremental—such as addition of the disabled to Medicare in 1972—rather than through a complete reexamination of the rationale for and desirability of the current system.

A new look at long-term care services for the elderly is especially needed now. The growth in the elderly population, especially the increase in frail elderly over age seventy-five, means that more services and more spending for services will be required in the future. A major conflict looms between expanding long-term care needs and the economic and budgetary constraints on public spending. Fragmentation of existing programs and lack of adequate alternatives to nursing home care will become more problematic in the future. Rather than patch things up with makeshift solutions, the aging of the population provides an opportunity to design a new system that will assure adequate and stable financing of long-term care and guarantee that the elderly can live out their lives with dignity, freed of worrying about the financial ruin that major illness can bring.

Strategies for Long-Term Care Reform

The various reforms of long-term care proposed over the last decade generally agree on the array of help necessary to enable the frail elderly and disabled to function independently in the community. Services ranging from transportation and chore services to skilled nursing care would be provided under almost all plans. The discord arises as reformers try to agree on the cost and the means for financing that care. What share of the financing should be borne directly by the individual receiving services or by his or her family? To what extent should care be provided and financed by the public sector? Underlying these questions are issues related to whether eligibility for publicly financed care should be based on income and how to avoid buying a lot of care that is now provided informally for free.

A variety of strategies for long-term care reform have been formulated and discussed over the last decade. The major approaches are promotion of private initiatives to increase savings or to acquire insurance coverage to protect against the risk of long-term care costs, development of comprehensive delivery systems that make long-term care more affordable and available, and provision of public coverage for long-term care.

Private Initiatives

In an era of looming federal deficits and intense pressure to reduce federal spending for social programs, private sector initiatives offer one possible solution to financing that could minimize federal expenditures by encouraging the elderly to use their own funds to purchase services directly or to buy private insurance to cover the cost of care. Creation of a private long-term care insurance market and use of home equity conversions and modifications of the tax code to increase personal resources and family support of long-term care are the predominant options in this approach.

Private Insurance for Long-Term Care

Unlike acute care, long-term care has not developed as a private insurance market. Today, for most Americans, nursing home care is not an insurable risk; less than 1 percent of over $35 billion spent on nursing home care is covered by private health insurance. Although private long-term care insurance is offered today on a very limited basis, expansion of such policies is viewed by many as a viable approach to improving protection of the elderly against financial ruin in the event of catastrophic or chronic illness. Stimulation of the private insurance market for long-term care coverage has received increased attention in recent years as an alternative to increasing the public role in long-term care.

Under the private insurance approach, policies covering community-based as well as institutional long-term care services would be marketed and sold to the elderly or their families for an annual or monthly premium. Like private insurance policies that the elderly buy to supplement Medicare's acute coverage, these policies could be purchased by individuals through commercial insurance companies or Blue Cross/Blue Shield or offered by companies as a retirement benefit.

Advocates of private insurance believe coverage is affordable for the middle- and upper-income elderly and that individuals would purchase coverage to avoid the necessity of exhausting personal assets to become eligible for Medicaid. It is estimated that prior to their admission to a nursing home, about 20 percent of Medicaid-supported residents had sufficient income and assets to purchase private insurance, if such policies had been available. The government would also save money if private insurance helped divert or delay eligibility for nursing home care under Medicaid.

However, the development of private long-term care insurance coverage for the elderly faces several significant barriers. First, a private insurance market requires that there be a substantial group of people who recognize the risk of chronic disability and who are willing to pay for insurance coverage to protect themselves against that risk. The elderly appear to underestimate their need for long-term care and may not be willing to pay $500 or more per year in premiums. By the time an elderly person is over age seventy-five and more likely to recognize the need for long-term care insurance, the cost of a private policy is likely to be prohibitive.

Second, insurers argue that the existence of Medicaid as a safety net for those who become impoverished in a nursing home undermines the private insurance role. It is argued that many people will not purchase private insurance because they feel their tax dollars have already supported Medicaid and the program should pay for them in return when they need nursing home care.

Third, premium pricing presents serious problems. The risk of institutionalization increases with age. If premiums rise with age, the cost of coverage could be prohibitive for the older age groups most in need of coverage. It would also be difficult to set premium levels at a rate that anticipates inflation and delivery system changes over time.

Fourth, the potential of adverse selection in the purchase of private coverage is another major obstacle. People most at risk are those most likely to purchase private insurance coverage. And since they are most at risk, they will tend to use services once insured. It will be difficult to develop actuarially sound premiums related to risk. Low-risk consumers may not consider long-term care coverage worth the price, leaving insurance coverage to the high-risk and costly consumers.

Lastly, most of the private plans currently available focus on nursing home benefits. Although the purchase of private insurance to protect against impoverishment in a nursing home would appeal to some people, most of the elderly would prefer insurance coverage that provided assistance to enable them to remain in their own homes. However, an attractive home care package used by many of the elderly could result in premiums that few could afford.

Although a few long-term care insurance plans are now offered in several areas of the country, it seems unlikely that the private insurance industry will become a dominant force in this field in the near future because of the uncertainty surrounding the profitability of insuring the risk of long-term care. Undoubtedly, the experience of the few plans that now offer such coverage will be closely monitored to assess the market potential.

Home Equity Conversion

The home equity conversion option is a mechanism to free up some of the elderly's assets so they have more funds to pay for either private long-term care insurance or the direct purchase of services. Three-quarters of the elderly own their own homes and most have no mortgage on their property. James Firman estimates the net home equity of older Americans to be approximately $550 billion. Yet despite the substantial equity on their homes, most elderly homeowners cannot obtain cash on their investment without selling the home.

Under the home equity conversion option, the elderly could use the cash value of their home as a source of income for the purchase of long-term care, while continuing to live in the home. Proponents maintain that over half the elderly homeowners in this country would be able to finance any long-term care services they needed for the remainder of their lives with home equity conversion.

However, the plan's success hinges on the elderly's willingness to trade the value of their home for more income to pay for long-term care. Many of the elderly might be reluctant to participate for fear of losing their home as a tangible resource that they can pass on to children and grandchildren. Others might fear loss of financial security. For those who do choose to take advantage of the home conversion option, there is no guarantee they will elect to use the cash for long-term care.

The potential gains for long-term care financing from conversions may never be realized.

Another drawback to this approach is that financial institutions have resisted offering this option because they are reluctant to evict elderly persons who outlive their loans. They prefer that the mortgages be federally guaranteed to protect both the homeowner and the institution. As a result, the actual experience with home equity conversions is extremely limited.

Tax Incentives for Long-Term Care

Tax incentives are another vehicle that could encourage private financing of long-term care. This approach would provide favorable federal tax treatment to those who save for their future long-term care needs or to families who care for a disabled parent or relative instead of placing the person in a nursing home.

One of the most popular ideas to stimulate savings is the creation of personal savings accounts for long-term care, similar to individual retirement accounts (IRAs). These private investment accounts could qualify for federal tax credits or deductions and could be used to finance in-home or institutional long-term care services. For example, people over forty could be permitted to put up to $1,000 a year in a private long-term care account. At age sixty-five, individuals could draw against their account to purchase long-term care services directly or to buy a private policy for long-term care insurance. At death, any funds remaining in this account could be willed to a relative or spouse's separate long-term care account. Requirements could be placed on use of the account funds to assure that the funds are used to purchase only long-term care services.

The private investment approach can be tailored to meet individual needs and reinforces individual and family responsibility. The decision to set up a long-term care account and the choices on what services are purchased are made by the purchaser and his or her family. Requirements on how the account funds can be used should help assure that the funds subject to the tax break are actually used to provide long-term care, but monitoring the expenditures will be extremely difficult.

One concern with these accounts is that the tax breaks to encourage the investments reduce the revenues to the federal government and thus are a drain on the federal treasury. Moreover, the tax incentives tend to favor the more affluent elderly, and many of the elderly may not have the financial resources to participate. Experience with IRAs for retirement income shows that most of those who took advantage of the tax breaks were upper income.

In addition to encouraging people to save for their own long-term care needs, tax incentives have been discussed as a way to encourage and maintain family assistance and support for the frail elderly. Tax deductions could be offered for the cost of in-home services or respite care or as additional personal exemptions for nonelderly taxpayers with older parents or relatives living in their home. Elderly parents who live apart from their adult children do not qualify for this credit regardless of the level of assistance provided by the children. To use the tax system to encourage greater family support, tax policy could recognize contributions from children in separate households and allow them to deduct the contribution from their taxable income.

Proponents of this approach argue that financial incentives in the form of tax credits or deductions would reinforce and expand private support for long-term care, but others maintain that tax incentives will just support the informal care that is already delivered free of charge and without financial incentives. As with long-term care accounts, this approach would also reduce federal tax revenues, and a large share of the tax credits would undoubtedly go to families that would have provided the care without new incentives.

Reforming the Delivery System

Improvements in financing without improvements in the delivery system can often frustrate the goals of reformers. No one wants to put more money into a system and not get more or better services. As an underpinning for improved financing, the long-term care system needs restructuring to improve the coordination and provision of services, especially in noninstitutional settings, and to assure a continuum of health and social services can be provided.

Early attempts at reform through organizational restructuring centered on the concept of a single entry point for delivery. The Medicare and Medicaid long-term care demonstrations undertaken in the 1970s and the National Channeling Project demonstration started in 1980 are examples of the coordinated case management model of long-term care reform. Under this approach, the case management agency provides an in-depth assessment of the long-term care services required by a person and then arranges for or provides those services. The agency serves as both a facilitator in arranging services and a gatekeeper in controlling utilization of services.

The new generation of long-term care delivery systems builds upon the case management and channeling approach, but adds integrated financing of services. Two examples of these new organizational approaches are the social health maintenance organization (SHMO) and the continuing care retirement community. These organizational structures can be used with private financing or could be coupled with various public financing options.

Social Health Maintenance Organizations

The social health maintenance organization attempts to extend the concept of prepayment for integrated acute care in health maintenance organizations to long-term care. The basic premise behind the SHMO is the voluntary enrollment of a defined elderly or disabled population and the guaranteed provision of an integrated package of both medical and long-term care services on a capitation rather than fee-for-service basis. The SHMO would be paid a monthly premium by the elderly or reimbursed by Medicare or some other third-party payer and would be at financial risk to provide needed care.

The proponents of this approach argue that the combination of prepaid capitation and centralization of responsibility for acute and long-term care will lead to a more coordinated and comprehensive service package and to more efficient use of resources by permitting the substitution of nonmedical social services for more expensive medical care. As the single entry point for a continuum of services for the frail elderly person, the SHMO serves as both a care coordinator and a gatekeeper to control unnecessary utilization. Another advantage of the SHMO is that it reorganizes the delivery system for the elderly without requiring relocation into a retirement community, sale of the family home, or other disruptions to normal life style.

A basic concern in the development of the SHMO model is the minimum size needed for the enrolled population to produce revenues to spread the financial risk. The target population will be small and may not produce a large enough enrollment base to ensure efficient spreading of risk and stable cash flow. Marketing to attract enrollees will be critical and especially difficult if the elderly have established care providers that they are unwilling to leave or if the premiums for SHMO enrollment are too expensive.

The newness of this concept leaves many questions unanswered. The SHMO concept has been developed since 1980 and is now being tested at four sites with 4,000 enrollees per site. These demonstrations will provide important information on the effectiveness of marketing techniques and the characteristics of those who elect to join as well as provide a test for the actuarial methods required to predict capitation payments for acute and long-term care for the elderly.

Continuing Care Retirement Communities

Continuing care retirement communities are a relatively new concept in long-term care organization and delivery. The community is a total living environment including housing, social services, health care, and meals in accord with a contract between the participant and the community. In essence, social, health, and housing insurance for life for an elderly person or couple are provided in return for an entrance payment and monthly follow-up fees.

Arrangements for financing and requirements for entry vary from one community to another. The congregate living facilities provided range from independent townhouse or apartment units to skilled nursing facility–type arrangements. Initially, the new member resides in his or her own unit. As health problems increase, the life care community provides an increased level of assistance, such as home help aides or home-delivered meals, and ultimately nursing home care.

In the typical community, the entrance fee and monthly payment are based on the person's dwelling unit size and not on the scope of services required. In 1981 the average entrance fee ranged from $35,000 to $65,000 with monthly fees of about $550. Although the fees cover the cost of housing, there are no ownership rights. The funds are pooled so that individuals who require few services subsidize the care of those with expenditures exceeding their monthly fee or support those who exhaust their ability to pay each month. In principle, no one should ever be thrown out of a life care community—the assurance of guaranteed care until death is central.

Today there are about 275 life care communities serving some 90,000 elderly people. Most are nonprofit corporations, often under church sponsorship. Less than 10 percent are proprietary, although one-third of the nonprofit communities are managed by proprietary companies. Indications are that this may be an area for proprietary company investment in the future.

Supporters of the life care community concept argue that this private sector approach of protecting against the unknown costs of long-term care also provides a solution to the fragmentation and institutional bias of the current system. Medicare continues to pay for acute care and the remaining long-term care needs are covered under the life care contract, but the delivery of acute care and long-term care services are integrated. People are assured they will live independently as long as possible and will then receive support services. The continuum of care is indeed a major selling point.

Yet these communities are not the solution for most elderly Americans. First, it is to the advantage of the community to market to the healthy and wealthy elderly and be selective in admitting new residents. Restrictions are often placed on maximum age to control adverse selection by ensuring that the young, and normally healthier, elderly are admitted. Life care is not a realistic option for the elderly who are ill or poor.

In addition, many people who would otherwise qualify will not want to live in a life care community since it requires physically relocating and consumes a substantial portion of their assets, leaving little to pass on to children or other relatives. Others will elect not to enter on the assumption that they will live out their lives without the need for the long-term care coverage offered by the community.

The financial structure of the life care community is a major concern since many of the residents are turning over a substantial portion of their life's savings and should be sure their investment is sound. Residents' fees must be accurately calculated to project future costs and fund future renovations. Unfortunately, almost 20 percent of the current communities are expected to have some financial problems in the future because of inability to predict future funding requirements.

The experience with life care communities is relatively new and much is still to be learned about the feasibility and attractiveness of this approach for organizing an integrated housing, medical care, and long-term care system for elderly enrollees. Although only 2 percent of the elderly are expected to reside in life care communities by 1990, this approach represents a reasonable solution for some elderly people.

Public Insurance

Another major strategy to address the long-term care needs of older Americans is to provide coverage through a publicly financed program. A public role in long-term care will still be important even if extensive private initiatives and sweeping delivery system reforms are pursued. The fact that Medicaid pays for over half of all nursing home care argues for a continuation of public funding for at least nursing home care because it is unlikely that private insurance would replace Medicaid spending. Private insurance would most likely substitute for direct spending by the elderly and their families rather than replace most public spending. A public role also assures that those without the opportunity and financial resources to utilize private options are not left destitute or without care.

A public role in long-term care can be structured in different ways. One model is to improve the Medicaid program to expand assistance to the low-income elderly and to provide more coverage of community care as an alternative to nursing home care. Another approach would be to move away from the means-tested Medicaid program and instead add long-term care benefits to Medicare. Under an expanded Medicare program, assistance would be offered to all elderly and acute and long-term care could be integrated. Finally, in the most comprehensive approach, a freestanding long-term care program, comparable to Medicare for acute care, could be established.

Medicaid Improvements

The strategy of improving Medicaid coverage of long-term care keeps public dollars focused on helping the most vulnerable of the elderly. Instead of providing assistance to all elderly, a Medicaid strategy targets on the low-income elderly because Medicaid is a means-tested program. In an era of limited dollars, targeted spending on the poor and frail elderly can provide meaningful assistance, whereas the impact of the same dollars would be substantially diluted if the benefits had to be spread across all the elderly. However, an approach that focuses on the poor requires that all funding come from the public coffers since the poor, by definition, are unable to finance some of the cost of their own care through cost sharing.

One option to improve financing for long-term care would

be to require states to extend Medicaid eligibility to all elderly with incomes below the federal poverty level and to permit other low-income elderly to obtain assistance from Medicaid by paying an income related premium. The elderly with incomes between 100 and 200 percent of the poverty level would be expected to pay a monthly premium based on the value of the long-term care coverage, but actual payments would not be allowed to exceed 5 percent of income. Under such a plan, the Medicaid benefit package would be expanded to include home health care, chore services, adult day care services, and respite care.

The advantage of the Medicaid improvement strategy is that it builds on an existing administrative structure and program. The mechanisms for establishing eligibility, processing claims, and paying providers already exist. By raising the income level and range of benefits for elderly in the community, the proposed reform would help to reverse the bias toward institutionalization in the current Medicaid eligibility and benefit structure. Limited federal dollars, especially new federal dollars, would be targeted first on those most in need and could later be expanded to cover additional groups.

The targeted nature of this approach is also a disadvantage. Because Medicaid is a means-tested program, no assistance is provided to the middle-class elderly until their medical expenses reduce their income to Medicaid eligibility levels. The incentives in the current system to transfer income and resources to children or relatives in order to qualify for Medicaid eligibility will continue. In addition, although this approach makes community-based care more available under Medicaid, it does little to expand coverage for nursing home bills. Finally, since states are required to share financing with the federal government, constraints on state spending could undermine expansion to the low-income elderly.

This Medicaid policy option is premised on moving Medicaid toward a more uniform eligibility and benefit structure under which the elderly in any state would be entitled to the same benefits. However, another policy option for Medicaid—

block grants for long-term care to the states—goes in exactly the opposite direction by reducing the federal role and providing greater discretion over long-term care to the states.

In 1984 a national study group on state medicaid strategies, composed of nine state Medicaid or public health directors, recommended shifting responsibility for long-term care to the states. In their proposal, the current Medicaid program would be replaced with a federally financed and administered primary care program and a state-administered block grant for long-term care.

In the block grant option, federal Medicaid funding for long-term care services is no longer based on matching payments for services to entitled individuals. Instead, a fixed sum of federal funds based on an allocation formula would be provided to each state for long-term care. In exchange for the limit on federal long-term care spending, states would be allowed broader flexibility to experiment with innovative approaches to the organization and delivery of services and would have full control over eligibility, the range of services to be provided, and payment of services.

Supporters of the block grant approach maintain that states would be better than the federal government at reforming long-term care systems because responsiveness to state and local conditions, coordination of multiple service delivery networks, and institution building within the long-term care community are more easily achieved at the state level. However, many view block grants as an abdication of the federal role in providing long-term care support to the elderly and fear that the lack of direct federal involvement would ultimately compromise federal funding for the block grant. Block grants would also end the entitlement to long-term care embodied in the current Medicaid program and perpetuate existing inequities in the care of the elderly.

Block grants, then, have appeal from a federal fiscal perspective and also remove the onus of responsibility for reform of the long-term care system from the federal government. This must be balanced, however, against the problems that would arise in actual implementation. The fiscal pressures and general politics of long-term care combine to make the block grant a less than ideal Medicaid reform option.

Medicare Expansions

Expanding Medicare coverage to include long-term care services is perhaps the most frequently discussed approach to improving publicly financed coverage for long-term care. The addition of long-term care services to the Medicare package of acute care services is a logical extension and makes Medicare coverage truly comprehensive. By building on the framework of the existing Medicare program, this approach provides the elderly with both health and long-term care services from a single program, avoiding the confusion and duplication that would arise from two separate programs.

Several proposals to expand Medicare coverage to long-term care have been advanced. Underlying each of these expanded Medicare options is a rejection of the view that Medicare should cover only acute medical care services. The proposals vary in scope of services added, requirements for beneficiary cost sharing, sources of financing, and administrative structure, but all would move Medicare closer to providing a full continuum of health and long-term care services for the frail elderly.

One plan, proposed by myself and Karen Davis of Johns Hopkins University, would restructure the existing Medicare program, put limits on total out-of-pocket costs by beneficiaries, and expand coverage to include skilled and custodial nursing home care and home health and related community-based long-term care services. The benefit improvements would be financed with greater premium contributions from the elderly on an income related basis. The new services would be subject to a coinsurance charge and to a maximum ceiling on out-of-pocket costs. In the original proposal, enrollment for long-term care benefits was at the beneficiary's option. However, mandatory enrollment could be required to avoid adverse selection.

A proposal recently advanced by a team of researchers at Harvard University also advocated expanding Medicare coverage of long-term care and restructuring acute coverage to improve beneficiary protection, promote primary care, reform provider payment, and simplify administration. Their plan would finance the coverage of extended nursing home care through a combination of Social Security payroll taxes, premiums paid by the elderly, and general revenues. Geriatric assessment teams would be used to determine eligibility for expanded long-term care services in the community. This ambitious plan is estimated to cost an additional $15 billion a year within ten years of implementation.

Another proposal, advanced by Anne Somers of Rutgers University, would increase publicly funded assistance to the elderly under Medicare by eliminating the current prohibition against custodial care and expanding current benefits to increase in-home and nursing home care. A disability definition would be used to determine eligibility for the expanded benefits. The additional benefits would be financed by pooling existing long-term care expenditures under Medicaid and Title XX and by requiring cost sharing. A companion program, either as part of Medicare or on its own, would provide comprehensive assessments and coordinate placement of those needing long-term care.

The advantage of all of these approaches for expanding Medicare coverage to include long-term care is that they build on an existing program and offer comprehensive benefits to the elderly under a single administrative structure. The single-program administrative structure would eliminate beneficiary confusion about covered services since Medicare would finance the full range of services. The goal of developing a continuum of care by integrating acute and long-term care would be achieved through administration of both types of benefits by a single program. Such integration would also facilitate the development of integrated delivery programs such as social HMOs.

A potential drawback is that the integrated approach could subject long-term care to an overly medical model. The current Medicare program and its acute care orientation may not easily adapt to an expanded sense of mission. Initially, there could be problems in defining and developing the expanded range of benefits.

Another drawback is that the expanded benefits of this proposal are likely to require new federal revenues. Because all elderly would be covered by a plan that expands Medicare, the additional costs of almost any proposal to provide comprehensive benefits would exceed $10 billion. Given the size of the federal deficit, new federal dollars are not likely to be forthcoming. Moreover, the annual budget pressure to cut overall Medicare spending will make an expansion of this type even harder to enact.

Income related premiums offer some promise as a means of generating revenue without unduly burdening the lower-income elderly. However, premiums must be kept at affordable and acceptable levels for the elderly which may not be sufficient to generate the revenue to cover program costs. Relying on cost sharing to meet the shortfall could seriously compromise the benefits of the expanded services and result in large out-of-pocket expenditures for the elderly near-poor.

A narrower, but more fiscally acceptable, approach for expanding Medicare coverage to long-term care may be to start with improvements in home-based services and a limited nursing home benefit with high levels of cost sharing. Assistance could then be phased in with the cost-sharing levels reduced over time. If a phased-in Medicare plan were coupled with immediate improvements in Medicaid coverage for the low-income elderly, a sound foundation for future comprehensive long-term care coverage would be laid.

Comprehensive Long-Term Care Insurance

The most extensive public reform of long-term care financing would be to create a comprehensive long-term care entitlement program, comparable to a national health insurance plan. Under such an approach, a freestanding government financed long-term care program separate from either Medicare or Medicaid would be set up. All elderly would be covered, eliminating the adverse selection problems of a private insurance strategy. The cost of providing comprehensive long-term care insurance could be partially borne by the beneficiaries by using either income related cost sharing or an income related premium, but much of the financing would come from tax revenue.

The advantage of a compulsory entitlement approach is that it covers all the elderly who meet the disability criterion, regardless of income, and spreads the risk across the broadest population base. Since long-term care is a principal cause of catastrophic health expenditures, universal long-term care coverage would protect the elderly from the risk of financial ruin from chronic health expenditures and nursing home care.

A public entitlement approach to long-term care would replace the means-tested Medicaid program with an alternative available to the middle-class elderly, who would no longer have to impoverish themselves before being eligible for benefits. It would also replace the state-determined eligibility and benefit policies under Medicaid with a national program with uniform eligibility and benefits. This would help to assure equitable treatment of all the elderly regardless of place of residence.

Expanding institutional and noninstitutional long-term care services under a financing program separate from Medicare would remove such services from the medical model and could encourage a more efficient mix of institutional and home care. A broad benefit package should promote the use of home-based services to avoid institutionalization.

This approach, however, has several disadvantages. It is an entirely new program that would require substantial lead time prior to implementation. Unlike expanding Medicare, this approach would require a new bureaucracy and the development of new relationships. A separate program for long-term care could also be confusing to beneficiaries who might not understand which program covered what service.

Providing benefits to millions who are without coverage today would require increased federal outlays. Although management and restrictions on provider payment levels as well as beneficiary cost sharing could help restrain costs, a substantial investment of new federal dollars would still be required. A federally financed compulsory long-term care entitlement program would have added from $28 to $50 billion in new federal outlays in 1985 alone, according to one estimate by the Congressional Budget Office. Some of the new federal costs could be offset by requiring states to contribute what they would have otherwise spent on Medicaid long-term care.

Another drawback of a comprehensive entitlement program is that the real demand for services is unknown. The assistance currently provided by families cannot be accurately estimated. However, it is assumed that a significant portion of families now supporting elderly members informally would seek payment for the care they deliver or obtain formal care if it were covered by insurance. Future needs for long-term care assistance are likely to increase substantially over current levels because of the aging of the population and changes in family structure.

Prospects for the Future

America is faced with a growing population of elderly citizens who will increasingly require long-term care services. Existing public and private insurance coverage for long-term care has serious deficiencies. Medicare coverage is limited to short-term acute home care and limited posthospital nursing home care. Medicaid pays for nursing home care, but only for the impoverished. Conventional private insurance policies provide essentially no coverage for these services. As a result, over half of the funding for long-term care comes from the personal savings and earnings of the elderly and their families. These gaps in long-term care coverage pose a major threat to the financial security and independence of tomorrow's elderly.

We cannot continue to ignore the implications of an aging population. Action must be taken now to put in place a long-term care financing structure and delivery system that can meet the demands of tomorrow's elderly and ease the burdens faced by today's elderly. Whether we accomplish reform by establishing a stronger role for the private sector, reorienting the delivery system, empowering more public interventions, or by pursuing a combination approach, we must begin now to build for the future.

The system of long-term care services we build for the future will be shaped by public debate, but will undoubtedly reflect the pluralistic traditions of the United States. A more active private sector involvement can be predicted, but it is doubtful that private long-term care insurance will be the dominant force in shaping long-term care coverage. A public role through some combination of Medicare and Medicaid is virtually assured. A freestanding comprehensive public long-term care program is highly unlikely given current fiscal pressures and the inertia that works against new public initiatives.

Initial steps at long-term care reform are likely to focus on stimulation of a private long-term care insurance market and improvements in Medicare and Medicaid. Medicaid should be provided to all poor elderly and the benefit package should be expanded to include a full range of home- and community-based services. Medicare should be expanded to include more in-home supportive services and some nursing home care. Broader use of social HMOs and life care communities should be encouraged, and other innovative delivery approaches should be developed and tested. These actions would serve to provide needed assistance to today's elderly and would provide the framework for building an adequate system for tomorrow's elderly.

Bibliography

Alpha Center, "Long Term Care Alternatives: Continuing Care Retirement Communities," *Alpha Centerpiece*, Bethesda, Md. (January 1984), 1–6.

Center for Health Policy and Management, *Medicare: Coming of Age. A Proposal for Reform.* Cambridge, Ma.: John F. Kennedy School of Government, March 1986.

Cohen, J., "Public Programs Financing Long Term Care." Urban Institute Working Paper no. 1466–18. Washington, D.C.: Urban Institute, January 1983.

Committee on Ways and Means, U.S. House of Representatives, *Background Material and Data on Programs within the Jurisdiction of the Committee on Ways and Means.* Washington, D.C.: U.S. Government Printing Office, 1986.

Davis, K., "Aging and the Health-Care System: Economic and Structural Issues," *Daedalus*, 115, no. 1 (1986), 227–246.

Davis, K., and D. Rowland, *Medicare Policy. New Directions for Health and Long-Term Care.* Baltimore: Johns Hopkins University Press, 1986.

Department of Health and Human Services, "National Health Expenditures, 1985." Washington, D.C.: HHS Press Release, 1986.

Feder, J., and W. Scanlon, "Problems and Prospects in Financing Long Term Care." Washington, D.C.: Center for Health Policy Studies, Georgetown University, December 1985.

Firman, J., "Reforming Community Care for the Elderly and Disabled," *Health Affairs*, 2, no. 1 (1983), 66–82.

Fullerton, W.D., "Finding the Money and Paying for Long Term Care Services: The Devil's Briarpatch, in *Policy Options in Long Term Care*, eds. J. Meltzer, F. Farrow, and H. Richmond. Chicago: University of Chicago Press, 1982.

Greenberg, J., and W.N. Leutz, "The Social/Health Maintenance Organization and its Role in Reforming the Long-Term Care System." Presentation at Conference on Long-Term Care Financing and Delivery Systems: Exploring Some Alternatives, sponsored by HCFA, Washington, D.C., January 24, 1984.

Health Care Financing Administration, *The Medicare and Medicaid Data Book, 1983.* HCFA Publication no. 03156, Washington, D.C.: U.S. Department of Health and Human Services, 1983.

Jacobs, B., and W. Weissert, "Home Equity Financing of Long-Term Care for the Elderly." Presentation at Conference on Long-Term Care Financing and Delivery Systems: Exploring Some Alternatives, sponsored by HCFA, Washington, D.C., January 24, 1984.

National Study Group on State Medicaid Strategies, *Restructuring Medicaid: An Agenda for Change.* Washington, D.C.: Center for the Study of Social Policy, 1984.

Somers, A.R., "Rethinking Health Policy for the Elderly: A 6-Point Program," *Inquiry,* 17 (1980), 3–17.

Weissert, W., "Size and Characteristics of the Non-Institutionalized Long Term Care Population." Urban Institute Working Paper no. 1466–21, Washington, D.C.: Urban Institute, September 1982.

Weissert, W., and W. Scanlon, "Determinants of Institutionalization of the Aged." Urban Institute Working Paper no. 1466–21, Washington, D.C.: Urban Institute, September 1982.

Winklevoss, H., and A.V. Powell, *Continuing Care Retirement Communities: An Empirical, Financial, and Legal Analysis.* Pension Research Council of the Wharton School. Homewood, Il.: Richard D. Irwin, 1984.

8

Health Care Costs: Technology and Policy

H. DAVID BANTA AND ANNETINE GELIJNS

Health care technology is associated with a number of societal implications, including its effect on health and health care costs. This is, however, not a one-way process. Patterns of health, the nature of the health care system, and social and economic developments also influence the development and dissemination of health care technology. The impacts of technology depend on a number of factors, including

H. DAVID BANTA is chair of the Commission on Future Health Technology in the Netherlands and a consultant for the World Health Organization. He has served in various capacities with the U.S. Congress Office of Technology Assessment and was on the faculty of the Mount Sinai School of Medicine in New York for several years. Dr. Banta has written numerous articles on the costs and policies of technology in health care in both national and international realms.
ANNETINE GELIJNS is a senior researcher for the Project on Future Health Technology and the Steering Committee on Future Health Scenarios in the Netherlands. She also has served on the Staff Bureau of Health Policy Development for the Ministry of Health. She has written several articles on future health technologies and health care systems.

its pervasiveness. This is in part due to the broad definition of health care technology: the drugs, medical devices, and medical and surgical procedures used in health care, and the supportive systems in which those services are provided.

Medical science has developed over thousands of years, but it was only in the seventeenth century that modern ideas of physiology and pathology were developed. During this period, science and technology became effectively linked for the first time. This change led, during the eighteenth and nineteenth centuries, to the development of an array of diagnostic tools still used today, including the stethoscope, the ophthalmoscope, and the blood pressure cuff. Wilhelm Roentgen discovered X-rays in 1895, and their medical applications were rapidly accepted. The development of bacteriology at the end of the nineteenth century and the beginning of the twentieth century made the prevention of disease through vaccination possible. The discovery and refinement of sterile surgical techniques and the development of anesthesia led to a flowering of surgery during the same period.

Despite this long history, there were few specific therapies before the 1930s. The physician's arsenal for treating major illnesses was limited to digitalis for heart failure, arsphenamine for syphilis, insulin for diabetes, quinine for malaria, vitamin C for scurvy, morphine for pain, horse serum antitoxin for diphtheria, and certain surgical procedures. The main task of the physician was to diagnose, to offer a prognosis, and to provide care and reassurance.

The development of technology stimulated changes in the organization and delivery of health care services. In the seventeenth and eighteenth centuries, medical practice was primarily centered in the home of the patient or physician. Institutional care was provided mainly for the poor and those with no or few relatives. In the nineteenth century, the picture changed, with urbanization and industrialization. Institutionalization was favored by these developments, as well as by advances in surgery and nursing care, hospital architecture, and control of hospital infections. The hospital, which fostered the centralization of health services, became the home for the newly developing technology. At the same time, the structure of health services has influenced the introduction and diffusion of technologies and, indirectly, their development.

The trend toward specialization beginning in the second half of the nineteenth century is one example of how technology affects health care delivery and health care delivery affects technology. A technological armamentarium associated with each specialty developed which required an infrastructure to bring patient, physician, and technology together. An example of this is the hospital radiology department, which was originally created as a home for X-ray equipment and is now a ready market for further developments in medical imaging.

After World War II, a centralized, specialist oriented and hospital oriented health care system evolved ready-made to incorporate certain kinds of technology. Large centralized laboratories, departments of radiology, intensive care units, and renal dialysis units were created in response to technological change.

Much of the growth in technology is directly related to the explosion of biomedical knowledge since 1950. Perhaps the most spectacular advances have occurred in cellular and molecular biology, beginning with the unraveling of the structure of DNA. The so-called biological revolution has fueled numerous technological innovations and revolutionized medical diagnosis. Therapeutic and diagnostic techniques that rely on new knowledge of recombinant DNA and monoclonal antibodies are now used in many disciplines of medicine. At the same time, a number of important new technological devices, such as lasers, computers, and various kinds of biomaterials, have been imported from other areas of science.

Improved diagnosis gives dramatic examples of technological progress. With the expansion of knowledge of the functioning of the cell, many new diagnostic tests have been developed. The typical genetic laboratory, for example, now provides about 300 tests. The development of diagnostic imaging, through computerized tomography (CT) scanners and nuclear magnetic resonance (NMR or MRI) scanners, has made it possible to look within the body noninvasively to visualize and diagnose abnormalities. It is also becoming possible to integrate anatomic information with metabolic information in ways that will further push back the frontiers of diagnosis.

Thus while there are still hospitals and physicians, and there are still sick people seeking help, the system of health care of today bears little resemblance to that of even the recent past. Technology has changed almost beyond understanding. Health care without high technology is almost unimaginable. It is an integral part of our modern way of life.

This is not to say that the role of technology in health care is without problems. The consequences of a health care system increasingly dependent on technology are profound. There is growing concern relating to the health benefits and risks of technology, its financial costs, and its social implications.

Benefits and Risks

It is difficult to assess the overall benefit of technology to health. Historically, improvements in nutrition and the physical environment have probably made a more important contribution to health than health care technology has. Health results from the complex interaction of the physical and social environments, the genetic inheritance of the individual, his or her personality, and the nature and effectiveness of the health care system.

Through a combination of socioeconomic developments and application of health care technology, rates of death and disease have changed dramatically. In the United States in 1982, one could expect to live twenty-seven years longer from birth than one could in 1900, largely because of the control of infant mortality. While advances at older ages are not so dramatic, the life expectancy for a person sixty-five years of age has risen 4.9 years over the same period. Infectious diseases have been largely controlled; in 1900 the ten leading causes of death included influenza and pneumonia, tuberculosis, gastritis, and diseases of early infancy. They have been replaced by chronic degenerative diseases. The most important diseases causing mortality in industrialized countries now are cardiovascular diseases, cancer, and accidents and violence. At the same time, chronic respiratory diseases and psychological diseases cause much morbidity and discomfort.

Health improvements began at least three centuries ago. These were surely not brought about by health care technology in any large part. In fact, looking at such conditions as tuberculosis, which was the greatest killer in western countries until approximately 1900, one researcher concluded that improvements in nutrition and the physical environment accounted for much of the change. There was a dip in the death rate from tuberculosis as early as 1838, a century before specific therapy was available, perhaps attributable in part to the improvement in nutrition related to the industrial revolution. Later, public health measures such as improved housing and sanitation were extremely important in curbing disease.

The now-predominant chronic diseases are complex and multicausal in their etiology. In contrast to many infectious diseases, where vaccines and antibiotics have made prevention or cure possible, chronic diseases have no effective preventive or curative measures. "Halfway technologies" are used to palliate manifestations of diseases whose underlying mechanisms are not understood. Historical examples of halfway technologies are the rehabilitation services and respirators created to treat poliomyelitis. With the introduction of effective vaccines, these technologies became obsolete almost overnight. Organ transplants, artificial organs, and many therapies for cancer are examples of halfway technologies in widespread use presently. These technologies are generally used after the disease has irreversibly damaged the organ. Halfway technology may contribute a great deal to functioning and quality of life, but because it often has to be applied as long as the person is alive, it is very expensive.

Although many individual technologies, such as penicillin, have doubtless saved many lives, they also present problems. All technology has risks. In many cases, they are small, and can perhaps be ignored where the benefits are significant. The point is that risks are important and need to be balanced against benefits, and this often is not done.

Perhaps drugs provide the clearest example. The case of thalidomide, which caused malformations in children whose mothers took the drug while pregnant, received much publicity. The epidemic of malformations caused a number of countries to tighten their regulation of drugs in the early 1960s. Another well-known case is that of diethylstilbestrol (DES) during pregnancy, which has caused vaginal cancer and other complications in children of these pregnancies. Less dramatic are side effects that sometimes accompany medications taken for high blood pressure: dizziness, impotence, and tiredness. Other technologies such as surgery also carry important risks, including the risk of death and of significant morbidity following surgery. Then there are the risks whose damage may not show up until years after the procedure, such as cancer caused by X-ray exposure.

It is difficult to balance risk against benefit because neither is completely understood in the case of any technology. Complications may develop years after a procedure, but the benefits are usually more immediate. Risks often occur at low rates that only become apparent when the technology is widely used. Benefits can be small but require careful study in large groups of people to be demonstrated.

Nonetheless, much more analytic work can, and should, be done, especially on the benefit side. Many technologies in current use have not been shown to be of substantial benefit. Indeed, many technologies in widespread use have later been shown to be worthless. Recent examples include internal mammary artery ligation and other operative procedures for coronary artery disease, lumbodorsal sympathectomy for hypertension, gastric freezing for peptic ulcer disease, and surgical approaches to prevent stroke. Careful evaluation of these technologies was not done until after they were in use.

The benefits of technology are becoming harder and harder to evaluate. The early procedures done to combat a particular disease often have dramatic effects, but when the procedure is used in a more widespread way its benefits may be small and very expensive. Technology is addressed more and more to functioning and to quality of life, which makes it difficult to evaluate. The end points are more subjective, and the benefits are smaller at the margin.

The ultimate policy challenge is probably to put benefits in relation to costs of care. Without this information, it is difficult to make meaningful decisions about a particular health care technology.

Financial Costs

Health care technology has become a policy issue in many countries primarily because of rapidly rising expenditures for health care. The wage and price inflation in health care has been markedly higher than the general inflation rate, and technological change appears to be a significant contributor to these rising costs.

A number of recent studies have attempted to quantify the impact of health care technology on costs. These analyses have been somewhat controversial, in part because of the complexities of the subject. The definition of health care technology is broad; thus, technology accounts for a major part of health care expenditures. These studies analyze the issue of costs from a number of different perspectives. Most fall into one of four categories: (1) the aggregate impact of technology; (2) the impact of particular technologies or classes of technology; (3) the impact of technology on a specific age group; or (4) the impact of technology on a specific disease entity.

"Service intensity" and the residual approach are the methods most commonly used to look at technology's aggregate contribution to health care costs. Total expenditures for health care reflect changes in population and health needs; overall wage and price inflation; wage and price inflation in health care in excess of general inflation; and changes in service intensity, that is, the quantity of inputs per unit of health care. The last two factors provide general indications of changes in health care technology and its effects on costs.

Using the service intensity approach, one study estimated that labor, supplies, and equipment accounted for about half of the daily charges for hospital care in the United States between 1951 and 1970. Another study estimated that from 1971 to 1981, 21 percent of the rise in costs could be attributed to increases in service intensity. The Office of Technology Assessment concluded that between 1977 and 1982 increases in intensity accounted for 24 percent of the rise in hospital costs per capita. The combined effect of increasing intensity and increasing health care prices in excess of the consumer price index accounts for approximately 16 percent of the increase in per capita health care expenditures during this period.

Changes in service intensity and excess wage and price inflation, however, are also influenced by forces unrelated to purely scientific and technological forces (that is, the introduction of new technology and improvements in existing technology). Examples of such forces include changes in reimbursement methods, attitudes of patients and clinicians toward technology, and the efforts of industry to market drugs and devices. Thus, examining the components of health care costs does not give an accurate picture of the overall contribution of technological change to costs, since this approach does not take into account the underlying reasons for technological change. It also ignores the patient benefits associated with costs increases or decreases.

The residual approach is closely related to the service intensity approach. Expenditures over time are regressed against a number of variables that influence supply and demand for health services. The unexplained residual is attributed to technological change. Using this approach, one study found that between 1930 and 1975 technological change reduced total health care expenditures in the United States at an annual rate of 0.5 percent. On the other hand, another study found that technological change raised expenditures at an annual rate of 6 percent between 1947 and 1967. The limitations of the residual approach relate to the sensitivity of any residual estimate of the variables chosen for inclusion, the time period

chosen (the differences in the two studies might be due to the
fact that cost-saving sulfa drugs were introduced in the earlier
period), and the narrow interpretation of technological
change embodied in the residual. For example, the increased
use of technology may to a considerable extent be attributed
to demand related factors such as changes in third-party payment, which means that technological change itself is underestimated in the results.

Another way to try to measure the impact of technology is
to consider particular technologies or classes of technology.
One study looked at the cost and operating data for seven
types of ancillary services (pathology, pharmacy, nuclear medicine, laboratory, diagnostic X-ray, therapeutic X-ray, and
blood banks) in approximately 1,500 hospitals and found that
about 40 percent of the increase in operating costs was due to
a higher use of these facilities per admission.

The costs of equipment are a relatively modest part of the
overall expenditures for health care. Purchases of medical
equipment in the United States cost about $17 billion a year,
about one-half of 1 percent of total U.S. health expenditures.
The cost of drugs was about $15.8 billion in 1981, also about
one-half of 1 percent of U.S. health expenditures.

One way to examine the costs of technology is to look at the
so-called big-ticket and small-ticket items separately. Big-
ticket technology includes CT scanners, open heart surgery,
and megavolt therapy. An example of small-ticket technology
is the autoanalyzer in the clinical laboratory. Health economist
Louis Groot estimated that big-ticket technology in the Netherlands accounts for 14.3 percent of total costs but concluded
that little-ticket technology might raise costs much more. This
is supported by analyses covering the period 1950 to 1970 in
the United States. Also, studies have found that between 1971
and 1982 little-ticket procedures appeared to contribute to
overall costs less than they did before 1971. Laboratory tests
did not contribute to rising costs, and new imaging techniques
were mostly substituted for older, more invasive procedures.
Some new and relatively expensive technologies did increase
costs. The following procedures accounted for much of the

rising costs: surgery on people admitted for myocardial infarction, Caesarean deliveries, respiratory distress syndrome of the newborn, and the provision of other intensive treatments for the critically ill (the latter, of course, use substantial clinical laboratory testing).

The costs of technology can also be examined by specific technology. Although some specific technologies are expensive, any one of them contributes relatively little to overall costs. For example, coronary artery by-pass graft was done about 170,000 times in the United States in 1982, with a net cost per procedure of about $15,000 and a total cost for the procedure of about $2.5 billion in 1982. Intensive care units cost about $4.8 billion in 1982, and end-stage renal disease (by dialysis and kidney transplant) cost about $1.4 billion. It costs about $250,000 a year to operate a computerized tomography scanner, and the United States has about 2,000 of them. CT scanning thus costs the United States about $500 million a year.

Some technologies are clearly money saving. The Office of Technology Assessment estimated that the Medicare program will reap cost savings from the pneumococcal vaccine after three to five years of use. Another apparently cost-saving technology is cimetidine, a drug for the treatment of peptic ulcer, in use since 1977. An economic analysis carried out in Rhode Island estimated that the reduction in surgery resulting from use of the drug brought about statewide savings of between $185,000 and $450,000. If these estimates are valid for the entire United States, the overall cost saving would be substantial.

When technology use is considered by age groups, the elderly are found to use relatively more health care technology and thus contribute more to costs. A number of analyses have focused on the "high cost of dying." In a review of these studies, Ann A. Scitovsky found that medical care costs at the end of life are indeed high. One study, for example, found that the 5.9 percent of U.S. Medicare enrollees who died accounted for 27.9 percent of total Medicare payments. Scitovsky concludes that the high cost of medical care at the end of life is not a recent development, but that the same situation existed fifteen or twenty years ago. She also concludes that

the data available at present do not support the frequently voiced or implied assumption that the high medical expenses at the end of life are due largely to aggressive, intensive treatments of patients who are moribund. Given the uncertainty of medical prognosis, it is not at all clear that resources were "wasted" in treating those who died.

Another group that incurs considerable expense is newborns with respiratory distress syndrome. These babies received increasing amounts of surgery between 1971 and 1982, and babies who had surgery received almost twice the resources provided to other infants.

Technology costs can also be analyzed by specific diseases. The costs of illness have been investigated by a number of researchers. One study, focusing on health expenditures by disease category, found that cardiovascular disease was the most expensive disease category for the United States in 1975, costing more than $13 billion (excluding cerebrovascular disease). Surprisingly, a number of diseases cost U.S. society more than cancer ($5.3 billion), including mental disorders ($9.4 billion); diseases of the respiratory system ($7.6 billion); diseases of the digestive system ($6.8 billion); diseases of the oral cavity, salivary glands ($7.8 billion); and accidents, poisoning, and violence ($6.8 billion).

Studies of the costs of illness are important and interesting, but they do not actually indicate the costs of technology. There have been few attempts to examine costs directly.

One study traced the changes in the costs of treating eleven conditions at the Palo Alto Medical Clinic in California. Between 1951 and 1964 the real costs of treating only two of the nine conditions studied fell: otitis media and pregnancy/delivery. From 1964 to 1971 the real costs of treating five of eleven conditions fell: pregnancy/delivery, breast cancer, closed reduction of children's forearm fractures with anesthesia, pneumonia without hospitalization, and duodenal ulcer without hospitalization. Those whose costs rose from 1964 to 1971 were otitis media, simple and perforated appendicitis, children's forearm fractures with cast only and with closed reduction but no anesthesia, and myocardial infarction.

The increases in diagnostic tests and therapeutic procedures were especially striking. Laboratory tests per case of perforated appendicitis rose from 5.3 in 1951, to 14.5 in 1964, to 31.0 in 1971. Inhalation therapy procedures per myocardial infarction rose from 12.8 in 1964 to 37.5 in 1971.

A 1981 update of that study found that the net effects of treating sixteen conditions from 1971 to 1981 were cost saving in eight, cost raising in seven, and neutral in one. However, in most cases the differences were small. The largest differences were in breast cancer and myocardial infarction, where new "big-ticket" technologies increased costs considerably. Another large difference was due to the increasing use of Caesarean section with its high costs.

Overall, researchers agree in their findings on the primary reasons for rising costs, namely: surgery for people admitted for myocardial infarction, delivery of a baby by Caesarean section, respiratory distress syndrome of the newborn, and the provision of other intensive treatments for the critically ill.

The findings on the use and cost of technology by specific disease deserve wide distribution and discussion. Perhaps efforts to effect the adoption and use of technology have been more successful than realized previously, and the real problem is with a few very high-cost technologies that are used. If so, the policy problem is greatly simplified.

In summary, the cost of health care technology is an important issue for all societies. Technology is costly, and its value needs to be demonstrated. Policy mechanisms should create strategies to ensure that investments in technology are made wisely and cost-effectively.

Social Implications

The social implications of health care technology are profound. In the aggregate, technology has transformed the health care system. Hospitals have grown up to house the burgeoning technology. Specialties have developed to provide certain technologies. These changes in the organization and delivery of care have enormous cost implications, but they have social repercussions as well.

Perhaps the most significant implication of technology is that while it has given providers new capabilities, it has resulted in a system that is often perceived as less caring. That is, the modern machines of health and medical care have, in a sense, dehumanized the health care system. With more and more functions automated and involving a machine, the effect on the nature of health care is profound. Of course, the growth of technology is fueled by a value system that says that information obtained by machines is more useful than that obtained by human beings.

While technological change in health care can have important social implications, social developments themselves influence both the development and use of health care technology. Two significant social trends that will affect technology are under way, and are to an extent in conflict with each other: medicalization and demedicalization. These trends are very complex, and we describe only some of their implications.

In past decades the influence of the family and organized religion decreased. The public has increasingly turned to the health care system, in part because of the lack of other resources to call upon for advice and support. This care-seeking behavior has fostered a process of medicalization, in which social problems are redefined as medical. Advances in medical knowledge and technology and the resulting improvements in prevention, diagnosis, and therapy have further stimulated this process. As an extreme example of this process, death has changed from a social event supported by family and church to a medical event taking place in a hospital. The changed values and attitudes toward death are reflected to a certain extent in the ways that technologies such as intensive care are used to prevent or postpone death, sometimes with great human and financial costs.

The dominance of the biomedical concept of health and disease, sometimes described as resulting from the Cartesian paradigm or from the classical theory of disease, has led to a certain role for health care technology in modern medicine. In general, advances in medical science and technology have resulted in markedly improved prevention, diagnosis, and therapy over the last decades. These advances have been visible to the public, and have great public appeal. Because of this, basic questions of values, beliefs, and meaning in modern societies are discussed more and more in terms of health and health care technology.

At the same time, however, a process of demedicalization seems to have begun. The process of demedicalization can be seen as partly a reaction to the expanding role of "sickness" in society, but it is also partly due to concerns about an increasingly machine oriented and sometimes dehumanized form of health care. In diagnosis, the trend is away from the patient's sensations and physician's observations and toward more "objective" evidence provided by laboratory procedures and mechanical and electronic devices. Physicians see patients more briefly and indirectly through a screen of high-tech care and machine-mediated diagnostic and therapeutic procedures. An increasing reliance on machines tends to lead to a loss of human skills, and the patient often complains that physicians are not so sensitive and caring as they once were. These considerations play a role in the recent trend toward the growth of alternative systems of care and the growth of self-care.

Some specific technologies have profound potential effects in their own right. The birth control pill, for example, is often credited with promoting the liberation of women and the sexual revolution. And genetic screening followed by abortion of fetuses with certain congenital or genetic abnormalities (such as Down's syndrome) can clearly save money for society. However, many would choose not to do the abortion for moral reasons.

Thus the interaction between society and technology is enormously complex and multidimensional. It is essential that we increase our understanding of these interactions so that we can rationally plan and deploy technology.

Future Perspective on Health Care Technology

The rapid pace of technological change during the past decades can be expected to continue—and may even accelerate. Many new diagnostic and therapeutic technologies can be anticipated. For example, there may be a whole array of new and improved vaccines (e.g., influenza) and new ways of administration (e.g., by nasal spray). There may be robotics for home care, neuroelectronic prostheses, brain grafting, new diagnostic kits using monoclonal antibodies, and lasers in cardiovascular surgery. The new technologies, of course, will raise concerns about health benefits and risks, increasing costs, and social and ethical issues. The changes in diagnosis are likely to be profound, with new tests being developed from the fields of biotechnology and medical imaging. New diagnostic procedures will not necessarily have much impact on health, but they will certainly add to costs. Many new therapeutic technologies could appear in the next few years. For example, artificial organs may be developed that will keep some people alive, but probably at great cost. At the same time, patterns of health and disease are changing, and these influence the needs and demands for technology as well. A major factor between now and the early twenty-first century will be the aging of the population. Because most chronic diseases are age related, many chronic degenerative diseases will increase in prevalence in the near future. There is likely to be an increase in psychosocial problems, chronic psychiatric diseases, and such chronic diseases as respiratory diseases, diabetes, and rheumatoid arthritis. As the population ages, the use of technology is likely to be more addressed to improving the quality of life.

Straight-line extrapolation of present trends, of course, does not necessarily give a realistic picture, since future health and health care needs will be influenced by changing environmental factors. A number of new diseases may appear, just as AIDS, legionnaire's disease, and toxic shock syndrome emerged only in the last few years.

Despite advances in knowledge and the development of definitive approaches to some diseases, much of health care technology will remain "halfway technology." Thus more questions of benefit versus risk and costs will be raised.

A number of forces will affect the nature and structure of the health care system in the future, including technology. As society moves increasingly into the preindustrial era, the population of most countries will become more heterogeneous and oriented to individuality. At the same time, it will depend more on organized services than in the past, when family or neighborhood provided more care and information. The demands on health services will be heavy, and will include demands for different types of services, even parallel methods of delivering care.

Issues of centralization versus decentralization are likely to take on increasing importance in the health care debate. The trend in the past has been toward centralization and institutionalization. However, the recent trend has been toward out-of-hospital care, even home care. Some highly specialized activities, such as heart and kidney transplants, must be concentrated in a few centers to control costs and assure adequate standards of quality. At the same time, however, some new technologies are fostering decentralization to physicians' offices or even to people's homes. Integration of computers, robotics, and telecommunication technology can enhance decentralization and home care. Diagnostic kits are fostering decentralization to clinic and home. Surgical technologies such as lasers are making some surgery more feasible in ambulatory settings.

As a consequence of these new technologies, the role of the physician and the overall number of physicians needed may change significantly in the future. The trend in centralized, larger organizations may be more toward seeing the physician as a functionary in a hierarchical structure. The development of scientific knowledge on benefits and risks of technology can foster this trend through the development of algorithms, new payment schemes based on evidence, and cost-effectiveness studies. This could mean the relative loss of clinical freedom for clinicians.

The introduction of new technology will certainly raise a number of complex social and ethical issues in the future. For example, it may be possible by 1995 to map most of the human genome. Genetic material could be collected at birth and comprehensive health-risk patterns generated that would identify not only purely genetic disease, but susceptibilities for such diseases as cancer and cardiovascular disease. How would the individual and society use this information? There could be fundamental changes in job selection and hiring decision patterns and in marketing behavior by companies offering health insurance.

Anticipating the rapidly growing armory of future health care technology, we will have to ask how this technology will be used, not only effectively and efficiently, but also humanely. How will the caring function fit into the health care system of the future? Which tasks will be performed by machines, and which tasks will be kept within the domain of people? The growing array of choices and conflicting goals merits broad public debate and eventual policy changes.

In considering these questions, one should bear in mind that attitudes toward technology are likely to change. Today's middle-aged people are tomorrow's elderly. Whereas today elderly people might be seen as not overly demanding concerning health care services and tolerating illness and pain rather well, tomorrow's elderly will probably be less tolerant and more demanding. With increasing educational levels and knowledge of health and health care, people will know their rights and will be more and more critical of the care that they receive. One aspect of these demands will surely be an increasing focus on quality of life. A long life has little meaning without reasonable physical and mental functioning.

The value of "life at any cost" is already being seriously questioned. Grave ethical questions occur at both the beginning and end of life. Some elderly people with no hope of regaining functions, or even consciousness, are now kept alive by machines. Smaller and smaller babies, often with the potential for serious mental and physical handicaps, are kept alive in intensive care, and as intensive care techniques improve, they are applied to more and more infants. Infertile couples undergo a great amount of intervention in attempts to have children. Technology has given us the tools, but society has not yet learned how to use them.

These technologies are likely to raise health care expenditures overall. Although some future technologies, such as vaccines, may lower costs, most will increase costs. This in turn will lead to increasing attempts to control costs. Developing alternatives to hospital and long-term care such as home care and ambulatory care may help curb costs—but they may also, overall, increase costs.

Ultimately, we will have to accept the fact that resources for health care are limited, which means that difficult choices will have to be made, and they are likely to be increasingly agonizing. Questions will be raised regarding equality and equity in access to care. Conflicts will surely grow between individual rights and demands and collective decisions. With growing pressures on health care resources, one response might be to allow less patient choice. Technology assessment will probably continue to develop as an aid to such decisions. Even so, many of the choices will be increasingly agonizing.

The move toward explicitly limiting resources for health care will also raise many problems of equality and equity in access to care. Conflicts will surely grow between individual rights and demands and collective decisions. With growing pressures on health care resources, one response might be to allow less patient choice. Attempts to resolve these issues will surely involve changes in existing policies.

Technology Assessment in Future Policy Making

An important policy issue facing the United States is how to deal with the problem of limited resources for health care. It is likely to take on increasing importance in the future as rates of chronic disease grow and new technology is created. Health care expenditures will undoubtedly increase, but they will not be allowed to increase indefinitely. It is just not possible to do everything for everybody.

The United States already has a health care delivery system full of inequities. About 37 million people have no effective health insurance, and so have limited access to health care. One approach to the problem is to treat health care like a good sold in the marketplace, like television sets. Those who can afford it can have it. Those who cannot will have to do without.

Although there are some who might endorse this approach, they are surely a minority. It would be morally unacceptable to the vast majority of people to let someone in a traffic accident die on the street because of lack of insurance. It also seems morally unacceptable to have an epidemic of measles in a poor area because some of its residents cannot afford a relatively expensive vaccine.

Yet something akin to this is already happening on a small scale. Heart transplant has now been shown to be an effective and cost-effective procedure at least compared with many other technologies in widespread use. More than 80 percent of Blue Cross and Blue Shield Plans and commercial carriers in the United States now include heart transplantation as a standard benefit. The official position of the Medicare program, however, is that heart transplantation is experimental. And only twenty-four state Medicaid programs and the District of Columbia pay for heart transplants. Thus many elderly, poor, and disabled people in the United States who might benefit from transplant cannot have it. Many of these people will die for lack of the procedure.

There must be a better way to distribute scarce health care resources. One possibility is to define a set of important services that will be available to everyone. Such decisions must be based on the value of the services, that is, the costs and benefits of the services. These services should undoubtedly include basic preventive services, primary care services, and specialized diagnostic and therapeutic services shown to be cost-effective. Heart transplant is an example of a technological service that appears to meet the last test.

The family of techniques for assessing the costs and benefits of technology has come to be called technology assessment. The objective of technology assessment, simply stated, is to understand the implications of health care technology. Technology assessment is addressed to policy questions and ethical dilemmas, and is intended to be an aid for policy making. It is an eclectic process aimed at producing the information that will be most helpful to decision making. In examining one technology, assessment may deal with questions of benefits and risks; in another, it may be concerned primarily with social effects. In most cases, however, financial costs versus health benefits are the prime issue. For this purpose, cost-effectiveness analysis and cost-benefit analysis are the most useful analytic tools.

Technology assessment is a growing discipline and is likely to take on increasing importance in the future. A number of countries are moving to establish national efforts in health care technology assessment. In the future, much more information on the consequences of technological change in health care should be available. The rapidity of social and technological change demands that attempts be made to identify and prospectively assess important technological developments. Indeed, a future orientation is not just a luxury—it is a necessity.

Technology assessment by itself, however, does not change anything. Policies toward health care technology are most important—that is, the way in which the information gained from technology assessment will be used.

A Policy Structure for Health Care Technology

Although "policies" can refer to actions of industry or professional societies, they here refer primarily to government-determined policies, which presumably have been formed to function in the broad public interest. All of the forces described in this chapter, and others, seem to indicate a growing government involvement in health care, with new policies and laws. Public policies will obviously sometimes be in conflict with the policies of industry or professional societies.

Until recently, many countries, including the United States, relied on a regulatory approach to control technology and costs. It largely failed because of the sheer numbers of technologies that have been created in recent decades and because of inadequate financial and political support. At the same time, the success of Canada and the United Kingdom in holding down health care costs through straightforward budgetary restrictions has focused attention on the payment method, in particular the health care budget, as a major policy tool for the present and future.

The potential impact of health policy in the United States today is probably greatest at the stage of basic research, whose funding is paid almost entirely by the public. Governments generally have not attempted to intervene to create policy at this stage of technological development, but have functioned under the assumption that the development of knowledge is itself a good thing. The allocation of the available money has been largely left to the scientists themselves, which, on the whole, is probably a wise philosophy.

However, government may intervene prior to a new technology's distribution to the general public. For example, governments regulate medical experimentation and testing in human beings and require proof of efficacy and safety before drugs can be marketed. In the United States, medical devices are regulated through premarketing programs. The government also intervenes in the development and manufacture of new health care technologies to strengthen the economy and promote exports, especially for drugs and equipment.

Government can also intervene in the diffusion of health care technology through straightforward policies that create licensing laws, certificate-of-need restrictions, and payment schemes. Perhaps the most important policies concern payment for services. In the life cycle of a given technology, payment is an issue when the technology has begun to diffuse into use. Payment for the services needed to deliver the technology is to a large extent under public control, and payment policy should be created to ensure the appropriate use of the technology.

Until recently, the Medicare program paid hospitals by the method of cost reimbursement, which encouraged hospitals to spend—and charge—more. In 1982 the method of payment was changed to a prospective payment system in which prices were determined in advance for hospital care for 468 diagnosis related groups (DRGs). This change has profoundly altered the financial incentives of hospitals. With time, other payers will probably change to prospective methods of payment as well, because private payers generally follow policies defined by some public programs.

Physicians are still paid predominantly on a fee-for-service basis. This method, like the old cost-based Medicare payment method, encourages more services or visits because the physician is paid for each service rendered. Physician fees are not necessarily closely related to the costs of providing given services. Fees for services based on new technology often are substantially higher than those for established services, especially the so-called cognitive services, which may require substantial diagnostic and therapeutic skill, patience, and time on the part of the physician. Visits where patients express worries or receive counseling are paid at an especially low rate relative to visits involving visible modern technology.

Summary and Conclusions

Health care policy in the United States has developed within the context of a pluralistic society, where the role of government has been limited. A more active governmental role in the future, however, is virtually guaranteed by virtue of the size and expense of the health care system and the rapid growth of an aging population. Technologies will surely develop to treat the chronic diseases that this population will develop.

But society's resources are limited, and not all of the technologies will be provided to everyone who might benefit. Choice will become more and more explicit—and the choices will not be easy. A set of policies created from the growing body of information gleaned from technology assessment must guide the adoption and use of technology in directions determined by the broad society.

It may be tempting to adopt a broad policy of budgetary

restraint similar to that used in Canada and the United Kingdom. Strict budgets can certainly constrain overall costs, but perhaps not in the most rational way. Society has the potential tools to guide rational technological developments in health care, and it must put them to use.

Perhaps the most significant health policy question facing industrialized countries like the United States is how to simultaneously control the costs of health care and encourage the development and use of beneficial technologies. Is it possible to have a system that promotes the use of cost-effective technologies for all citizens? In an attempt to answer this question, technology assessment will take on greater importance. In time, more and better information will be available to guide the choices that will have to be made.

The overriding problem at the present time, however, is that there is no consensus on directions for the future. This remains a critical problem that must be addressed.

9

Final Report of the Seventy-second American Assembly

At the close of their discussions, the participants in the Seventy-second American Assembly, on *Health Care and Its Costs*, at Arden House, Harriman, New York, November 13–16, 1986, reviewed as a group the following statement. This statement represents general agreement; however, no one was asked to sign it. Furthermore, it should be understood that not everyone agreed with all of it.

The twentieth-century vision of American citizenship embraces participation by all in the benefits of our wealthy society. Over time, health care has become a part of this vision. Indeed, medical progress has come to be an emblem of American innovation and success. As the Thirty-seventh American Assembly on *The Health of Americans* proclaimed in 1970, "Access to adequate health care for all in the United States must be recognized as a basic right."

In the ensuing sixteen years, American society has changed in ways that challenge this vision. As a nation, we spend faster than we earn. As a people we are growing older; more of us live alone than before. Our work force now includes more part-time, low-paid, and other workers with marginal health care coverage. Technology creates new possibilities as well as unanticipated risks. These forces also are reshaping the American health care system.

The Thirty-seventh Assembly observed a crisis in health care that could be solved "only by a national commitment to prompt action of a sweeping nature." The nation has addressed many of the problems articulated by that Assembly through development of new technologies, the training of more physicians, and the implementation of innovative forms of delivery. However, the most profound difficulties—cost, quality, and access—persist. Indeed, they are in some ways linked to what we have achieved.

Health care costs have continued to rise despite two decades of growing concern and efforts by private and public actors to reduce both annual increases and aggregate costs. New approaches to cost containment have emerged from these policies. Increasingly, public and private purchasers have focused on price and utilization control as the central mechanisms of control. Powerful payers gained discounts on behalf of large pools of consumers. This price-centered policy rests on the assumption that more efficient production and distribution of health care will result.

As each purchaser scrutinizes the aggregate cost of care for the population it covers, medical care is now treated as a commodity. The result is a profound challenge to our historic system of implicit cross-subsidization. Traditionally cross-subsidized products of the health care system included: the provision of care to the poor, support of medical education, and the sustenance of an environment where medical research and technology could flourish. These are now threatened and may be lost. Our past failure to solve the cost problem forces us to face these and perhaps more perplexing problems in the future.

Health care for the uninsured is particularly problematic in a price-centered world. With eroding public and private commitment to care for the medically indigent, where fewer people are covered and less adequately, the importance of historic cross-subsidies is put in higher relief. Some institutions, long

devoted to the care of disproportionate numbers of poor and
near-poor patients, may not survive. The vision of a medically
just society is at risk as a result of recasting medical care as a
price-distributed commodity.

This change has, however, heightened concern for efficiency
and quality of care. Unfortunately, we lack adequate systematic
and scientific means for both providers and consumers to evaluate quality of care.

In addition, profound organizational change characterizes
our environment. Institutions that traditionally have been devoted to the delivery and finance of care are in flux. The
magnitude of change is evidenced by the growth of alternative
providers; the decline in inpatient utilization; the reduction of
the importance of the hospital to the medical care system; the
reconfiguration of the relationship among physicians, hospitals, and payers; the melding of identities between finance and
delivery illustrated by health maintenance organizations
(HMOs) owned by health insurance companies, and preferred
provider organizations (PPOs) owned by physicians and/or
hospitals, and insurance companies owned by hospitals; and
the significant market presence and general acceptance of for-
profit providers. These changes are simultaneously celebrated
and decried. They hold potential for increased efficiency,
effectiveness, and improvement in the quality of care. We are
mindful, however, of the potential problems. The pursuit of
lower cost may have produced incentives for insurers to avoid
some risks and for providers to avoid some patients (the most
poor and, ironically, the most sick).

As we contemplate the future, it is important to note one
characteristic of the American system of health care. Unlike
other western democracies, we never nationalized health coverage. This reflects both the American ambivalence about the
role of government and the value we place on mixing private
and public action. Our past reflects the coexistence of voluntary, public, and for-profit hospitals; a system of charitable,
private, cooperative, and government financing; and attempts
by hospitals, employers, unions, physicians, payers, and government to control the future of health care. In addition, state

and local governments have become active participants in the search for innovations; they have demonstrated new capacities and introduced a wide range of reforms. It is unproductive to characterize the past as one that has been dominated by either government or private initiative; it is misleading to cast the contemporary dilemma as a stark choice between public or private, "regulation" or "competition." Americans appear comfortable with their pluralistic approach to solving problems.

This uniquely American way of solving problems will continue to characterize our approach to health care, because there is no clear consensus on the relative importance of health care in the package of individual rights enjoyed by every American. We do agree, however, that not all the health care provided is necessary (meaning that some Americans receive more services than they need) and all that is necessary is not provided (meaning that some Americans do not receive adequate care). We agree that not providing care for those who need it should be unacceptable in a rich society committed to decent and humane life for all its people.

The participants of the Seventy-second American Assembly make the following recommendations for national action:

1. Making quality health care available to all members of our society remains a national goal. However, there are limited resources to be spent on health care in our society. For some of our spending, we are not receiving results in health status improvement or maintenance that are worth their cost. The efficiency is not optimal in delivery of individual and aggregate services. There are difficult questions of individuals' claim to societal resources. Health care expenditures must be evaluated within the context of the full spectrum of societal goals. We strongly urge a higher profile of national discourse on the level and distribution of health care spending. There should be a strong public and private effort to reduce the long-term rate of growth in health care spending, and consideration

should be given to measuring success in this endeavor against the rate of change in some external indicator.

2. The Assembly believes that the nation must take action to secure access for all Americans to basic medical, surgical, and preventive services. The Assembly calls on the federal government to seek this objective by passing legislation that would:

- Reform Medicaid eligibility and set federal standards of participation for all individuals with incomes under the federal poverty line;
- Assure that non-Medicaid eligible individuals who are uninsured receive coverage for basic health care services and specify the benefits to be included in the plan;
- Set maximum copayment requirements;
- Require all employers not offering basic health insurance to provide coverage to their employees, with special consideration given to the problems of small employers, marginal employers, and employers of part-time workers; and
- Establish a mechanism analogous to unemployment insurance to assure that individuals do not lose health insurance coverage during temporary spells of unemployment.

The Assembly strongly believes that states should have flexibility in implementing these recommendations.

The Assembly recognizes that its proposal would involve a commitment of additional federal and/or state funds to expand the Medicaid population and subsidize certain employers and others who on their own cannot obtain health care benefits. The Assembly recommends that consideration be given to financing this greater effort through a variety of mechanisms including:

- General revenues;
- Earmarking taxes on alcohol and cigarettes;
- Value added taxes; and
- Savings resulting from improved efficiency.

3. We support the broadly increasing efforts to promote health and prevent disease, including expanding coverage of screening and preventive care, enforcement and expansion of existing legislation on environmental standards, and accident pre-

vention. Research to define which programs pay off in real health impact is especially needed. Education of the public through the schools, workplace, and media is essential to support responsible behavior, such as smoking cessation and seat belt use.

4. The Assembly believes that there is too much emphasis on institutionally based services for long-term care. Mechanisms should be developed to shift the emphasis of chronic and long-term care toward formal home care and community-based services. Family support systems that in the past were available to provide long-term care are insufficient to meet today's needs.

Medicare beneficiaries often have little knowledge of benefits with respect to long-term care. More information should be provided regarding the limits of the Medicare benefits package. Steps should be taken to expand access by exploring public and private options for financing services, such as:

- Creating a contributory program within the Medicare system;
- Community-based care with case-managed systems;
- Reverse annuity mortgages; and/or
- Social health maintenance organizations (SHMOs).

5. This Assembly urges public officials and the legal, medical, and insurance professions to take steps to reduce the incidence of malpractice, to introduce new forms of dispute resolution and injury compensation, and to pass more uniform laws among the states.

6. Much attention has been given to health improvements attributable to new technology. Some have clearly saved money; many have required substantial additional expenditures. To balance progress and cost containment, we recommend that states monitor the diffusion of new equipment and procedures. Federal support should be expanded for assessing technology and promoting information and consensus on appropriate uses of technology.

The rapid pace of technology development in the past has been a function of a combination of the profit motive and readily available payment for capital-intensive innovative services. New payment arrangements (per admission, per capita) will continue to reward cost-saving technologies and development. Those public and private agencies devoted to technology assessment should give special attention to the pace at which new technology is harvested from basic and clinical research.

7. The nation has exhibited a firm commitment to the discovery and application of new knowledge through support of basic science and technology. The Assembly endorses this historic commitment and affirms the importance of continued federal support of basic biomedical research.

8. The Assembly believes that there is a national oversupply and maldistribution of hospital beds and number of physicians. The Assembly urges states to develop appropriate mechanisms to address these problems with the objectives of improving efficiency, equity, and access to care.

9. We recognize the right of patients to refuse medical treatments they find disproportionately burdensome. Providers should be relieved of liability in such instances.

10. The Assembly encourages the collection and analysis of data by states consistent with national guidelines in the areas of morbidity, mortality, utilization, quality of care, and expenditures. Researchers, businesses, unions, and the public should be encouraged to use these data. There should be disclosure requirements on information necessary to assess quality and the cost of care. These efforts must assure the protection of patients' confidentiality.

11. It is increasingly important that we develop a national analytic capacity to monitor the changes occurring in the medical care system. Basic research around the question of medical practice, with particular emphasis on indicators related to quality and access to care, should be undertaken.

12. Physician services have been an important factor in the increasing costs of medical care. The Assembly recognizes the lack of information currently available about controlling the costs of physician services. More attention and further study should be given to innovative and equitable forms of financing.

Participants
The Seventy-second American Assembly

HENRY AARON
Senior Fellow
Economics Studies Program
The Brookings Institution
Washington, D.C.

†DAVID AXELROD
Commissioner
Department of Health
State of New York
Albany, New York

HOWARD BAUM
Harriman Scholar
The Johns Hopkins School of
Medicine
Baltimore, Maryland

MARK BENEDICT
Minority Staff Director
Subcommittee on Health &
Long-Term Care
Select Committee on
Aging
Washington, D.C.

RICHARD BERMAN
Health Care Consultant
New York, New York

BRIAN BILES, M.D.
Staff Director
Subcommittee on Health
Committee on Ways &
Means
U.S. House of Representatives
Washington, D.C.

†Delivered Formal Address

PETER BOUXSEIN
Counsel
Subcommittee on Health &
The Environment
Committee on Energy &
Commerce
Washington, D.C.

JOHN C. BURTON
Dean
Graduate School of
Business
Columbia University
New York, New York

W. DOUGLAS CAMPBELL
Majority Health Staff
Director
Committee on Labor & Human
Resources
U.S. Senate
Washington, D.C.

RONALD H. CARLSON
Associate Administrator
Planning, Evaluation &
Legislation
Health Resources & Services
Administration
Department of Health &
Human Services
Rockville, Maryland

GARY J. CLARKE
Deputy Director for
Health
Department of Health &
Rehabilitative Services
Tallahassee, Florida

MARC A. COHEN
Harriman Scholar
Research Associate, Health
Policy Center
Heller School, Brandeis
University
Waltham, Massachusetts

DONALD R. COHODES
Administrator
Federal Programs
Division
Blue Cross & Blue Shield
Association
Chicago, Illinois

A. MICHAEL COLLINS
Assistant to the General
President
International Union of
Operating Engineers
Washington, D.C.

JAMES E. DAVIS, M.D.
Speaker, House of
Delegates
American Medical Association
Chicago, Illinois

SUSAN FEIGENBAUM
Associate Professor of
Economics
Claremont McKenna College &
Claremont Graduate School
Claremont, California

ROBERT H. FINCH
Chairman
Viratek Incorporated
Pasadena, California

*Discussion Leader
**Rapporteur
†Delivered Formal Address

RUTH FINKELSTEIN
Harriman Scholar
School of Hygiene and Public
Health
Johns Hopkins University
Baltimore, Maryland

†DANIEL M. FOX
Professor of Humanities in
Medicine
State University of New York at
Stony Brook
Stony Brook, New York

MARCEL FRENKEL, M.D.
Editor
*Journal of Medical Practice
Management*
Department of Opthalmology
College of Medicine
University of Illinois
Chicago, Illinois

STEPHEN W. GAMBLE
President
Hospital Council of Southern
California
Los Angeles, California

ELSIE I. GRIFFITH
Chief Executive Officer
Visiting Nurse Service of New
York
New York, New York

**FRANCES HANCKEL
Associate Hospital
Director/Planning &
Marketing
Temple University
Hospital
Philadelphia, Pennsylvania

WILLIAM S. HOFFMAN
Director
Social Security Department
International Union, United
Automobile, Aerospace &
Agricultural Implement
Workers of America—
UAW
Detroit, Michigan

CLARENCE L. HUGGINS,
M.D.
Cleveland, Ohio

*KAREN M. IGNAGNI
Assistant Director
AFL-CIO Department of
Occupational Safety, Health &
Social Security
Washington, D.C.

JOHN K. KITTREDGE
Executive Vice President
The Prudential Insurance
Company of America
Newark, New Jersey

*RICHARD M. KNAPP
Director
Department of Teaching
Hospitals
Association of American
Medical Colleges
Washington, D.C.

DAVID KORN, M.D.
Vice President & Dean
School of Medicine
Stanford University
Stanford, California

*Discussion Leader
**Rapporteur
†Delivered Formal Address

†RICHARD D. LAMM
Governor
State of Colorado
Denver, Colorado

SIDNEY S. LEE, M.D.
President
The Milbank Memorial Fund
New York, New York

ALLEN W. MATHIES, JR.
President & CEO
Huntington Memorial Hospital
Pasadena, California

KENNETH McLENNAN
Vice President & Director of
Industrial Studies
Committee for Economic
Development
Washington, D.C.

TRACY E. MILLER
Executive Director
The New York State Task
Force on Life and the Law
New York, New York

**JAMES MORONE
Professor
Department of Political
Science
Brown University
Providence, Rhode Island

*JOHN W. MURPHY
Executive Director
Flinn Foundation
Phoenix, Arizona

H. RICHARD NESSON, M.D.
President
Brigham & Women's Hospital
Boston, Massachusetts

DAVID NEXON
Majority Health Staff
Director
Labor & Human Resources
Commission
U.S. Senate
Washington, D.C.

JOHN B. O'DONNELL
Executive Office of Human
Services
Department of Public
Health
Boston, Massachusetts

JOHN J. PARIS, S.J.
Professor of Ethics
College of The Holy
Cross
Worcester, Massachusetts

JUDITH PERES
Director
Health Policy
The Villers Foundation
Washington, D.C.

STEVEN C. RENN
Department of Health Policy &
Management
The Johns Hopkins Medical
Institutions
Baltimore, Maryland

ALLAN ROSENFIELD, M.D.
Dean
School of Public Health
Faculty of Medicine
Columbia University
New York, New York

*Discussion Leader
**Rapporteur
†Delivered Formal Address

THOMAS G. RUNDALL
School of Public Health
University of California at
Berkeley
Berkeley, California

DAVID J. SANCHEZ, JR.
Associate Professor
Family & Community
Medicine/UCSF Mexus
Program
University of California at San
Francisco
San Francisco, California

LEONARD D. SCHAEFFER
President
Blue Cross of California
Woodland Hills, California

WALTER B. SCHAUERMANN
Director
Office of Health Program
Systems
Bureau of Data Management &
Strategy
Health Care Financing
Administration
Baltimore, Maryland

CAROL SCHEMAN
Director
Federal Relations
American Association of
Universities
Washington, D.C.

PAUL SHULLENBERGER
Assistant Director
MacArthur Fellows
Program
MacArthur Foundation
Chicago, Illinois

JAMES R. TALLON, JR.
Chairman, Health Committee
New York State Assembly
Albany, New York

WILLIAM J. TODD
Assistant to the Vice President
for Health Affairs
Woodruff Health Sciences Center
Emory University
Atlanta, Georgia

**JANE K. WHITE
Managing Editor
Health Affairs
Chevy Chase, Maryland

EDWIN C. WHITEHEAD
Chairman
Whitehead Associates
Greenwich, Connecticut

**Rapporteur

ROSALIND WHITEHEAD
University Health Partners
Greenwich, Connecticut

DANIEL WIKLER
Professor of Philosophy &
Medical Ethics
Department of History of
Medicine
University of Wisconsin
Medical School
Madison, Wisconsin

RAYMOND L. WILSON
Senior Vice President
Nationwide Insurance
Columbus, Ohio

KENNETH WING
School of Law
School of Public Health
University of North Carolina
Durham, North Carolina

About The American Assembly

The American Assembly was established by Dwight D. Eisenhower at Columbia University in 1950. It holds nonpartisan meetings and publishes authoritative books to illuminate issues of United States policy.

An affiliate of Columbia, with offices in the Helen Goodhart Altschul Hall on the Barnard College campus, the Assembly is a national, educational institution incorporated in the state of New York.

The Assembly seeks to provide information, stimulate discussion, and evoke independent conclusions on matters of vital public interest.

American Assembly Sessions

At least two national programs are initiated each year. Authorities are retained to write background papers presenting essential data and defining the main issues of each subject.

A group of men and women representing a broad range of experience, competence, and American leadership meet for several days to discuss the Assembly topic and consider alternatives for national policy.

All Assemblies follow the same procedure. The background papers are sent to participants in advance of the Assembly. The Assembly meets in small groups for four or five lengthy periods. All groups use the same agenda. At the close of these informal sessions participants adopt in plenary session a final report of findings and recommendations.

Regional, state, and local Assemblies are held following the national session at Arden House. Assemblies have also been held in England, Switzerland, Malaysia, Canada, the Caribbean, South America, Central America, the Philippines, and Japan. Over one hundred fifty institutions have cosponsored one or more Assemblies.

The American Assembly
COLUMBIA UNIVERSITY

Index